WHERE THE CITY MEETS THE SOUND

THE STORY OF SEATTLE'S WATERFRONT

BY JENNIFER OTT

HistoryLink / Documentary Media

Seattle, Washington

WHERE THE CITY MEETS THE SOUND: The Story of Seattle's Waterfront

by Jennifer Ott

Copyright 2025 by HistoryLink

All rights reserved. No part of this book may be reproduced or utilized in any form without the prior written consent of HistoryLink.

First Edition
Printed in USA

HistoryLink
admin@historylink.org
www.historylink.org | (206) 447-8140

Documentary Media LLC
books@docbooks.com
www.documentarymedia.com | (206) 935-9292

Author: Jennifer Ott
Editing and book production: Tori Smith
Photo research: Elisa Law
Book design: Marilyn Esguerra
Editorial Director: Petyr Beck

Available through the University of Washington Press
uwapress.uw.edu

ISBN: 978-1-933245-74-4

Library of Congress Control Number: 2025938243

This book was made possible with the support of:
The. Port of Seattle
The City of Seattle
King County
Washington Department of Archaeology and Historic Preservation

Front cover photo by Jean Sherrard. Back cover images courtesy Museum of History and Industry (top) and Paul Dorpat (bottom). Inside cover images courtesy Seattle Municipal Archives.

CONTENTS

INTRODUCTION		6
CHAPTER 1	Becoming dᶻidᶻəlalʼič	10
CHAPTER 2	Becoming Seattle	18
CHAPTER 3	In Search of a Transcontinental	32
CHAPTER 4	Engaging the Economic Flywheel	42
CHAPTER 5	The Floodgates Open	62
CHAPTER 6	Wrestling with Growth	80
CHAPTER 7	Negotiating Depression and War	96
CHAPTER 8	Old Waterfront, New Ships	114
CHAPTER 9	Creating a Destination	128
CHAPTER 10	Envisioning a Waterfront for All	148
CHAPTER 11	Becoming a Waterfront for All	170
ACKNOWLEDGMENTS		196
CREDITS		197
SELECTED SOURCES		201
INDEX		204

Introduction

ON FEBRUARY 28, 2001, a 30-second earthquake measuring 6.8 on the Richter scale rocked the city of Seattle. On the central waterfront, it rattled the Alaskan Way Viaduct carrying cars on its elevated decks. It jolted the Alaskan Way seawall running the entire length of the central waterfront and holding Elliott Bay back from hundreds of acres of filled land along the shoreline. It jangled the nerves of the hundreds of thousands of people who drove on the Viaduct each day and the engineers who knew its weaknesses. Had the quake originated closer to the surface, it would have been catastrophic, and the near miss left many feeling even more apprehensive about the "big one" that is inevitably going to rupture along the region's seismic fault lines.

When the immediate danger passed, Seattle had an infrastructure emergency. The earthquake, soon named "Nisqually" after its epicenter location 30 miles under the Nisqually River delta just north of Olympia, left the Viaduct and the seawall structures compromised and at risk of failure if even a small subsequent quake hit. If those structures failed, the consequences would ripple out through the region. The ground west of Western Avenue would be washed away in just a few tides, destroying the city streets and leaving buildings and the Alaskan Way Viaduct teetering on their pile foundations, if standing at all. A key piece of the region's transportation network, the Viaduct, would be rendered unusable. The busiest Washington State Ferries dock would be out of commission. The electrical

View of the old Alaskan Way Viaduct looking south with demolition just starting, 2019.

grid and communications networks would be disrupted throughout the Northwest. And many lives could be lost.

The situation demanded a swift response, and city and state agencies took immediate action to shore up the structures. But those were temporary solutions at best. Less than a minute of shaking had created large, expensive, and urgent problems. Seattle is not known for its rapid decision-making, however, and fixing the beloved but neglected central waterfront would take stamina; herculean feats of public organizing, engineering, and problem-solving; and a little arm-twisting and back-room dealing.

Twenty-four years after the Nisqually earthquake, the stretch of shoreline from King Street to the Olympic Sculpture Park has been entirely remade and a new iteration of Seattle's central waterfront is emerging. The Viaduct is gone and Alaskan Way realigned, a new seawall provides a solid foundation and a new "highway" for salmon, Waterfront Park offers a swath of new public spaces where people can gather and play, Overlook Walk bridges the steep hillside that separates the shoreline from Pike Place Market, newly rebuilt Colman Dock reconnects the ferry dock with the streetscape, Pioneer Square Habitat Beach returns an intertidal zone to the city's front porch, and redesigned streets reconnect Pioneer Square to the water.

This newest iteration of the central waterfront is a culmination more than a reinvention. It is a product of all that came before, and it makes space for people and stories that have been historically excluded. Street signs along Alaskan Way and Elliott Way, from Dearborn Street to Bell Street, mark the Indigenous name for the area, dᶻidᶻəlalič (often Anglicized as Dzidzilalich). For the first time, non-Natives have officially recognized Coast Salish people's presence on the waterfront. The original shoreline is marked with pavers in the streets in Pioneer Square. The former work of the waterfront—cargo handling, fishing, transporting people, and industry—is visible in the loading docks preserved along Alaskan Way, the transit sheds on the piers, the ferry terminal at Colman Dock, and the interpretive signs and art works found throughout the new park.

The variety of stories gives a sense of the complex history of the waterfront. Each era has left a legacy that shapes how people know and experience the shoreline today.

The variety of stories gives a sense of the complex history of the waterfront. Each era has left a legacy that shapes how people know and experience the shoreline today. Glaciers, mudflows, earthquakes, and erosion created hills, a river valley, and the bay. The Coast Salish people, the ancestors of the Duwamish, Muckleshoot, Suquamish, Snoqualmie, Tulalip, and other tribes, developed deep relationships with the land and other elements of the non-human world that continue today. The Indigenous people shaped the landscape the non-Natives experienced when they first arrived in the 1850s and have remained part of the social and cultural fabric of the region.

The non-Native settlers that came to build a city radically and rapidly reshaped the entire waterfront. First, they created a port town with a wharf for sailing ships. As the ships grew in size and number, the waterfront grew, with new piers crowding the shoreline and train trestles covering the tidelands. Seawalls made it possible to create dry, level ground where there had been a sloped beach.

In the midst of constant earthworks and construction, the people who lived, worked, and traveled through the waterfront shaped the culture of the neighborhood. Longshoremen, steamer captains, ships' crews, shipping companies and fisheries supplies, labor and racial unrest, immigration, and daily and seasonal ebb and flow of ship passengers brought people from a wide range of backgrounds together. The city grew up around this nucleus of activity and its influence was felt in the business district, the neighborhoods where waterfront workers lived, and in the news media that reported on the comings and goings of the ships and cargo moving through the port. One of Seattle's most famous restauranteurs, Ivar Haglund, built his image by crooning songs about "acres

View looking south down Alaskan Way during the final stages of construction on the new waterfront, 2024.

of clams" and carting a pet seal around town in a baby carriage. The waterfront was busy, noisy, and rough, but for a century, it was the center of the city's economy and identity. As that importance faded after World War II, Seattleites began to envision its future.

When the ships outgrew the central waterfront, leaving the piers underutilized, state highway planners took advantage of the newly available space to build an elevated freeway and the long process of repurposing the piers and the enormous pier sheds began. But comprehensive solutions to waterfront redevelopment failed in the face of high costs and seemingly insurmountable disadvantages like car and train traffic, and the steep bluff rising up from Western Avenue north of Seneca Street.

The story of the Seattle waterfront is the story of welcoming and excluding, upheaval and transformation, renovation and reinvention. Part of the story is about bringing people together and building community. But another part is about dividing people, often by race, sometimes by class, and ruining lives and communities. That complex history is deeply embedded in the collective consciousness of the people who live here. Even when no longer visible, as in the case of dᶻidᶻəlaľič, or when functionally obsolete, like the piers' enormous transit sheds, the story remains vital to the city's sense of place.

When the opportunity arose after the 2001 earthquake for a wholesale reallocation of space on the strip of land where the city meets the sea, high costs, competing visions, and conflicting priorities led to a prolonged debate over the future of the waterfront. How much history to preserve? How to protect the environment effectively? How to bring Indigenous people into the conversation when they had been excluded for more than a century? How much to invest? What was too idealistic? Too conservative?

After more than two decades, decisions have been made and dust has settled. Seattle's central waterfront has been transformed. The threads of the future will now be woven into the fabric of the past.

CHAPTER 1

Becoming dᶻidᶻəlal'ič

The land was low, at extreme high tide the salt waters sometimes ran across the bay to the marsh behind. . . . Back of the marsh on the beach was an (I)ndian camp and a small stream of fresh water came down the hill. . . . At low tide the canoes were hauled on shore and the Indians crossed over on foot . . . the waves having thrown up a gravelly beach somewhat higher than the marsh leaving always a dry trail.

— DAVID KELLOGG, "THE MAKING OF A MEDICINE MAN"

Contemporary Puget Sound shore wetlands flora not far from Elliott Bay.

ELLIOTT BAY'S ORIGIN story is full of grinding ice, flowing water, erupting volcanoes, crashing lahars, and unending cycles of erosion and deposition. The scale of earth moving is nearly incomprehensible. Throughout the history of this region, geological forces have caused massive disruptions and the people living here have adapted to them, relying on deep networks of relationships across the region for stability. Native people who have lived on the bay and surrounding lakes and rivers embody the continuing cycles of disruption and adaption in stories of dukʷibəł, the Transformer, who shaped the landscape and created the plants, animals, and humans we know today. The stories help convey how this place "works," how it changes but remains the same. Change doesn't necessarily represent loss; it can simply be a transformation.

The collision of continental plates and repeated glaciations were followed by volcanic eruptions out of Təqʷuʔməʔ (Mt. Rainier) and massive mudflows known as lahars. The watershed's rivers then carried the debris downstream, slowly filling in the Green and Duwamish River valleys' floors and pushing the southern extent of saltwater northward over thousands of years. By about 1,000 years ago, the mouth of the river reached the present shoreline on Elliott Bay and the region's geography looked much as it does today.

While the Duwamish River's mouth is roughly in the same location today, nearly everything else about Elliott Bay's shoreline has been altered since the 1850s. Prior to non-Native settlement, an enormous estuary with a small delta riven with channels extended across the southern portion of the bay. Thousands of acres of tideflats wrapped around the southeastern lobe of the bay along the base of Beacon Hill. Shallow water extended northwestward from the river mouth, along the eastern flank of the Duwamish Head. In the middle of the bay, the seafloor plunged to depths of 600 feet. On

In this DNR map of the Puget Sound region showing the extent of the ice sheet, the approximate areas of greatest water embayment after the ice age are visible in dark blue-green. These areas were slowly filled over time.

A massive ice sheet covered what is now the city of Seattle to a depth of over 3,000 feet and shaped the diverse topography we see today.

THE STORY OF SEATTLE'S WATERFRONT 11

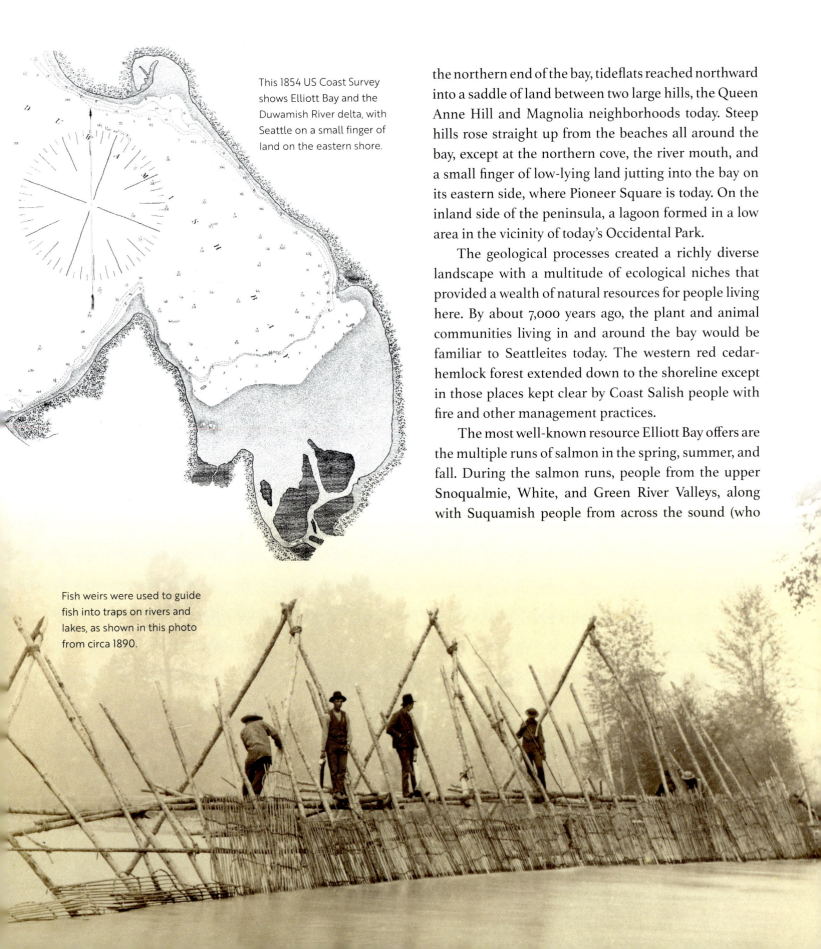

This 1854 US Coast Survey shows Elliott Bay and the Duwamish River delta, with Seattle on a small finger of land on the eastern shore.

Fish weirs were used to guide fish into traps on rivers and lakes, as shown in this photo from circa 1890.

the northern end of the bay, tideflats reached northward into a saddle of land between two large hills, the Queen Anne Hill and Magnolia neighborhoods today. Steep hills rose straight up from the beaches all around the bay, except at the northern cove, the river mouth, and a small finger of low-lying land jutting into the bay on its eastern side, where Pioneer Square is today. On the inland side of the peninsula, a lagoon formed in a low area in the vicinity of today's Occidental Park.

The geological processes created a richly diverse landscape with a multitude of ecological niches that provided a wealth of natural resources for people living here. By about 7,000 years ago, the plant and animal communities living in and around the bay would be familiar to Seattleites today. The western red cedar–hemlock forest extended down to the shoreline except in those places kept clear by Coast Salish people with fire and other management practices.

The most well-known resource Elliott Bay offers are the multiple runs of salmon in the spring, summer, and fall. During the salmon runs, people from the upper Snoqualmie, White, and Green River Valleys, along with Suquamish people from across the sound (who

The geological processes created a richly diverse landscape with a multitude of ecological niches that provided a wealth of natural resources for people living here. By about 7,000 years ago, the plant and animal communities living in and around the bay would be familiar to Seattleites today.

did not have a large river or lake within their traditional territories) came to Elliott Bay to fish. Through family and trade relationships, they could be incorporated into the cooperative fishing efforts managed by Duwamish families. Many of these relationships and fishing practices continue today.

Those runs provided food security for the Coast Salish people in their abundance. Salmon could be smoked or dried and preserved for the long winter months. That reliable bounty allowed local villages to be fairly large relative to Indigenous communities in other parts of North America.

Over thousands of years Coast Salish people living on the bay shaped the plant and animal communities with fire, cultivation, selective harvesting, hunting, and fishing. They also developed social networks and spiritual practices that helped them sustainably manage the seasonal abundance, and relationships dictated salmon fishing locations and practices. Likewise, family-based connections to berry patches, or cattail and grass stands, facilitated cooperation in harvesting resources as they ripened or matured. The interconnectedness of the region's communities provided security in the event of local scarcity.

Over the millennia, Native people living around Elliott Bay have developed deep knowledge of and relationships with the plants and animals found

LUSHOOTSEED

Lushootseed is the traditional language of the Coast Salish people who live in the Seattle area. Place names are written in the Lushootseed orthography utilized by the Waterlines Project Map. Dzidzilalich, seen on street signs on the waterfront, is an Anglicization of the Lushootseed spelling dᶻidᶻəlal'ič [pronounced: dzee-dzuh-lahl-litch] and can be translated as "Little Crossing-Over Place."

PLANT AND ANIMAL RESOURCES ON ELLIOTT BAY

The area around Elliott Bay once offered a richness of habitats that is hard to fathom given the simplification that has come with urbanization. Forests, tidelands, estuaries, nearshore and deep water, river, and prairies. From the largest elk to the smallest mussel, towering western red cedar to trailing blackberry, every kind of plant and animal could find a niche and thrive. The Duwamish people who lived here developed a complex understanding of and deep relationships with the non-human world over thousands of years. Archeologist Lynn Larson explored the range of plants and animals that made this such a remarkable place for the Duwamish people who lived here and their more distant friends and relations in her study *Traditional and Historic Use of the Seattle Waterfront by Muckleshoot Indian Tribe Ancestors*.

There were the more well-known delicacies, such as clams, crabs, salmon, and cod that flourished in the vast tideflats and bay. But the freshwater, saltwater, beaches, and uplands supported a plentitude of other species. The marshes upriver from the river mouth teemed with waterfowl, including ducks and geese. Under the sand, four kinds of clams—butter, Venus, littleneck and horse—basket cockles, and moon snails could be easily gathered with specialized digging sticks and put into large loosely woven baskets that allowed water to drain. Mussels, oysters, barnacles, and frilled dog winkles covered the rocks. In the waters, there were too many fish species to count, including dogfish, smelt, halibut, herring, and three kinds of perch as well as wolf eels, harbor seals, and octopus.

The shoreline was dominated by thick forests with hemlock, Douglas fir, western red cedar, big leaf maple, and alder trees in their overstories, and vine maple and dogwood below them. Salal, mushrooms, native blackberries, red currant, Oregon grapes, salmonberry, and several species of ferns formed a thick, rich understory. Interspersed with the forest, several large prairies provided

Coast Salish basketmaker, circa 1900.

Larson catalogued myriad uses for trees:

Cedar	**Maples**	**Fir**
housing materials	ladles	fuel
canoes	platters	harpoons
clothing	mat smoothers and creasers	salmon spears
baskets	combs	dipnet handles
mats	spearheads for hunting fish and duck	poles for fish weirs
diapers	fish clubs	cradleboard
sails	tools	tump lines

habitat for plants needing more sunlight, such as camas and some berries. In marshy areas, cranberry plants grew. These plants produced delicious food and provided medicines.

Like fish and shellfish, plant species are too numerous to list, as were their uses, which ranged from soaps and arrow shafts to cooking tools, cough medicine, and fish nets. Plant species also provided a multitude of foods that could be paired with the game animals living on the prairies and in the forests, including elk deer, bear, and cougars. Small animals, such as squirrels, skunks, and rabbits abounded then as they do today. Birds, including pheasants and ruffed grouse, could be roasted and eaten, along with their eggs, while their feathers were valued for their beauty.

Beyond their usefulness, plants and animals brought a spiritual richness to life on Elliott Bay. Duwamish people developed deep relationships with the non-human world over the millennia they lived at West Point, on the rivers, at dᶻidᶻəlal'ič, and at babaqʷəb. They cultivated plants and shellfish beds and developed hunting and fishing practices that ensured enough food for everyone while maintaining healthy animal populations.

One significant aspect of the redevelopment of the central waterfront has been the recognition by non-Natives of Native people's continuing relationships to dᶻidᶻəlal'ič and other area villages, which is maintained through fishing on Elliott Bay, activities and events held on the waterfront, and personal connections to the shoreline and uplands.

Duwamish adze with iron blade, collected in Seattle, 1920.

there. They have passed that knowledge and connection down to younger generations through storytelling and spiritual practices. In the precontact era, the knowledge was shared while wintering in permanent villages on the shores of Puget Sound, area rivers, and lakes. Each year, after spending much of the spring, summer, and fall traveling to hunt, gather plant materials, trade, and visit relations, the families who lived on Elliott Bay returned to the villages that encircled the harbor.

Just outside the bay, there was likely a village on the prairie at Alki Point. Muckleshoot tribal elders remember going there into the 1920s. Other winter villages in the surrounding area were located at Shilshole Bay where the Ballard Locks are today, šilšul; two along the Black River around Renton, both called sq̓ʷuʔalq̓ʷuʔ; and sluʔqiɬ, near today's Ravenna Park, at the former northern extent of Union Bay.

Duwamish anchor made of wood and stone, photographed in 1903.

One of the reasons winter villages were located on waterways was the ease of travel by canoe around the region. In a landscape of thickly forested hills and marshy lowlands, travel by water was infinitely easier. Canoes could be paddled up to beaches, pulled up onto shore, and stored above the tide line. The more challenging topography could be bypassed entirely by traveling on the relatively placid rivers and lakes.

The Coast Salish had several types of canoes, each designed for specific uses and types of waterways. The largest canoes, Nootka, were used for moving large numbers of people and quantities of goods over long distances on open water like Puget Sound or the Pacific Ocean. Salish canoes were smaller but also used for carrying people and

THE STORY OF SEATTLE'S WATERFRONT 15

cargo on larger water bodies such as the Sound and Lake Washington. Shovel-nosed canoes could move easily on rivers and smaller lakes, allowing paddlers to fish and hunt waterfowl.

Dᶻidᶻəlaličʼ, which can be translated as "Little Crossing-Over Place," was especially well-situated between saltwater and freshwater, in a harbor at the foot of several routes into the interior. A trail led over the hills to Lake Washington. Canoes could be left at either end for later use. A chain of waterways, from Lake Washington to the Sammamish Slough to Lake Sammamish, led to the foot of the Cascade Mountains and the hunting and gathering grounds found there, along with spiritually significant places. Lake Sammamish also provided access to the Snoqualmie River valley that offered routes to the upper elevations of the Cascades on that river's forks and up the Skykomish River towards today's Stevens Pass. From the Duwamish River, the Black and Green Rivers provided easy routes to the Cascade foothills and Təqʷuʔməʔ. The waterways also connected the Duwamish to a trade network extending up to Alaska and out to the outer coast.

Non-Natives arriving after the 1850s radically altered this landscape and the human communities that were deeply intertwined with it. Despite that, tribal members today retain their connection to dᶻidᶻəlaličʼ. It co-exists with Seattle. The Indigenous people who lived there are remembered and honored; the tribal communities' connection to place is maintained, along with its role in their collective and personal identities. Muckleshoot Indian Tribe Historian Warren King George explained,

> "One of the things that I truly believe in my heart, one of the things I value the most about our history and culture is, that no matter how much impervious surface is created, no matter how big of a skyscraper is built, it doesn't erase, it doesn't take away any of the culture, any of the history, any of our tie, . . . it doesn't impede any of our cultural rhizomes, they still grow there. They're there. There is nothing that modern society can do to cover that up, sweep it, or burn. Our ties to . . . dᶻidᶻəlaličʼ [Dzidzilalich] . . . are true and strong. There's nothing that's going to extinguish that memory, that connection, it's never going to be severed. Now we've been displaced all the way thirty miles up, as the crows fly, thirty miles from sdzidzelʔaličʼ, and I still feel that I belong there. There is a presence there. . . . It provides me an opportunity for continuity, it gives me that sense of belonging, like a refreshment. Like when you get thirsty, you have a glass of water. Well, if I need to add a growth ring, I need to go to Seattle. I need to go, just to be. There's lots of things to do in Seattle. One of the things is to be able to experience that area, the same way my ancestors did."

The tribes' understanding of how this place works and how humans can live here in relationship with the non-human world has been carried forward across the generations and, after nearly two centuries of disregard and repression, it is now being recognized by non-Natives as key to charting a sustainable path forward for human and non-human life on Elliott Bay.

Top: Salmon or sealing canoe showing sections carved separately and then joined together.

Bottom: Nootka-type sealing canoe line drawing adapted from Makah carver Greg Colfax by naval architect James Cole.

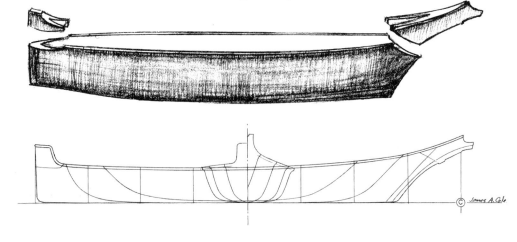

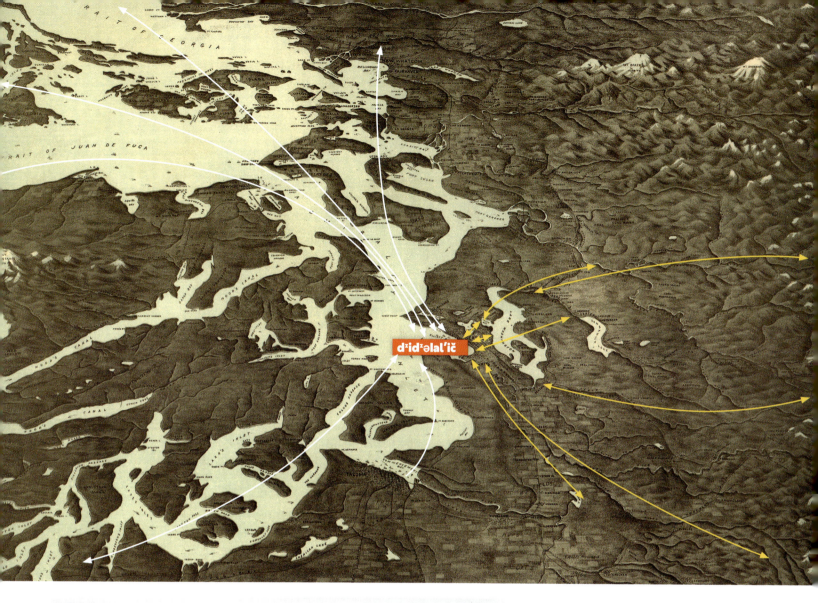

Above: Water and overland trade routes to and from dᶻidᶻəlaliʼč, overlayed on Charles Baker's 1891 bird's-eye view of Puget Sound.

Left: Indigenous people from around the region often came to Elliott Bay in oceangoing canoes to visit, trade, and, after non-Native settlement, work. This woman, likely from British Columbia, was photographed on the Seattle waterfront in 1898.

THE STORY OF SEATTLE'S WATERFRONT **17**

CHAPTER 2

Becoming Seattle

"I came to the coast impressed with the belief that a railroad would be built across the continent to some point on the northern coast within the next fifteen or twenty years, and located on the Sound with that expectation."

—ARTHUR DENNY

THE REMARKABLE NATURAL WEALTH of the Puget Sound region attracted attention from non-Native people looking to expand European and American empires beginning in the 1790s. They nosed their ships into Puget Sound and explored what its waters and lands could offer. Over the late eighteenth and early nineteenth centuries, the fur trade drew non-Natives to the Sound, but the colonists shifted away from pelts to the many other natural resources that could be extracted from the region and sold around the globe by the 1850s. As that trade developed, so did a new town on Elliott Bay. Almost immediately, the new arrivals began to reshape the landscape and the waterways to meet the needs of new technology and a new economy. They added a new layer on top of the geology and the Native peoples' imprints, one that adapted the place to new technology—sailing ships and steam sawmills, and a new ideology—capitalism. The shoreline development was chaotic and ad hoc, with very little

Painting by unknown artist showing Seattle's waterfront in 1874.

capital and hardly enough workers to realize the town's enormous potential.

The first non-Natives to take a close look at Elliott Bay came in the 1840s as the British and Americans competed to gain permanent possession of the lands north of the Columbia River. The Americans sent the United States Exploring Expedition to survey Puget Sound under the leadership of Captain Charles Wilkes. In 1841, he and his crew assessed the potential of each of its harbors, taking soundings to determine water depths, noting their utility for ships and cargo handling, and sometimes giving them English names, as he did with Elliott Bay. He describes the harbor in his report:

> *"The anchorage is of comparatively small extent, owing to the great depth of water, as well as to the extensive mud-flats; these are bare at low water. Three small streams enter at the head of the bay, where good water may be obtained. I do not consider the bay a desirable anchorage; from the west it is exposed to the prevailing winds, and during their strength there is much sea."*

The expedition report includes a detailed map of the harbor, with soundings recorded. It appears to be a blank slate, ready for development, with none of the existing Duwamish villages on the bay or river marked on the map.

Detail from US Coast Survey map of "Duwamish Bay," 1879.

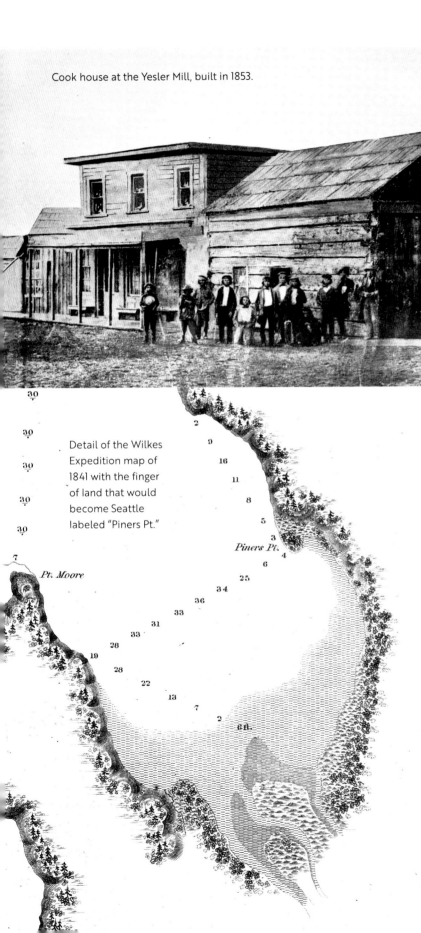

Cook house at the Yesler Mill, built in 1853.

Detail of the Wilkes Expedition map of 1841 with the finger of land that would become Seattle labeled "Piners Pt."

The Americans won control of Oregon Territory from Great Britain in 1848, but several years passed before any colonists gave Elliott Bay a closer look. Drawn north by a chance encounter on the Oregon Trail with someone who had visited Puget Sound, a group of Americans traveling on the *Exact* from Olympia landed at Alki Point on November 13, 1851. The members of the Denny Party, as they have been known since, were the Arthur and Mary Ann Denny family, the John and Lydia Low family, the Carson and Mary Boren family, the William and Sarah Bell family, Louisa Boren, David T. Denny, and brothers Charles and Lee Terry. They had been propelled westward by the promise of free land under the Oregon Donation Land Act of 1850, which granted 320 acres to adult American citizens, and 640 acres to married couples, provided they lived on their claims for four consecutive years.

The Denny Party, like other early non-Native settlers, did not let the fact that the land had not yet been ceded by Native people through treaties with the federal government slow their efforts to claim Elliott Bay and its surrounding land. In fact, their inability to register legal claims until the treaties were signed worked to their advantage because it allowed them to adjust their property lines twice over the next couple of years as they located the best townsite and incorporated the later arrivals of Henry Yesler (who brought the first steam-powered sawmill to Puget Sound) and David "Doc" Maynard.

Although the Denny Party initially landed at Alki Point, they soon moved across to the more protected side of the bay, which also had better access to deep water, where sailing ships could approach the shore. The site they claimed overlaid dᶻidᶻəlaľič. While it is often asserted in written histories that the village was largely deserted in 1852 due to the impact of introduced diseases, a reminiscence by B. F. Shaw printed in a 1904 newspaper describes his visit to the bay in 1850: "On seeing an Indian village located on a large sand spit, which was alive with moving Indians, we ran in and landed. In less than a minute after our boat touched the sand, out they all came and rushed down to the beach."

The Coast Salish people living in the region were deeply involved in the new settlement and its economy from the beginnings of Seattle as a non-Native town. Duwamish people continued to live in their village area on the point of land alongside the saltwater lagoon. They worked alongside Doc Maynard to cut down trees and split it into firewood, fish for salmon and salt it to preserve it for transport to California, and to make barrels. When Yesler established his mill in 1853, Native men helped operate it.

Native people also did a variety of other jobs that supported the new town's establishment. The men provided transportation and made deliveries to outlying settlements with their canoes. Women worked in town where they provided domestic help and sold berries, fish, and other foods, including potatoes. Potatoes had been introduced by the Hudson's Bay Company and were readily adopted, likely because of their similarities in their cultivation, preparation, and nutritional value to a traditional food, camas.

Wage labor and trade with newcomers were compatible with Native people's existing seasonal movements and offered opportunities for Native people to expand their networks of relationships. As historian Vera Parham has explained, "For American Indians, acquiring rights to land and resources as well as wealth through trade was a powerful goal in life, similar to the goals of the new immigrants, though the reasons for acquisition were generally to represent spiritual powers and social status, not for capitalist gain."

Beyond their labor and trade relationships, Native people ensured the success of the new settlement

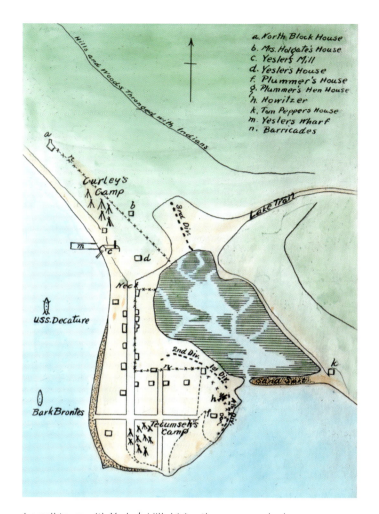

A small town, with Yesler's Mill driving the economy, had grown up adjacent to the Duwamish longhouses on the point by the 1850s.

by sharing their knowledge with the newcomers. As historian Linda Nash noted, "They learned from Natives which berries to eat, which to avoid, and where to find them. They followed Native trails, mimicked Native material practices, learned from them about the better fishing spots and edible plants, and relied on Natives to canoe them up rivers."

In 1852, the Denny party at Alki sold a load of logs to the captain of the *Leonesa,* bringing in some welcome cash into the local economy. Yesler's Mill offered an opportunity for lumber, a value-added product, to be sent to San Francisco and other markets. When it began operating, Olympia's *Columbian* newspaper exclaimed,

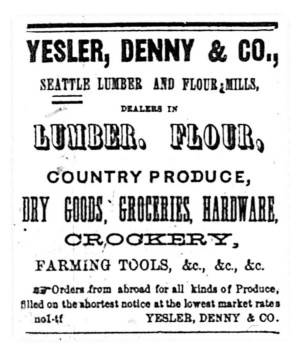

Advertisement for Yesler, Denny & Co., *The Seattle Gazette*, 1864.

"Huzza for Seattle! It would be folly to suppose that the mill will not prove as good as a gold mine to Mr. Yesler, besides tending greatly to improve the fine town-site of Seattle, and the fertile country around it, but attracting thither the farmer, the laborer, and the capitalist. On with the improvements! We hope to hear of scores of others ere long."

The mill was located on the shoreline in the middle of town—near where Yesler Way and First Avenue meet today. The adjacent harbor was essential to its functioning. First and foremost, the harbor allowed Yesler to load lumber onto sailing ships. This was important because, as Daniel Jack Chasan has pointed out in his history of Puget Sound, *The Water Link*, "no one within 500 miles of Seattle needed trees" in those years. Lumber could only be sold in more distant markets like San Francisco.

In addition to allowing ships to get reasonably close to the mill, the bay also provided an effective way to get logs to the mill once the area immediately around it was logged off. All around Puget Sound, hills rising from the shoreline made it possible to roll or drag logs

This 1878 Peterson Bros. photograph taken from Yesler's Wharf looking northeast shows some of the bluffs and steep terrain that rose up directly from the tidelands.

downhill to the water and float them to the foot of Mill Street. Yesler held them adjacent to his wharf until he was ready to pull them into the mill.

Very quickly, the newcomers began to reshape the landscape with their activities. The shoreline and interior lagoon provided handy locations for dumping sawdust. As Yesler dumped the refuse from the mill, and others in town added their garbage, the shallow areas became "made land." This effect was accelerated by the dropping of ballast around the wharf, which was both convenient for the ship captains and helpful for filling in the shoreline. With fewer than 200 non-Native people in Seattle, and just a few thousand around the Sound, there was not much market for imports and no railroads connecting the port to distant cities. Instead, ships filled their holds with enough rocks to maintain stability before leaving their home ports then dumped that ballast in Elliott Bay before loading lumber from the mill.

Most of the shoreline on the central waterfront where ships could get closest to shore ran up against steep bluffs, leaving little dry land for industry or commerce. When the settlers began to "make land"

> Very quickly, the newcomers began to reshape the landscape with their activities. The shoreline and interior lagoon provided handy locations for dumping sawdust. As Yesler dumped the refuse from the mill, and others in town added their garbage, the shallow areas became "made land."

THE STORY OF SEATTLE'S WATERFRONT 23

Three ships moored at Yesler's Wharf in 1875 (left to right): side-wheel steamer *Pacific*, steamship SS *Salvador*, and bark *Harriet Hunt*.

with the sawdust and ballast fill, they were creating much-needed level land adjacent to the deep-water part of the harbor. In other parts of the bay, tidelands separated the shore from deep water. Just north of Yesler's Mill, the hill rose up, making water access difficult. South of what would become King Street, the tideflats hemmed in development.

Over time, Yesler's Wharf grew wider and an extension branched off to the northwest. Buildings lined its sides. Some housed water-dependent businesses, but not all. Some just needed space to operate once the lots on the limited, solid, level ground filled up. The wharf's sprawl was the beginning of a network of streets constructed out of wood planks on pilings with buildings built on piling foundations elevating them over the tidelands. In time, the trestles, pilings, and planking would support the entire waterfront west of Western and Elliott Avenues, from King Street to Bay Street.

Beginning in November 1853, Seattle had regular steamer service, with a terminal at the outer end of Yesler's Wharf. The *Fairy* operated by Captain D. J. Gove, ran weekly between Olympia, Steilacoom, Alki, and Seattle. Steam-powered vessels had been on the Sound since the 1830s when the British Hudson's Bay Company brought the *Beaver* to the Northwest to carry goods and people between their forts, including Fort Steilacoom, near the company's large farm on the south Sound. The *Fairy* and other small steamers that followed in the 1850s allowed American settlers to move around the region more quickly and reliably. Over the next several decades, more of these steamers would operate on the Sound and launch what became known as the Mosquito Fleet—a veritable swarm of small steamers that moved people and goods around the region.

With the establishment of Washington Territory in 1853, came a territorial governor, Isaac I. Stevens. His two most pressing tasks were locating a northern route for a transcontinental railroad to connect Puget Sound with the East Coast, which he did while enroute to his new post, and securing treaties with Northwest tribes. The treaties would resolve property ownership and allow settlers to file claims legally. In the Treaty of Point Elliott, signed

Log booms next to Yesler's Wharf (left), circa 1888.

with multiple tribes at a gathering near Mukilteo in 1855, Duwamish tribal leaders ceded the lands around Elliott Bay. The treaty included provisions for tribes to have continued access to their "usual and accustomed" places for hunting, fishing, and gathering, a key element in their ability to maintain their traditional ways of life. However, it also required that they live on reservations.

What had been an accommodating arrangement between the Duwamish and non-Native settlers on Elliott Bay became an armed conflict when the stark terms of ownership and removal were laid down on paper. Where the Duwamish had made room for settlements, the Americans moved to displace the tribes and block their use of dᶻidᶻəlalʼič and other villages around the bay. This, coupled with settlers' violence against Native women, led to the outbreak of the Treaty War on Puget Sound in 1855.

On January 26, 1856, Native people attacked Seattle from the woods above the town. Having been forewarned by other violence in the region and alerted to the imminent danger by Native allies, Seattle's small population retreated to a fortified blockhouse they had built for protection. In a vivid example of historian Linda Nash's description of the non-Native settlers as "government-backed speculators," the US Navy ship *Decatur* anchored offshore on Elliott Bay and defended the settlement with its cannons, repelling the attack.

The war ended in the late summer, with changes to reservation locations and other concessions from Stevens. While Stevens intended for a complete removal of Native people from white settlements, their actual post-war movements were more complex and complicated. Some Duwamish moved to the Muckleshoot and Port Madison Reservations. Neither reservation was on their traditional lands, but many had family connections to those communities. Some stayed in the midst of Seattle into the 1890s. Siʼahł and another Duwamish leader, Suquardle, moved north to Belltown just after the war. Siʼahł would soon move across the water to the Suquamish Tribe's Port Madison Reservation, where he lived in the enormous longhouse on Agate Passage known as Old Man House. Some lived in cabins north of Pike Street. Quite a few remained involved in the town's economy, working for wages and trading or selling goods, and continuing to fish and to gather plants and shellfish on the parts of the tidelands not yet covered by piers or fill. When salmon were running in the bay, Duwamish and other Coast

Painting by Emily Inez Denny of the 1856 battle showing cannon fire from the *Decatur*.

Salish people erected temporary shelters on the beaches to smoke the fish.

After a lull in development following the war, Seattle's economy picked up again because it was one of the last American ports on the route north to Canada. When the Fraser River gold rush started in 1858, Americans came through Seattle on their way to and from British Columbia, bringing a burst of economic activity. As the population of the region increased, more goods started to come into the city, including food, clothing, tools, mining equipment, milling machinery, and the like. Seattle was becoming the region's market town. Moving people and goods across its docks was key to Seattle's future ambitions.

As Seattle grew, new people added texture to the fabric of the community. Without railroad connections or direct shipping service, most newcomers arrived from other West Coast ports, such as San Francisco or Portland. Or they made their way overland to Olympia, at the southern end of Puget Sound and then bought passage on a ship headed to Seattle. Some ships' crewmembers elected to stay in Seattle when their ship sailed, like Manuel Lopes, originally from the Ivory Coast. Lopes landed in Seattle in 1858, becoming the city's first Black settler. Others came from the East Coast, Midwest, and Europe.

Seattle's first direct connection to Asia and to all the potential trade and immigration associated with it, was Chen Cheong and his wife, Gin Come. They did not stay long, leaving behind just a record of their 1867 marriage and their portrait from that day. Not long after, Chun Ching Hock set up residence and a store, Wa Chong Company, near Yesler's Wharf, right in the thick of the business district. The Wa Chong store had goods from China and Chun Ching Hock augmented his import business with labor contracting. Through his contacts in San Francisco, he could find Chinese workers for Seattle employers who needed more hands to construct buildings, roads, and, eventually, railroads and canals. In a pattern that can be seen across the United States from the colonial era forward, the flywheel of capitalism

Chen Cheong, shown here in 1867 with his wife, Gin Come, was among the first Chinese merchants to shape the Chinese American community in Seattle.

Advertisement for the Wa Chong & Company store started by Chun Ching Hock in 1868.

couldn't get going without enough money and labor to power it. That has often meant reliance on an imported working class that can be exploited. In the South, that was African slavery. Across the West, because of the connection to China through Pacific Rim trade routes, it was Chinese laborers who built railroads.

In Seattle, there were not enough men in the area to build the infrastructure needed to support businesses that would attract trade and more settlers, like mining and sawmills. Businessmen turned to labor contractors like Wa Chong Company to supply low-wage workers. The Chinese workers would have preferred to work for equal wages, but once they were in the United States, white settlers' prejudices and discrimination undermined the Chinese workers' ability to demand them. It was difficult to refuse work and return to China from most West Coast ports, and essentially impossible from Seattle.

Before long, Chun Ching Hock had stores in other towns on Puget Sound, and inland as far west as Montana, where he sold imported goods and provided laborers. He and other Chinese labor contractors created the nuclei of Chinese immigrant communities in Northwest cities and towns over the latter half of the 19th century.

Seattle first incorporated in 1865. Although its population was only about 1,000, civic leaders had high hopes this outpost of the American empire would gain a reputation as a "real" American city, which would

THE STORY OF SEATTLE'S WATERFRONT   27

Woo Gen (left) and Chun Ching Hock (center with cane), Wa Chong Company, 406 Main Street, Seattle, circa 1905.

GENERAL STORES

One of the businesses on the wharf, a general store operated by Yesler, sold goods on commission for ship captains sailing back and forth between San Francisco regularly. The captains would sell from their ships while the ships were being loaded and then leave what supplies remained with Yesler to sell for them. This solved one of the biggest problems Seattleites faced in building an economy. They needed capital to prime the pump, but investing in enough goods to fully stock a store was a risky move in a town with little hard cash. Many of the settlers subsisted on their homesteads and invested any income they had on improvements to their homes and farms. The commissioned goods provided a stopgap method of getting money moving through the local economy.

encourage more emigration and immigration and cement its position as the Queen City of the Northwest. While fostering economic and political development, civic leaders also encouraged social development. Religious institutions, social clubs, and schools all helped recreate the mores of the Midwestern towns where many of the newcomers had come from. To cement that identity, the city's first leadership, the Board of Aldermen, passed Ordinance No. 5, which said

> "No Indian or Indians shall be permitted to reside, or locate their residences on any street, highway, lane, or alley or any vacant lot in the town of Seattle, from a point known as the South side of Chas. Plummer's ten-acre lot to a point known as the South side of Bell's land claim."

There is no evidence that the ordinance led to wholesale removal or exclusion of Native people, likely because that would have been impractical. Their knowledge of the region and their availability to work in forests, mills, and homes were essential to the functioning of the town. Regardless of its efficacy, the ordinance marks the first formal attempt to exclude Native people from dᶻidᶻəlaĺič and erase the village from the shoreline.

Seattle's city government dissolved in 1867. When it reincorporated in 1869, the new city council did not pass a similar law. It is hard to say if that is because the residents felt more secure in their town's American identity, or because many Native people had moved to the edges, north to babaqʷb, or to the south bay and river villages and so seemed less threatening to the white settlers. It is clear, however, that white settlers still needed Native people's labor to propel the economy forward. In 1878, the *Puget Sound Argus* ran an editorial that read

> "A proposition . . . is suggested by the Seattle 'Dispatch' [Puget Sound Dispatch] to send the coast Indians to Alaska. We would ask why move them at all, particularly the Indians about Puget Sound? They are becoming more useful to white people every year; and now that canneries are

commencing to be established on the Sound these Indians can be of great use."

During the 1860s, Yesler's Mill and associated operations remained the economic driver for Seattle. Yesler partnered with businessmen from San Francisco, Seattle's largest lumber market, who supplied capital for him to expand the mill with a new top saw to increase capacity from 10,000 to 15,000 board feet per day. He also added a gristmill to grind grain and continued to operate the wharf. In 1869, he rebuilt the mill again and increased its capacity to 20,000 board feet per day—enough lumber to build three small houses.

Demand for coal soared as steamships, factories, and the post-Gold Rush population boom in San Francisco all increased demand for power to run machinery and engines and heat homes. Coalfields lay relatively close to the port, as the crow flies, but quite distant via waterways. In 1862, Lyman B. Andrews tried to bring coal into the city from where Issaquah is now. He carried it to Lake Sammamish then loaded it on a scow and traversed the lake to the slough at its outlet, then down the length of Lake Washington, and over the hill into town. He didn't even try to use the Duwamish River, with its shifting shoals and strong tidal influence that could leave boats and barges stranded at low tide. Heavy forests, steep hills, and other obstacles made an entirely overland route from the foothills infeasible.

The next year, Philip H. Lewis and Edwin Richardson found coal significantly closer to Seattle at what is now known as Coal Creek, near Renton. A group of Seattleites formed the Lake Washington Coal Company in 1866 to develop the mine. They tried using mules to carry it overland to the port, with minimal success. In 1870, the company reorganized as the Seattle Coal & Transportation Company and invested in a hybrid tram-scow-railroad route to the city. A wooden tramway from the mine carried coal cars down to the lakeshore where they were loaded onto a scow. A steamer then pulled the scow north to the Montlake Isthmus, where they pulled the coal cars across the narrow strip of land to another scow on Lake Union, where another steamer pulled it to

Ordinance No. 5, passed shortly after the city of Seattle's first incorporation, was a formal attempt to exclude Native people from dᶻidᶻalalʼič.

THE STORY OF SEATTLE'S WATERFRONT **29**

This detail of the 1878 bird's-eye view map shows the growth of the businesses on Yesler's Wharf.

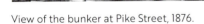

View of the bunker at Pike Street, 1876.

Saloon on Yesler's Wharf, 1872.

the south end of the lake. There, a locomotive hooked up to the cars and pulled them to a bunker built out from the bluff at Pike Street. Ships pulled up to the bunker and the coal dropped down into their holds.

The bunker was the first waterfront development north of Yesler because, in this case, the bluff adjacent to the shore was a benefit, not an impediment. Loading coal onto ships was still labor-intensive, however. It involved six men at the top to operate the chutes, four heavers in the hold who pushed the coal out to four coal pushers who dispersed it into the far edges of the hold. In 1870, according to Clarence Bagley's history of Seattle, the *Moneynick* sailed with the first load of coal from King County to San Francisco. By the end of the year, about 50 tons of coal per day were moving from the mines to the bunker.

A similar process took place at Yesler's Wharf with lumber handling, which required skilled workers to ensure that every available space on each ship was filled with lumber and that the weight was evenly distributed. Usually, a ship's crew loaded a ship under a local stevedore's supervision. Millworkers delivered the lumber to the pier by handcart. The crew loaded it into slings, which were hoisted over the deck and lowered into the hold. Spars or poles were lashed to the deck. For a coastwise ship going to California, it took about two weeks to load the hold. For a larger, trans-Pacific ship, it could take two months to stow a load of lumber.

By the early 1870s, the area around Yesler's Wharf was filling with new structures. Oregon Steam Navigation began service on the *Wilson G. Hunt* to Seattle on its Olympia to Victoria, British Columbia, route. In October 1869, Bailey Gatzert opened a branch of the Walla Walla-based Schwabacher Brothers & Company on Commercial Street at Mill Street (today's First Avenue and Yesler Way). A cooper shop operated at the foot of Columbia. Craig & Hastings produce dealers worked out of the wharf at foot of Washington Street. One shipyard was at the foot of Cherry and another at the foot of University Streets. Saloons were tucked in all along the waterfront. Wharves and warehouses jutted out from Washington and King Streets. Wrapping around the point, on the northern edge of the tideflats, the Hall & Paulson and Stetson & Post mills sat at the foot of Commercial Street, Seattle Gas Light Co. was at the foot of King Street, and Mechanics' Mill was at the foot of Second. All of the businesses operated on top of pilings driven into the tideflats.

The town's economic momentum was growing, but it still lacked some key elements it needed to really hit its stride and become a port city. Chief among them was a railroad. Seattleites would spend the better part of two decades trying to land a transcontinental railroad terminus.

Seattle's first railroad hauled coal from Lake Union to the bunker at Pike Street, December 1871.

CHAPTER
3

In Search of a Transcontinental

"Not a few of those on the train had been residents of Seattle for twenty and twenty-five years, and the struggles and hopes and experiences of that time made the event of today one of mutual congratulation and sincerest joy."

—NEWSPAPER ACCOUNT OF FIRST RUN OF THE SEATTLE & WALLA WALLA RAILROAD ON MARCH 7, 1877

E.S. Glover's bird's-eye view of Seattle, 1878.

BY THE LATE 1860S, Seattle had a well-established maritime connection to San Francisco and a nascent trade relationship with Alaska and British Columbia, but it was still just one of numerous West Coast ports trying to dominant the Pacific Rim trade. The vast, sparsely populated area between the coastal towns and the Midwest and East Coast, and the absence of overland transportation more effective and reliable than oxen-drawn wagons, stymied development of local industry. Instead of handling manufactured goods, the ports generally served as depots for the transfer of their region's natural resource wealth to places where the lumber, coal, fish, and furs were needed. Over the 1870s and 1880s, Seattleites eagerly pursued a railroad connection to the East that would launch it as a hub of regional, national, and global maritime trade.

Civic leaders in Washington Territory's ports first looked to the Northern Pacific Railroad as their best hope. In 1869, the company renewed its efforts to build a railroad across the Great Plains and Rocky Mountains to a Pacific Northwest port that would provide a connection to Pacific Rim ports. Two parties set out from Minneapolis to review the route Isaac Stevens had identified in 1854. One party went to the Dakotas and eastern Montana while the other, led by Thomas Canfield, traveled to Washington. The Canfield Party included William G. Moorehead of railroad investor Jay Cooke & Company, Northern Pacific engineers William M. Roberts and William S. Johnson, and Samuel Wilkeson, a "writer of distinction employed by Jay Cooke & Co. to describe the route of the Northern Pacific Railroad."

Upon reaching Puget Sound in July, the Canfield Party assessed candidates for a western terminus. They had considered Portland, but the treacherous bar at the mouth of the Columbia River stood between its port and the ocean. Too many boats and lives had been lost to the unpredictable currents there, so they traveled on to Olympia and explored Puget Sound harbors for three days aboard the *Wilson G. Hunt*. The party was joined by Arthur Denny from Seattle and James Swan, an influential resident of Port Townsend. Swan had been in Washington territory since 1852 and was involved in admiralty law and development of maritime legislation, so he had some authority on shipping matters.

Behind the scenes, Swan offered to prepare a report for Canfield on each of the harbors and their relative suitability as a terminus location. Canfield accepted the offer, and Swan investigated the deficiencies and merits of Olympia, Nisqually, Steilacoom, Tacoma, Seattle, Point Elliott (Mukilteo), Holmes Harbor and Penn Cove (both on Whidbey Island), Bellingham,

Northern Pacific Railroad workers at a crossing of the Green River, 1885.

Fidalgo and Guemes Islands, Port Discovery on the Strait of Juan de Fuca, and Port Townsend. For each harbor, he catalogued the space available for anchorage and port facilities, access routes, shoreline development potential, assets for city building, such as freshwater resources, exposure to weather (primarily winter winds), and relative distance to mountain passes and the open ocean.

Not surprisingly, Swan recommended Port Townsend. But Canfield took the report and drew his own conclusions. He saw the benefits Seattle offered with its deep water and central location, but he also asked Swan to look further at Port Townsend, Whidbey Island, and

Bellingham. He had already decided the railroad would follow the Columbia River through eastern Washington Territory to Portland, which was far more established and offered immediate business to the railroad. Following that route also avoided most of the broad, arid, and sparsely populated expanse of central Washington. From Portland, the railroad would run a branch line north on the west side of the Cascades to Puget Sound until a more direct route across the Cascades could be built and the terminus fully developed.

In June 1872, the Northern Pacific asked Seattle and Tacoma to present offers to secure the terminus. Their deficiencies relative to the northern harbors were outweighed by their central location on Puget Sound. Both harbors would serve the railroad's needs equally well, so the railroad pitted them against each together to gain the best advantage. Seattle's residents pooled their resources and offered 7,500 town lots, an additional 3,000 acres of land, $50,000 in cash, $200,000 in bonds, and space on the central waterfront for its tracks and a passenger depot. White River farmers north of Tacoma sweetened the Seattle pitch by offering land in their valley for the railroad right-of-way. Tacoma offered to sell 1,200 acres of shoreline to the railroad at cost and options on 1,500 more, riparian rights to the tideflats, and proximity to 10,000 acres of level uplands.

On July 14, 1872, the Northern Pacific announced its choice of Tacoma for the terminus. Tacomans rejoiced. Seattleites gnashed their teeth in anger and frustration. The decision had hinged on several factors: Tacoma had fewer established local interests giving the Northern Pacific more freedom to shape the port to its advantage. It was also a more realistic option because of the railroad's never-ending financing issues, Congressional deadlines for opening the line, and the extra distance to Seattle from Portland.

In the end, it might have been in the long-term best interests for Seattle to have lost the initial battle for the terminus. Had they given all the assets in their offer and virtual control of the harbor to the Northern Pacific, the city's fortunes would have been more tightly tied to the somewhat shaky railroad. The limited space available on Seattle's central waterfront would have only amplified the railroad's power.

Seattleites did not wallow in their despair for long. Three days later they held a town meeting and re-pledged their original offer of land and money to build

Map showing the Seattle & Walla Walla rail line coming from the south. Also visible is the Seattle Coal Company route from Lake Union to Pike Street, 1874.

a railroad from Seattle to Wallula, on the Columbia River, via Snoqualmie Pass. There, the railroad would intersect with the Northern Pacific's main line, connecting to all points east. They issued stock in the Seattle & Walla Walla Railroad the next night, naming it for what was then the largest town in the territory. The following summer, a work party built twelve miles of railbed toward Renton. Given the limited pool of workers and the ongoing work of building the city and its economy, many residents found it challenging to devote days to work on the Seattle & Walla Walla so they hired Chinese workers who had recently worked on the Northern Pacific line. In a forewarning of the Chinese expulsions to come in the 1880s, some white workers attempted to run the Chinese off, but the sheriff stepped in to defend them.

A nationwide economic panic in 1873 put construction on hold as the economy contracted and capital dried up. As the hard times eased, activity in the port increased. The Seattle Coal and Transportation Company put a larger locomotive on the tracks between Lake Union and the bunkers in June 1875, increasing the average daily volume of coal to 100 tons. In mid-1875, Pacific Mail Steamship Company began regular service between Seattle and San Francisco.

Despite these boosts to the local economy, the Seattle & Walla Walla Railroad, Seattle's best chance at moving goods through the port, struggled to make any progress. James Colman, a businessman and waterfront property owner, saved the day by investing $20,000 in the railroad, inspiring others to contribute, and took over construction management. By early 1876, the railroad trestle extended south across the tideflats to the tracks laid after that first work party in 1874. In February 1877, the first trains carried coal from the mines at Coal Creek and Newcastle to a coal wharf with bunkers at the foot of King Street. The train began running just in the nick of time. Teredos

Ships moored at the King Street coal bunkers. Top: circa 1880. Bottom: circa 1890.

THE STORY OF SEATTLE'S WATERFRONT **35**

(shipworms) and gribbles (a wood-boring isopod) had eaten through the Pike Street bunkers' pilings and it collapsed on June 11, 1877. All coal handling moved to the Seattle & Walla Walla's bunkers.

In 1880, Henry Villard, who owned Oregon Steam Navigation Company and had recently gained control of the Northern Pacific, bought the Seattle & Walla Walla, changing its name to the Columbia & Puget Sound Railroad. The tracks extended to the Black Diamond mines in south King County by 1883, increasing the volume and quality of coal coming into

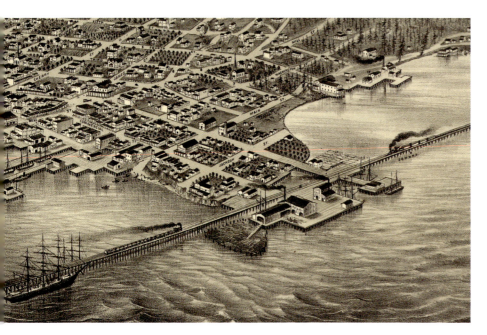

Detail of Glover's 1878 map showing the coal and lumber facilities at King Street.

Seattle for export. Villard promised to connect Seattle with the Northern Pacific in Pierce County, and the city council gave him the right-of-way on city-owned land along the shoreline. Villard had to negotiate with private property owners in his path, too, resulting in an oddly curved track alignment that earned it the nickname "the ram's horn."

In 1884, the Northern Pacific completed the Puget Sound Shore Railroad. It ran from a connection to the Northern Pacific's line just east of Puyallup, through the White and Duwamish River Valleys, then across the tideflats to King Street. Its economic impact was blunted by another recession that year which left the Puget Sound Shore in economic shambles and the rails unused.

In another attempt to get a transcontinental connection, Judge Thomas Burke and Daniel Gilman spearheaded construction of a new railroad coming into the waterfront from the north, through Interbay. The Seattle, Lake Shore & Eastern was intended to go around Lake Washington to Bothell and then south along Lake Sammamish to Issaquah and over Snoqualmie Pass, headed for points east. It needed pier access, but there was no suitable land available on the central waterfront. The city council established a new "street," in January 1887, Railroad Avenue. It ran over the tidelands and west of the Columbia & Puget Sound/Puget Sound Shore "ram's horn" right-of-way. The city granted the Seattle, Lake Shore & Eastern a franchise on the new pathway, giving that railroad a direct connection to the piers and de facto control over other railroads' access. This led to tensions with the Northern Pacific.

The development of Railroad Avenue on the waterfront also created a new problem. Trains had to come into the city from the north or south because of steep hills, and Lake Washington blocked a direct east-west approach to the waterfront. Additionally, the vast tideflats immediately south of town made it impossible to locate railyards anywhere but in the middle of the waterfront, right in the busiest part of the city. The tracks created a dangerous obstacle for people and freight moving between the business district and the piers. Wagons had to dodge trains and pedestrians had to thread their way around and between the trains or risk maiming or death if they went between the rail cars because the trains often moved without warning. Newspapers during this era have frequent stories about lost limbs and other gruesome, often fatal, injuries on Railroad Avenue.

WHERE THE CITY MEETS THE SOUND

Log train at a pier at King Street, circa 1888.

Looking north from Union Street along the Seattle, Lake Shore & Eastern Railroad in 1888, one can envision today's Alaskan Way.

By mid-1889, the waterfront was in disorder, with the railroad disputes just one piece of a larger conflict. Without zoning or even consistent alignment of piers and train trestles, the waterfront was unplanned and inefficient. Then, on June 6, 1889, a fire started at the corner of Front Street and Madison Street in a cabinet shop. The flames spread rapidly through the wooden structures jammed together along Front Steet and on the piers. Before the day was over, more than 40 city blocks and all the piers, except for Schwabacher's at the foot of Union Street, had burned to the ground. Miraculously, no one was killed.

At the first post-fire community meeting, Judge Cornelius Hanford urged the removal of the Northern

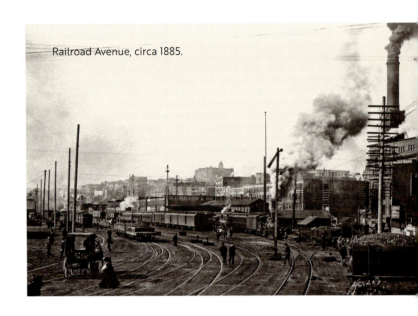

Railroad Avenue, circa 1885.

KIKISOBLU

Born about 1828, Kikisoblu was the eldest daughter of the Duwamish and Suquamish leader Si'ahl, for whom Seattle is named. She married twice and had three children and lived in several places around Puget Sound before moving to Seattle as a widow. Her home for a number of years was near what is now the Pike Street Hillclimb. While in Seattle, Kikisoblu earned a living by taking in laundry and selling clams.

In some ways, non-Native residents accorded her patronizing respect. They renamed her "Princess Angeline" in a nod to her "royal" lineage as a descendant of Si'ahl and helped her build at least one of her cabins on the hillside where she lived with her grandson, Joe Foster.

On the other hand, they treated her as an exotic mascot—a sentimental symbol of Seattle's "lost Indian past." She was one of the town's most-photographed residents during the 1880s and '90s, and her portrait adorned souvenirs for decades. Kikisoblu seems to have used her fame to her advantage, charging for photographs taken of her and accepting settler families' modest benevolence when she became too frail to work.

Many residents turned out for the grand funeral arranged by the city upon her death in 1896. At her request, she was buried in Lake View Cemetery on Capitol Hill, near her friend Henry Yesler and other city founders.

Kikisoblu walking on Seneca Street, sitting for a portrait, and at her home on Pike Street and Western Avenue with her dog, circa 1890s.

Pacific's ram's horn because of the trouble it caused for organizing the space west of Western Avenue and aligning new piers effectively. The community members at the meeting unanimously approved the proposal. They argued that neither the Puget Sound Shore nor the Columbia & Puget Sound had met the terms of their franchises, so they had forfeited their rights-of-way. Before that conflict could be settled, however, a dispute between the newly formed state government and the city over public ownership of tidelands had to be resolved.

The state constitution, adopted when Washington achieved statehood in 1889, required that the area between the inner and outer harbor lines remain in public ownership to maintain unimpeded navigation on city waterfronts. In 1890, the legislature formed the Harbor Lines Commission to survey tidelands adjacent to incorporated cities and establish the harbor lines. In Seattle, it proposed lines that would essentially nullify the entire existing waterfront layout because Railroad Avenue fell within the swath of public ownership for much of its length and the privately owned piers extended into the proposed public harbor area.

Had the proposed harbor lines been adopted, the amount of available space for railroads and piers would have been significantly reduced, making it difficult, if not impossible, to move people and cargo on the central waterfront, and thereby limiting Seattle's economic development. The Harbor Lines Commission refused to budge; the state constitution clearly stated that tidelands must remain in public ownership. Seattle's waterfront businesses simply outwaited the Harbor Lines Commission. The Commission dissolved in 1893 according to the date set in its originating legislation, with Elliott Bay's harbor lines unresolved.

Looking south on Front Street at the start of the Great Fire, June 6, 1889.

Aftermath of the fire at Western Avenue and Columbia Street.

Seattle businesses reopened in tents after the fire, 1889.

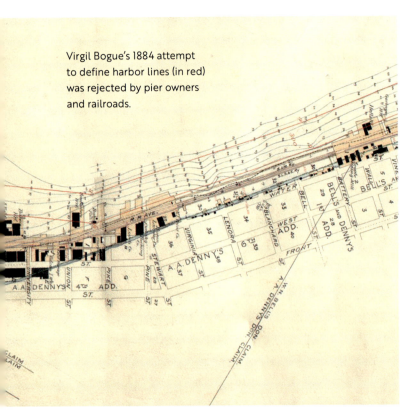

Virgil Bogue's 1884 attempt to define harbor lines (in red) was rejected by pier owners and railroads.

The legislature formed a new commission in 1894 and hired engineer Virgil Bogue to lay out a waterfront plan that would preserve as much public tidelands as possible, retain the Railroad Avenue alignment, and allow for existing private piers. He created a plan that was accepted by the Commission and the Secretary of War (who had authority over navigable waters) but was immediately challenged by the railroads and pier owners.

The issue dragged on until Secretary of War Russell Alger stepped in to resolve it just before leaving office in 1899. He set the inner harbor line at the end of the existing pier lines, essentially privatizing a portion of tidelands and recognizing the city's railroad thoroughfare. As railroad historian Kurt Armbruster noted, "This wiped out virtually all the public waterfront access the first Harbor Lines Commission attempted to create. The railroads would remain in charge of Railroad Avenue."

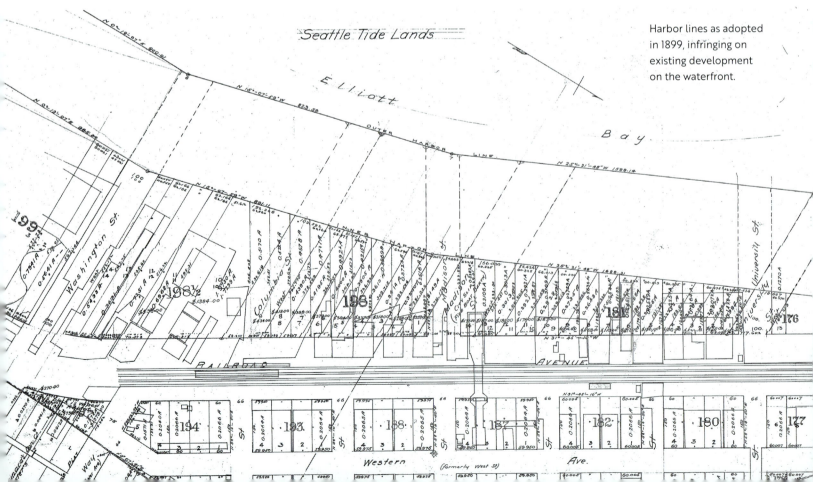

Harbor lines as adopted in 1899, infringing on existing development on the waterfront.

Once the harbor lines were resolved, the city re-platted the tidelands and shifted pier lines and waterfront parcels west of Railroad Avenue and north of Yesler Way to a 45-degree-angle alignment. The realignment improved port traffic flow by allowing ships to enter and leave the slips with minimal turning given that the entrance and exit routes to Elliott Bay ran northwest-southeast. It also maximized the length of the new piers by extending the distance of usable seafloor within each parcel.

While the Harbor Lines Commission process unfolded, a series of sales and incorporations introduced new demands for portions of Railroad Avenue. The Northern Pacific's service was spotty at best. So, in November 1889, Thomas Burke led efforts to attract James J. Hill's Great Northern Railway that was coming across the Great Plains from Minnesota. Hill needed a western terminus and Burke proposed Hill take over the Seattle, Lake Shore & Eastern to reach Elliott Bay. In early 1890, Hill's Seattle & Montana Railroad bought land from the Seattle, Lake Shore & Eastern in Smith Cove. Burke helped the railroad acquire additional land on Salmon Bay near Ballard and on the Elliott Bay tideflats.

On March 8, 1890, using language drafted by Burke, the city council designated the western 60 feet of Railroad Avenue for the Seattle & Montana's tracks. The Northern Pacific immediately stepped forward for a similar allotment. As Armbruster described it, the council was frozen like "deer in the headlights" in the face of the demand because not enough right-of-way was left to meet it, but they didn't want to alienate the Northern Pacific which still provided the city's only actual transcontinental connection.

Once again, as he had with the Seattle & Walla Walla Railroad in 1877, James Colman guided the city to a solution. He proposed that Railroad Avenue be reorganized to make space for all the railroad tracks, rather than having the Northern Pacific's on the ram's horn and the others on Railroad Avenue. In April 1894, the city council passed an ordinance to that effect, but it would be another year before the railroads settled all their disputes with each other. The ram's horn was fully decommissioned, and the cacophony of tracks and trains brought into modicum of order.

Sorting out the railroad access was one key element in developing the port, but there were other factors that could make or break Seattle's economic success. The people who lived and worked on the waterfront played a significant role in the functioning of the port too, and in the 1880s and 1890s, they would bring labor strife, racial conflict, and yet more jockeying for space on the central waterfront for a wide variety of activities.

Detail of Augustus Koch's 1891 bird's-eye view showing the railroads along the waterfront. The beige spaces along the shore are all pier structures elevated on pilings.

Chapter 4

Engaging the Economic Flywheel

"The American idea is what I like."

—WOO GEN, CHINESE IMMIGRANT DESCRIBING WHY HE IMMIGRATED TO THE UNITED STATES IN 1873

J. J. Stonor's bird's-eye view of Seattle, 1884.

Chinese men make slings to lift horses aboard a ship headed to the Philippine American War, 1899.

Cargo and passenger handling, commercial infrastructure, and industrial output had to grow exponentially to support the continued growth of the city. Railroad service was just one part of the infrastructure Seattle needed to become a major port. It also needed larger piers, more rational use of space on the tightly packed central waterfront, and a skilled labor force. The city experienced growing pains as activity on the waterfront diversified and more people got involved. Tensions rose over who would control working conditions and who would be allowed to make their homes in the city. Labor unrest and racial conflicts, that led to expulsions of Chinese and Indigenous people, shaped the culture of the waterfront in the 1880s and 1890s.

As shipping increased, more men found regular work on the waterfront loading and unloading ships. Though often referred to as one occupation, longshoring, there were several jobs involved in moving cargo on the piers. Riggers set up the slings used to hoist cargo over the side of a ship. Stevedores stowed the cargo in the ship's holds. Longshoremen moved the cargo on the piers, often using hand trucks. These teams of workers moved breakbulk cargo—goods in boxes, barrels, bales, sacks, and baskets—on and off the ships. Each man was expected to carry up to 200-pound loads up a gangway if the cargo could not be hoisted in slings. The cargo hooks they carried allowed them to drag cargo into place and were an extension of the longshoremen's hands to such an extent that the hooks became symbolic of the entire occupation.

When a ship arrived, longshoremen assembled on the pier for the "shape-up" and the shipping company's stevedoring boss would pick a crew and set the rate of pay. Decades of conflict between workers and shipping companies would stem from the indignities of the shape-up process, with its uncertainty of work and pay and the relative weakness of the workers.

THE STORY OF SEATTLE'S WATERFRONT **43**

The first strike on the Seattle waterfront took place in June 1886 when longshoremen stopped work because of low wages. The region was still emerging from an economic recession in 1885, but as prosperity returned, shipping companies refused to raise wages. On June 9th, the local longshoremen's committee called for an increase to 40 cents per hour during the day and 50 cents per hour at night. Three days later, the workers voted to establish the Seattle local of the Stevedores, Longshoremen and Riggers Union of Puget Sound. The union was affiliated with the Knights of Labor and espoused its "an injury to one is an injury to all" philosophy. That worker solidary only extended to white dock workers, however. Its constitution explicitly excluded Asian workers, a reflection of the pervasive anti-Chinese sentiment on the West Coast. White workers did not want to join forces with the Chinese in support of higher wages for all workers because they didn't believe the Chinese workers deserved equal pay. Thus divided, they were easier to manipulate and leverage against each other, allowing employers to continue to hire Chinese workers at the lower pay.

Knights of Labor organizers came into this atmosphere in Seattle and used those antagonisms to whip up a mob to expel the Chinese as they were doing elsewhere up and down the Coast. The city council set the stage for the expulsion by passing an ordinance in 1885 that required a minimum cubic air space per occupant of a hotel room. The ordinance was targeted at Chinese workers who saved money by sharing rooms.

The mob used violations of the ordinance as a pretext for forcing Chinese residents out of their homes in Pioneer Square on the morning of February 7, 1886, and onto the Oregon Improvement Company's Ocean Dock where the *Queen of the Pacific* was preparing to sail for San Francisco. When the ship reached capacity, the remaining Chinese had to wait in the city until another ship could be utilized. In the meantime, civic leaders, including Thomas Burke, Henry Yesler, and James T. Ronald, called for calm and order in dealing with the Chinese immigrants. This appeal was not so much to protect the Chinese workers' civil rights, but to stop the extralegal actions of the mob and to protect a much-needed labor force. A riot the next day led to one death and multiple injuries. Martial law and state militiamen restored order. One of Chung Ching Hock's Wa Chong Company business partners, Woo Gen, was interviewed in 1924 about his life. He recounted staying

Telegram from Secretary of Washington Territory Owings to Governor Squire requesting troops to quell the anti-Chinese unrest in Seattle, February 9, 1886.

in his home with his gun and axe at the ready in case the mob came to his door.

On the 14th, Chin Gee Hee, was quoted in the *Seattle Daily Post-Intelligencer*:

> "I think all the Chinamen will go if they can get their fares paid. The Chinamen are very poor. Since the Queen [of the Pacific] left I have opened a free eating house, where every hungry Chinamen who has no money can eat two meals a day. I feed about sixty for nothing. I know there is a feeling against the Chinese staying here, and I tell them to go, but how can they go without money to buy tickets?"

This second attempt to ouster non-white residents, just twenty years after the ordinance to exclude Native people, added a layer to race relations in Seattle that illustrates again how white Seattleites wanted to control who lived in the city but did not really have the capital or labor force to get the city on its feet economically. The discrimination against the Chinese was ironic, given that civic leaders were building Seattle's identity and future on trade with China and other Asian countries. Some Chinese continued to live and work in the city after the 1886 expulsion, but the hostilities and the federal Chinese Exclusion Act of 1882, which largely blocked new Chinese immigration, limited the size of Seattle's Chinese community for decades.

While Chinese immigrants were being pushed onto the Ocean Dock, they were likely observed by the Indigenous community living at Ballast Island, on the landward side of the pier. Created by ballast unloaded from ships, the peninsula of land grew out from the shore in the 1870s and 1880s between the Oregon Improvement Company's Ocean and City docks. It became the last place near dʸidʸəlaʔič where Native people could gather as the city grew.

The riot as depicted in the March 1886 issue of *Harper's Weekly*.

Militia in Pioneer Square during the anti-Chinese riots, 1886.

THE STORY OF SEATTLE'S WATERFRONT

Ballast dump near Washington Street, circa 1880 (top). Indigenous encampments on Ballast Island, circa 1890 (bottom), and 1895 (opposite).

In addition to Duwamish and other Coast Salish tribal members, members of outer coast tribes, First Nations people from British Columbia, and Alaska Natives also set up camp on the patch of bare ground. They came through Seattle on their way to Washington's hop fields in the Duwamish-Green, Puyallup, and Snoqualmie River valleys. Seattle provided a central location for people to meet, much as it had for generations of Native people, when they came to find farmers in need of pickers or to buy goods with their earnings. In September 1878, the *Weekly Pacific Tribune* reported:

> *"The slip at the foot of Washington Street was filled with Indians (sic) canoes to-day, and the stores and business streets, for the most part, have been crowded with Indians all day. These are the lower [northern] Sound and Northern Indians, who are just returning from their annual pilgrimage to the Puyallup hop fields, and are stopping over at Seattle for a day or two to spend their money and lay in their winter's supply."*

The space on Ballast Island was not freely shared, nor were the Indigenous people left alone to go about their business. Newspaper accounts record numerous instances of harassment and violence. Periodically, the Oregon Improvement Company would order everyone to leave. On April 1, 1892, the *Seattle Post-Intelligencer* reported:

> *"The Indians who have for years made Ballast Island (sic) their camping ground were unceremoniously ejected by the Oregon Improvement Company yesterday. The company regards them as a nuisance, and, as they are not a source of revenue, had no compunction about removing them.*

At 7 o'clock in the morning a squaw man [white man married to a Native woman] who talks Chinook [jargon] fluently was delegated to notify the siwashes [a racial slur for Native people] that they must get out or they would be forcibly put out.

About 1 o'clock in the afternoon a locomotive ran down the siding toward the Ocean dock and stretched a rope clear around the island with a slip-knot next to the road. Then the engine, in the presence of a great crowd of spectators, backed out again, dragging the rope with it. The circle of hemp grew smaller around the doomed encampment until it finally dragged tents, shanties, canoes and the whole miscellaneous make-up of an Indian settlement into the water... The crowd watched the proceedings with mixed feelings, many denouncing them as unnecessarily harsh."

While this story is distressing to read, even across more than a century of time, it is also important to understand it is evidence of how people survive wholesale displacement and massive cultural change. As Warren King George, Muckleshoot Tribal Historian, explained in 2017:

"Don't feel bad for them, don't pity them. These people were strong people and they did what they had to do to survive. Whether they starved to death or whether they found love there or whether they paddled five hundred miles or downstream two miles. This place was what they had. They utilized what they had at the moment, at that time. And Ballast Island just happened to be that place, where no law governed, and where no European neighbor was willing to go there because it was worthless to them. But to Native Americans, to our ancestors of this area, to Elliott Bay people, to Duwamish River people, to Lake Washington people, that was a place we found a little niche."

Ballast Island retains cultural significance today, even though it was relatively short-lived and hasn't been visible since the late 1890s.

Following the 1889 fire, the city seized the opportunity to bring some order to the waterfront and set the stage for future growth to a degree that would have been nearly impossible to do piecemeal. Immediately, the city cleared the slate by pushing the refuse from the burned buildings, trestles, and piers onto the beaches surrounding the Pioneer Square district. On the west side, the absence of a seawall limited the permanence of the fill, but on the lagoon side, it hastened the process of creating solid ground. New, fireproof, stone and brick buildings arose on a more orderly street grid and new piers grew out from the shoreline. South of Yesler Way, Railroad Avenue was widened to accommodate more train tracks. Additionally, construction of Railroad Avenue West, extending out to West Seattle, made the southern tideflats and West Seattle's shoreline easier to develop.

THE STORY OF SEATTLE'S WATERFRONT

Waterfront businesses north of King Street, circa 1893.

The new development soon reached the Oregon Improvement Company dock and Ballast Island was covered by planking in the mid-1890s. Settlers' demand for land stretched around the bay and on March 7, 1893, a man named Watson, who may have been an agent of a local land company, burned the longhouses at t'uʔəlaltxʷ on the west side of the mouth of the Duwamish. As explained by Ed Carriere, Suquamish elder, in 2017:

> "So they drove our people out by burning their big houses down. And then they finally got us out of Seattle and moved us over here to Suquamish. They just took over Seattle, but that was our land. One Indian family [Seetoowathl and his wife, Mandy Seattle] stayed out there and wouldn't move. They were on the shores of the river . . . and wouldn't move and the . . . families that came to Seattle, let that couple starve to death out there. These rich Seattle people just let them starve to death out there rather than going out there trying to help them."

The violence of the displacement was passed down in stories to descendants, as shared by Gilbert King George, a Muckleshoot elder:

> "My mother told me of the days when this area was claimed, and [her] playmates' homes were destroyed for relocation purposes. I always remember because she was so puzzled by what happened to her friend's home. She got up the next day, there was a pile of ashes there. Whole families were removed. Relocated. So you have to wonder, you know, what are the mental impacts on a mother and a father, grandparents, who have to literally pick up their family and have to move."

Coast Salish beach camp in Belltown, circa 1880s.

Native camps on the Seattle waterfront, circa 1990.

Woman weaving basket at a beach camp in Seattle, circa 1900.

Top: Indigenous families working in hop fields in Western Washington, circa 1890-1900.

Bottom: Native people selling baskets and other wares in downtown Seattle, circa 1906-1912.

50 WHERE THE CITY MEETS THE SOUND

Operated by the harbormaster, the gridiron was a stationary platform adjacent to the shore where scows could land, floating over it at high tide and resting on it at low tide. It provided a low-cost option for moving bulk materials like gravel, lumber, and bricks. The smaller scale of the gridiron and its public ownership made it a popular place for the smaller vessels to tie up, echoing the long use of that area as a landing place for dᶻidᶻəlalʼič.

By the mid-1880s, Budlong's boathouse at the foot of Columbia was one of several docks for small vessels along the shoreline. The West Seattle Land & Improvement Company ferry was operating at a pier at the foot of Main Street. Colman Dock's warehouse stored hay, grain, and feed brought in from around Puget Sound, and the G.G. Wiley Cement, Lime & Plaster Company operated there. A pier was wedged in south of Yesler's Wharf and was occupied by a succession of businesses including Stone and Barnett, Crawford and Harrington, Crawford & Smith, and Harrington & Smith.

FISH MARKETS

FISHERMEN'S TERMINAL IN SALMON BAY is famous for its Alaskan fishing and crabbing fleet, but fishing schooners tied up at the fish piers around the foot of Pike Street from the 1900s into the 1990s. They brought in hundreds of thousands of pounds of halibut, cod, rockfish, sablefish, and other species from Puget Sound and the banks off the outer coast of Washington. In just one day in August 1931, The Seattle Times reported that, "The vessels and their catches of halibut in pounds follow: *Seattle*, 52,000; *Akutan*, 60,000; *Orbit*, 20,000; *Sylvia*, 14,000; *Unimak*, 5,000; *Bernice*, 9,000; *Republic*, 25,000; *Maddock*, 14,000; *Faith*, 6,500; *Prosperity*, 6,000; *Aloha*, 16,000; and *Velero*, 2,000. The *Unimak* also brought 6,000 sablefish, the *Faith* 3,000 sablefish and the *Velero* 4,000 red cod."

Each time a boat returned to harbor after a couple of weeks out to sea, the local newspapers would publish lists of their catch and how much the fish sold for at the Seattle Fish Exchange or the Fishing Vessel Owner's Association Exchange, both on Pier 8. Fish wholesalers like Ainsworth & Dunn, or Chlopeck Fish Company, then sold the fish fresh to fish mongers on the piers such as Palace Fish, Whiz Fish, and Grand Trunk Fish. Many of the fish monger companies were owned by Sephardic Jews from what is now Turkey who settled in Seattle in the early 20th century, such as Solomon Calvo's Waterfront Fish & Oyster and another unidentified market in the images to the right.

The wholesalers also sold to fish mongers in Pike Place Market and to stores around Seattle, or they loaded frozen fish into refrigerated railcars bound for the East Coast and southern states. Canned fish and shellfish were sold around the world.

The fish piers spawned a host of related businesses in the area around today's Piers 54 and 55. Companies like Pacific Net & Twine and Fisheries Supply Company supplied the fleet, and Diamond Ice & Storage kept the fish cold. American Can Company, further north on the waterfront, provided the tin cans used to package salmon, tuna, and shellfish.

Halibut fishing boats alongside New England Fish Company dock, 1912.

San Juan Fishing and Packing employees, circa 1935.

Workers weigh the catch at San Juan Fish Co. at the foot of Pike Street, circa 1905.

Chlopeck Fish Co. packing warehouse, at the foot of Wall Street, circa 1907.

As the city and activity on the waterfront grew, some industries moved out to other parts of the Elliott Bay waterfront and other waterways around the city. Prior to the fire, several sawmills processed timber on central waterfront piers. Yesler's Mill closed in the early 1870s, but Mechanics' Mill took its place on the wharf, the Oregon Improvement Company operated a mill, and the Seattle Lumber and Commercial Company operated a sash and door factory at the foot of Marion. After the fire, mills moved south to the tideflats or north to Ballard. New piers were built out from the shore with larger berths and transit sheds for storing freight, leaving less room for the saloons, tanneries, and other small-scale industries that had previously tucked in around the shipping facilities. The boathouses largely moved off the central waterfront, too, because fewer people hired small boats as the Mosquito Fleet steamers offered an easy and reliable alternative for local travel.

In addition to the larger shipping piers, new fish wholesalers and canneries proliferated on the central waterfront in the 1890s. Many of the early non-Native fishermen in Seattle were from Eastern and Southern Europe, like elsewhere on Puget Sound, and a nascent fishing industry developed during the 1870s. In 1877, racial and ethnic tensions flashed in a newspaper editorial in the *Seattle Post-Intelligencer*, which lamented how the Slavs and Greeks lacked ambition

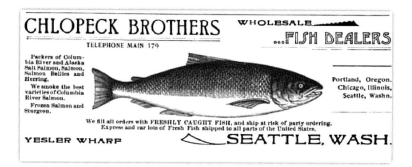

and primarily fished for the local market instead of looking farther afield to the California market and embracing new canning technology that had been recently introduced from the Columbia River.

Though the newspaper blamed the fishing industry's slow start on character flaws in the southern Europeans, the idea of distant fish markets was fairly new for Seattle. Salted fish had not been well-received in San Francisco and barely brought a high enough price to make a profit. Canning was introduced to Seattle in the early 1880s leading to an explosion in the number of fishing boats and canneries, many of them owned by native-born Americans and northern European immigrants. Exports skyrocketed in the 1880s and 1890s. By 1893, Boston Fishing Company operated a pier at Pine Street, Hunt & T.C. Campbell packing company operated nearby on the inland side of Railroad Avenue, San Juan Fish Company was at the foot of Spring Street, and Chlopeck Brothers were at the foot of Yesler. Puget Sound Fish Company canned oysters and clams at the foot of Washington Street.

In 1896, Ainsworth & Dunn built a pier at the foot of Pike Street for their fish, hay, and feed business. The two owners, Elton Ainsworth and Arthur Dunn, had started their business in 1888 with a wagon they drove around town selling fish to homes and businesses. Their Seattle Fish Company had expanded enough by 1896 to warrant construction of the large pier. Part of it was occupied by Willis Robinson, who sold hay sourced from farms in Skagit County. The Northwestern Steamship Company also used the dock as terminal for its ships running between Seattle and Victoria. Other transportation companies like Alaska Steamship, Blue Star Navigation, and Columbia River & Puget Sound Navigation, provided passenger and cargo service from other piers to around the Sound, along the Strait of Juan de Fuca and on Hood Canal, up the coast to Alaska, and to ports on the Pacific Rim and beyond.

As Seattle grew into the region's market town in the 1890s, it also became a labor hub. Stevedoring companies, like Griffiths & Sprague, opened labor bureaus in Seattle. Other labor contractors soon joined them. Employers from across the region listed jobs with the contractors because the loggers, sailors, farmworkers, miners, fishermen, longshoremen, and

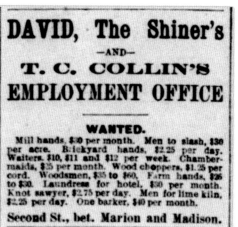
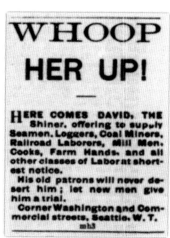

The ebb and flow of workers attracted middlemen who connected workers with jobs for a fee. One such contractor, Dave Fletcher, known as Dave the Shiner, capitalized on the wide array of acquaintances he made as a shoe shiner to build his labor contracting business. As an African American man, Fletcher likely initially started his shoeshine stand because it was one of the few occupations open to Black men. He started in the 1880s with advertising jobs he had on offer in the paper and directing people to contact him at his stand. By 1890, he had enough business to open his own employment office at 2nd Avenue South and Washington Street.

laborers who came to the city to spend their hard-earned money provided a ready supply of workers when their funds inevitably ran low again.

Many labor contractors started small and built up their network of employers and workers over time. It didn't require much money to get started, but ready access to large numbers of people was essential. Contractors located in Pioneer Square because it was filled with businesses catering to poor, unmarried, transient men, such as brothels, bars, gambling houses, and cheap hotels. These men were the most likely to sign on for jobs in the forests, mills, and mines, and on cargo ships and fishing boats. As cannery workers came into town after the salmon runs ended in Alaska, they could be hired to work in farm fields or coal mines.

The combination of the labor contractors, the transient workers, low-cost accommodations, and the activities offered in the neighborhood shaped the character of Pioneer Square as a rough-and-tumble district where many city laws were nullified with bribes for police officers. Some Seattleites would try to limit the "attractions" and encourage Christianity, sobriety, and respectability, but as John Geoghagen would write in his 1924 study of the transient work force,

> *"It may be that strict regulation of the places of amusement and close supervision of those agencies that tend to make profit out of commercialized vice will relieve the situation somewhat, but in order to meet this problem adequately there will be need for much more heroic action than is called for by an ordinary local program."*

Pike Street Wharf, 1905.

FIRE STATIONS

Following the Great Fire in June 1889, civic leaders planned improvements to the city's fire protection. A *Post-Intelligencer* editorial called for, "a good water service in the heart of the city, a fire patrol boat for service along the city front, an electric fire alarm system with new and improved appliances for the fire department," and asked, "Will our people wake up to the gravity of the situation, or will they wait for a second fire?" They did, in fact, wake up, and one of their first actions was to procure a fire boat. In late 1890, Seattle Dry Dock and Shipbuilding Company delivered the *Snoqualmie* and berthed it at the foot Madison Street. It could pump 7,000 gallons a minute and, with the right hoses, reach buildings on 4th Avenue.

The first fire station on the pier opened in January 1891. It was, like other fire stations in the city at that time, a simple, single-story, wooden structure. After the turn of the century, the city replaced many of its early stations with larger structures and a new two-story station with a fire hose tower opened on the pier in 1901. In 1917, a larger structure was built with a unique feature—it was "portable." It appeared to be brick, but actually it had a brick veneer and a foundation built so that it could be rolled onto the street when its pilings needed to be replaced, or moved to a new pier if the Madison Street location proved unfavorable. That clever innovation did not serve the building well, however, and it had to be vacated in early 1961 due to its rapidly deteriorating foundation.

As planning for its replacement got underway, a new interest in the waterfront as a tourist attraction was emerging. Several nearby piers had shifted from cargo and passenger handling to retail uses and the city council and Design Commission wanted the new building to contribute to the waterfront's tourist appeal. After a couple of years of debate over style and features, a station opened in 1963. Its modern design incorporated large windows that allowed tourists to see into the building and view the firefighting apparatus stored inside. The building was sited where there would be room for visitors to walk out to the water side of the pier and view the fireboat tied up to the adjacent float.

Fire station built after the Great Fire of 1889 at the foot of Madison Street.

There have been more fireboats than buildings at the pier. The fireboat *Duwamish* began service in 1909. Built by the Puget Sound Shipbuilding Company, it had far more capacity than the *Snoqualmie*, pumping 22,800 gallons per minute. It was decommissioned in 1984 and is now moored at the Historic Ships Wharf at the Museum of History and Industry on Lake Union. The fireboat *Alki* served from 1927 until 2013. In 1985, the *Chief Seattle* took the place of the *Duwamish* and is currently moored at Fishermen's Terminal in Salmon Bay. Fireboat *Leschi*, commissioned in 2007, is currently moored at Fire Station No. 5, along with *Fire One* and *Fire Two*, smaller boats introduced for their nimbleness and speed in 2006 and 2014, respectively. The *Leschi* can pump 20,000 gallons of water per minute and is outfitted to respond to chemical, biological, radiological, nuclear and explosives incidents.

Fireboats *Duwamish* and *Snoqualmie* at the pier behind the fire station, 1910.

Stevedoring company McCabe & Hamilton introduced the first cargo handling mechanization on the waterfront. The portable conveyor belt could be moved around the docks and inside transit sheds. It could only lift boxes and bales of cargo to upper storage levels, or to workers on top of stacks of goods, but the handling of breakbulk was so labor-intensive and time-consuming any improvement in reducing labor costs made a meaningful difference to profit margins.

LOADING SHIP BY ELECTRIC CONVEYOR.

Above: View of development filling level land around the tidal lagoon from Beacon Hill, 1895.

Columbia & Puget Sound Depot at the foot of Main Street, 1904.

He argued that the success of the logging camps and mines and canneries relied on men without family ties, homes of their own, or expectations of regular work. Their carousing and unstable lives were a logical outcome of that work environment and wouldn't change unless the companies that hired them found a different way to maintain their work forces.

While the Great Northern line was under construction in the early 1890s, James J. Hill announced plans for a shipping firm that would carry cargo from Asian ports to Seattle and that lumber would be carried on the railroad at 40 cents per ton. This remarkably low price for that time would make Washington lumber marketable in the Midwest and East. The Great Northern's tracks over Stevens Pass opened in early 1893 and the first passenger train pulled into Seattle on June 22nd, finally making Seattle a transcontinental terminus.

With the arrival of the Great Northern, it appeared that Seattle was finally on its way to becoming the "Queen City" of the Puget Sound and the Northwest. Plans were afoot for a park system; neighborhood subdivisions were being platted left and right, and the business community prospered. The city's hopes were put on hold, however, by the Panic of 1893, a nationwide recession. Capital dried up, development ground to a halt, and activity on the waterfront slowed drastically.

Longshoremen on the waterfront faced a wage cut in January 1894 when the Pacific Coast Steamship Company reduced their rates and put ship crews to work unloading cargo from the hold to the pier, reducing the need for longshoremen. The company also gave hiring control to their pier foremen. The union called a strike in mid-January, but it was short-lived because too many people in need of work were willing to cross the picket line. When the strike ended in early February, the union's membership and power declined significantly.

In August 1896, a glimmer of future prosperity appeared with the arrival of the Nippon Yusen Kaisha Line's *Miike Maru* from Yokohama. Operated in conjunction with the Great Northern Railway, it marked the beginning of the first regularly scheduled passenger and cargo service between Asia and the United States. Seattle had one competitive advantage over other West Coast ports: It was about more than 300 miles closer to Asia because of its northern location. In much the same way that planes between Seattle and Europe fly over the Arctic to take advantage of the shorter distance, relative to traversing the wider arc over North America and the Atlantic Ocean, ships can travel over a smaller arc of the globe via the North Pacific Ocean. This advantage, along with Seattle's two transcontinental railroads, made it an appealing trans-shipment port for cargo moving between Asia and Chicago or the East Coast.

Top: *Miike Maru* moored at Schwabacher's pier, 1896.

Bottom left: Port of Seattle advertisement showing trans-Pacific routes to global ports, 1925.

Bottom right: Nippon Yusen Kaisha Line calendar.

The newspapers reported on the crowd—15,000 people lined the docks to welcome the ship—and the festivities welcoming the *Miike Maru*. The fireboat *Snoqualmie* carried the Chamber of Commerce reception committee and 200 other prominent Seattleites to the entrance to the harbor near Magnolia. There, "small craft of all kinds and description" joined a boat parade back to the central waterfront piers. The *Miike Maru* fired a twenty-one-gun salute and "innumerable Japanese rockets" were fired "to beautiful effect."

In hindsight, it is remarkable to read about the excitement generated by the *Miike Maru*'s arrival and know that an even larger event was on the near horizon. Just a year later, the Klondike Gold Rush would trigger another massive transformation of Seattle's waterfront.

THE STORY OF SEATTLE'S WATERFRONT

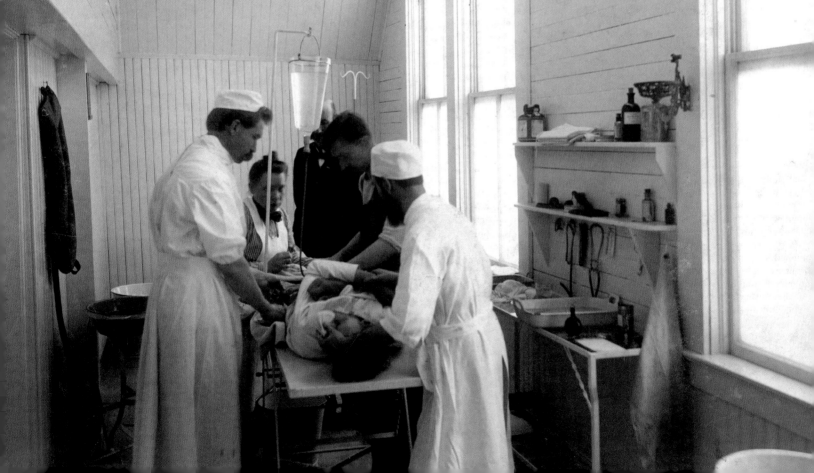

WAYSIDE MISSION HOSPITAL

Little medical infrastructure existed in Seattle to treat the injuries that came with industrialization and intoxication on the waterfront, and there was little in the way of a social safety net. When Dr. Alexander de Soto landed in Seattle in the 1890s, the waterfront was a tangled web of railroad tracks, ships, mills, and saloons, and mounting casualties. De Soto, an immigrant from Spain via New York City, helped establish the Seattle Benevolent Society in 1899 with the aim of opening a hospital in the steamship *Idaho* that was berthed at the foot of Jackson Street. He and the ship's owner, Captain Amos O. Benjamin, another member of the society, hatched a plan to raise the ship onto supports to prevent it from bobbing on the waves, then convert it into a hospital.

Before its official opening in 1900, the *Seattle Post-Intelligencer* reported that,

> "The latest patient at the hospital is Jack Corbett, who pretends to be a brother of James J. Corbett, the pugilist and ex-champion of the world. He is suffering from the effects of the morphine habit. He called at the hospital yesterday and asked to be taken in. The floating hospital is crowded, there being not a bed to spare."

The hospital treated all manner of injuries sustained on the waterfront and around town, alcoholism and drug addiction, and illnesses. The hospital is mentioned frequently in the newspapers for the more sensational cases, like bar fights, shootings, suicides and suicide attempts over financial and emotional distress, wagon accidents due to runaway horses, and all sorts of injuries caused by trains moving unexpectedly, many of them fatal.

In 1904, the Society revoked Dr. de Soto's lease for the hospital due to dissatisfaction with his management. Fanny W. Cannon and Marion Baxter took over its operations until the hull grew too leaky and the Oregon Improvement Company needed the berth for its own operations. The hospital moved to Sarah Yesler's former home at 2nd Avenue NW and Republican Street where it operated until the new city hospital opened at 5th Avenue and Yesler Way in 1909.

Top: Article on the Wayside Mission Hospital in a 1903 issue of *The Commonwealth*.

Opposite top: The *Idaho* stationed at Pier C, at the foot of Jackson Street.

Opposite bottom: Dr. de Soto and staff performing surgery, circa 1900.

THE STORY OF SEATTLE'S WATERFRONT

CHAPTER 5

The Floodgates Open

"Now is the time to go to the rich KLONDYKE country, where according to last reports, the gold is as plentiful as sawdust."

—THE NORTH AMERICAN TRANSPORTATION & TRADING COMPANY'S ADVERTISEMENT IN *THE SEATTLE TIMES*, JULY 24, 1897

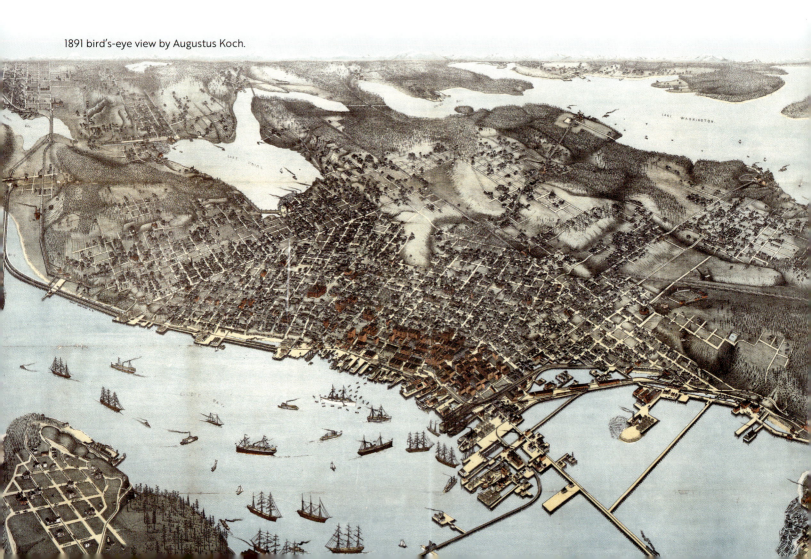

1891 bird's-eye view by Augustus Koch.

ON JULY 17, 1897, Seattle newspaper headlines shouted the news that "a ton of gold" was aboard the SS *Portland*, soon to arrive at Schwabacher's pier. It was a dream come true for Seattle's business community. San Francisco's history had demonstrated the power of a gold rush—after 1849 it blossomed into a metropolis and developed a sphere of influence that rippled out into new investments and ventures. In Seattle's case, the discovery of gold in the 1890s in the Klondike River basin in Canada's Yukon Territory opened the floodgates. Seattle was the nearest American port and goldseekers arrived by the thousands looking for supplies, advice, and transportation. The Klondike Gold Rush, the *Miike Maru*, and growth in the timber industry coalesced at the turn of the century to propel a burst of development on the waterfront. Everything got bigger—the piers, the volume of cargo, the number of passengers, the scale of operations, and the size of the ships.

One of the first changes brought by the Gold Rush was the transformation of Seattle into a supply depot. As historian Linda Nash explained, "The city morphed into a kind of giant warehouse, gathering mass quantities of food and manufactured goods from around the region and across the country." As the closest American port with railroad service to the rest of the United States, it was the most logical place for goldseekers to outfit themselves before venturing to Alaska and Canada. They bought clothing, boots, mining tools, tents, foodstuffs, and books to guide them to the gold. They took lessons in driving dog sleds and gold panning and otherwise prepared themselves for the rigors of the Far North.

Boxes of gold arriving at the Seattle waterfront, 1899.

Map of Alaska marked with "Gold Fields," 1898.

THE STORY OF SEATTLE'S WATERFRONT **63**

Team of sled dogs in front of the Yukon Mining School in downtown Seattle, 1898.

The steamer *Willamette* leaves Seattle with 800 passengers, 1898.

The foundation for Seattle's role in the Gold Rush began in the 1880s when regular shipping service to Alaska began. The Pacific Coast Steamship Company ran the *Eureka* to Sitka. Then, Charles Peabody, George Lent, George Roberts, Melville Nichols, and Walter Oakes organized Alaska Steamship Company in 1895 to serve the nascent mining district around Circle City, Alaska Territory, on the Yukon River, with the steamer *Willapa*. Companies in Seattle, like Schwabacher's and Cooper & Levy, developed inventories of supplies the goldseekers needed. When miners found gold in the Klondike in 1897, it was easy for the shipping companies to pivot to new routes and for suppliers to increase their inventories.

Almost immediately after the *Portland* arrived, the number of coastwise steamships serving Alaska multiplied. Smaller steamers built in Seattle made one-way trips to Alaska to join the fleet of boats ferrying goldseekers up rivers to the limits of navigation, shortening the overland portion of the trip as much as possible. Seattle's piers groaned with the weight of passengers and cargo, along with the throngs of people there to wish them well or to welcome them back and marvel at their newfound wealth. Some ships carried *boxes* of gold from the goldfields. Port warden statistics document millions of dollars of gold coming into the port annually. Ships in port increased from 305 in 1896 to 1,376 in 1899. The returning miners also stimulated the city's growth. Many chose to settle in Seattle, investing their profits in homes and businesses. Some fueled the economy by spending their money freely in the bars and brothels of Pioneer Square.

As the non-Indigenous population of Alaska also grew, so did its demand for goods from Washington. Seattle's piers filled with businesses to supply that demand. John Agen established the Alaska Butter & Cream Company in 1899 and moved to a pier at the foot of University

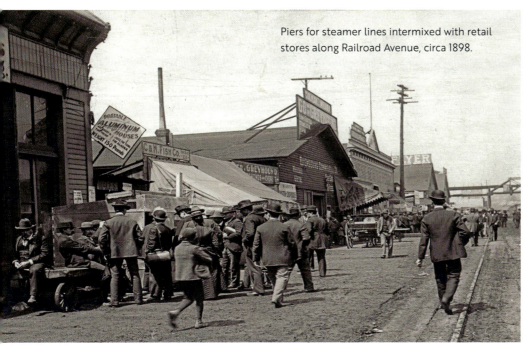

Piers for steamer lines intermixed with retail stores along Railroad Avenue, circa 1898.

Top-right: Schedule for passenger service on the steamer *Fleetwood*, 1889.

Above: Postcard of the stern-wheeler *Greyhound* on Puget Sound.

Street in 1902. He sourced produce from farms around the Sound and used an innovative tin can packaging to keep the butter fresh during the long trip north. Likewise, cattle, horses, and sheep—some raised in the Puget Sound lowlands, others in Eastern Washington— were shipped north to provide transportation and food. According to Linda Nash, the settlers' "personal success and happiness hinged on the flow of goods *through* the town, which depended upon the exploitation of various Northwest resources and their export *out* of town."

Demand for transportation around the Sound also increased dramatically with the introduction of "homeseeker" fares on the Great Northern and Northern Pacific trains. This inexpensive way to cross the continent to establish a home and find work in the burgeoning industries of the Northwest created a larger stream of people coming overland into Seattle and the surrounding area. Mosquito Fleet steamers connecting settlers to Seattle and its market made it possible to make a living on a small farm at a distance from the city. New steamer companies developed to meet the increased transportation demand, including the Puget Sound Navigation Company and the Kitsap Transportation Company.

THE STORY OF SEATTLE'S WATERFRONT

COLMAN DOCK

In the 1850s and 1860s, Yesler's Wharf was the only place to land a vessel that couldn't be pulled up on the beach. The Oregon Improvement Company built its Ocean and City Docks nearby in the early 1880s, providing four berths. After the 1889 fire cleared out all the piers south of University Street, larger piers took their places to serve the larger steamships as the city grew. Smaller steamers found space around existing piers, but quickly more space was needed.

James Colman had a boathouse just north of Yesler's Wharf that was about 40 feet by 60 feet. He expanded the dock in 1886 and 1890. Several businesses operated out of it, including a hay wholesaler. Small steamers could land there and discharge passengers and some cargo. As the 1890s progressed, the area near the foot of Marion Street became the center of the steamer traffic on the waterfront. In April 1893, the Seattle and Tacoma Navigation Company leased the Hatfield-Colman Dock at the foot of Madison and Marion for its steamer runs to Everett with the *Greyhound* and to Tacoma with the *Gatzert*. The dock would be known as Colman Dock going forward. Next door, also at Marion Street, the *Flyer* ran to Tacoma on Thursdays and Sundays from the Commercial Dock.

In 1908, Colman Dock underwent a large redevelopment. It extended further out into the bay to make room for fourteen slips and improved passenger facilities.

The first Colman Dock, circa 1903.

Interior of Colman Dock just after redevelopment in 1908. An interior balcony took passengers to a passenger waiting room.

Colman Dock with slips full of passenger steamers, circa 1909.

It featured a new dome-roofed waiting room and a clock tower on the west end of the pier. The interior of the pier had space for cargo handling on the lower level where it was easy for wagons and railcars to enter the pier from Railroad Avenue and to load cargo into the ships' holds. Passengers entered the terminal and walked onto the ships from the upper level. A new pedestrian walkway from the upper-level crossing over Railroad Avenue and Western Avenue to First Avenue was constructed in 1909. Office space for transportation companies lined the upper level of the north side of the pier. Charles Peabody's Puget Sound Navigation Company, which would soon merge with Joshua Green's La Conner Trading and Transportation Company and Thompson Steamboat Company, was known as the Black Ball Line. It dominated the ferry business on the Sound, eventually making the successful transition to auto ferries and outlasting all of its competitors.

When the new Colman Dock opened in February 1909, *The Seattle Times* ran an article praising it as "the most striking and conspicuous feature of Seattle's horseshoe-shaped waterfront." It included a reprint from *The Marine Review of New York and Cleveland* with admiring comments on the design and functionality of the new pier.

Traveler's Guide, published in January 1891, lists a remarkable number of steamers operating out of piers up and down the waterfront. A passenger could travel to Tacoma from Schwabacher's at Union Street, or to Tacoma, Olympia, and other south Puget Sound ports from Yesler's Wharf and the City Dock. Steamers to Victoria, Port Townsend, Port Angeles, Neah Bay, Whatcom County, Anacortes, La Conner, and Snohomish County left from Yesler's Wharf, the Union Pacific Dock, Baker's Dock at University Street, City Dock, Badere's Wharf at Spring Street, or the Harrington Dock and Hatfield Dock at Washington Street. The Puget Sound islands of Vashon, Whidbey, Bainbridge, and the San Juans could be reached on steamers from Yesler's Wharf, Baker's at University Street, the Hatfield Dock at Washington Street, or the Hatfield-Colman Dock at foot of Madison.

In 1905, the Great Northern Steamship Company joined 54 other steamship lines operating out of Seattle carrying goods and people between Asian ports and Seattle, where the freight was transferred to Great Northern trains headed east. The company's ships, the *Minnesota* and the *Dakota*, were enormous. They dwarfed the volume of cargo handled by the Nippon Yusen Kaisha's *Miike Maru*. Newspapers reported the *Minnesota*

A new clock tower was built after an ocean steamer crashed through the end of Colman Dock in 1912.

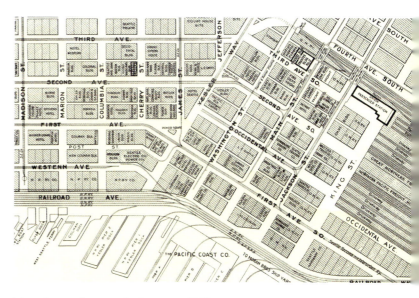

Map of new railway track alignments, 1905.

THE STORY OF SEATTLE'S WATERFRONT

was the largest ship then afloat, with 26,000 tons of cargo, including cotton, general merchandise, iron and steel, machinery, 75 railroad flatcars, and 141 passengers. It left Seattle on its first trip on January 23, 1905, headed to Asian ports by way of Manila. Two piers were constructed in Smith Cove at the north end of the harbor to accommodate the ships' length and volume of cargo.

The Great Northern's James J. Hill wanted to build a depot for passengers and piers for cargo on the central waterfront, but City Engineer Reginald H. Thomson opposed any construction of new terminal facilities on Railroad Avenue because of the gridlock that would come with increased trains, passengers, and cargo. In exchange for permission to build facilities south of Jackson Street between First and Fourth Avenues, Hill agreed to build a tunnel under downtown between Railroad Avenue at Pike Street and Jackson Street at 4th Avenue South.

The city council approved the Great Northern passenger depot in January 1900. The Northern Pacific then proposed its own depot on the waterfront. Great Northern threatened to leave town if it was allowed to be built. Haggling ensued and in August 1902 an agreement reached to reorganize both railroads' track alignments, build a shared passenger depot, and share the use of the tunnel, which opened in 1906. A short section of track, Railroad Way, was built to connect the new railyard on the tideflats south of Jackson to the waterfront. With these new facilities, trains could maneuver *around* the waterfront instead of being limited to the narrow, crowded shoreline between King Street and Pike Street.

King Street Station opened at the south portal of the tunnel on May 10, 1906. The railroads' old station on the waterfront closed, shifting a major source of train traffic and pedestrians to Pioneer Square. Great Northern built a row of warehouses along what

Railyard south of King Street, with the Smith Tower (left) and King Street Station (right), circa 1915.

Businesses along the piers at University Street, 1899.

WATERFRONT PIERS IN 1900

The Northern Pacific Railway owned eleven blocks of tidelands between Yesler Way and University Street. It built Piers 1, 2, and 3 and leased them to numerous companies. Over the course of the 1900s and 1910s, commission houses and warehouses filled the blocks along Western Avenue. Here are a few of the main business along the piers in the first decade of the 20th century from North to South:

- Pioneer Sand and Gravel (foot of Cedar, later operated by Roslyn Coal)
- Chlopeck Fish Company (foot of Vine)
- Wall Street Pier: cargo handling
- Oriental Dock (foot of Lenora/Virginia): Galbraith and Bacon
- Virginia Street Dock (foot of Virginia): cargo handling
- Gaffney Dock (foot of Pine): Western Alaska Steamship Company
- Pier 8 ½ (foot of Pine): San Juan Fish Company, Whiz Fish Company, and Ocean Fish
- Boston Fish Company and Hunter and T. C. Campbell Packers (foot of Pike/Union)
- Ainsworth & Dunn Dock (Pike Street Dock): Fish, hay, and feed company, along with H.W. Baker & Company's warehouse and Hicks Company's machine shop; also Northwestern Steamship Company terminal, Robinson Hay warehouse, and Seattle Fish
- Schwabacher's (foot of Union)
- Pier 6 (foot of Union): Agen's Alaska Butter and Cream Company, later the Chicago, St. Paul, and Milwaukee Railroad
- Pacific Net & Twine (across Railroad Avenue to additional warehouses at University Street)
- Pier 5 (foot of University St): Alaska Steamship Company, managed by Arlington Dock Company
- Pier 4 (foot of Seneca Street): Known as White Star Dock for one of its tenants, an Alaskan shipping company; also Frank Waterhouse and Company, managed by Arlington Dock Company
- Pier 3 (foot of Spring Street): Galbraith and Bacon, a hay and grain company; Kitsap Transportation Company
- National Building (foot of Spring): Built for Northern Pacific Railway and leased to National Grocery Company
- Mutual Creamery (foot of Marion)
- Pier 2 (foot of Yesler Way): Whatcom Line, La Conner Transportation Company, and the Port Orchard Line
- Pier 1 (foot of Yesler and Washington): Luckenbach Steamship, a coastwise shipping company

Pacific Net & Twine delivery wagon on Railroad Avenue, 1908.

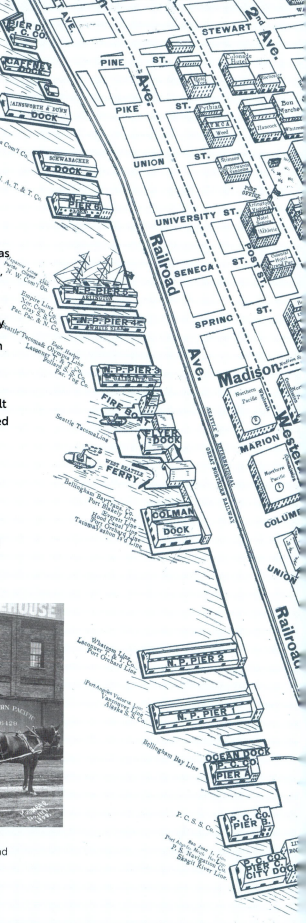

Houses on the hill below Belltown neighborhood, circa 1895.

was then the southern shoreline of Seattle south of Jackson Street. Later, when the seawall was built south of King Street in the 1910s, its freight facilities would pivot to a north-south alignment and the Northern Pacific would build its warehouses to the west, south of King Street.

Many of the pier owners built warehouses and commission houses on the inland side of Railroad Avenue. These multi-story buildings provided holding space for cargo coming into Seattle for local distribution. As the regional population increased, more companies began to import goods and equipment for the newly established farms and industries around the region. There was also a significant volume of farm produce coming into the city for sale in its neighborhoods and for export to Alaska. The warehouses were built to handle heavy loads and accommodate light industry, with massive post-and-beam construction designed to carry about 250 pounds per square foot, compared to about 50 pounds per square foot for a typical office building.

The waterfront north of Pike Street began to fill with piers in the 1900s, displacing people who were living in that area. Insurance maps and census figures indicate that the cabins there were small and somewhat makeshift. The community was made up of people from a range of backgrounds. A number of Native people had built cabins over the beach and up the hillside. The tribal associations of the Native people who are listed in the census are not identified. We do know that Kikisoblu, also known as Princess Angeline, and her grandson Joe Foster, lived on the hillside at the foot of Pike Street, below where the Pike Place Market is today. She was the daughter of Si'ahł, but she had not settled at Port Madison with him when he moved. We do not have any written records of her reasons for wanting to live in Seattle, but it seems likely that her connection to dᶻidᶻəlaľič played a role in her choice.

In February 1902, *The Seattle Times* announced that 18 new piers were completed or under construction, gushing that:

"So radical has been the change made in the construction of the new piers that Seattle has practically a new water front. Anyone who left the city two years ago and, coming back by steamer, would hardly know the place. Instead of the old irregular line of wharves and bunkers, there is now a complete change of piers, constructed along similar lines and in general conformity with each other, that form one of the most noticeable features of the city to strike the eye of the visitor approaching by steamer."

The cargo handled over the piers increased in volume and variety. In addition to the continued export of natural resources like lumber and coal, automobiles, furs, cannery supplies like tin for cans and food for workers also passed in and out of the city. The city landing at Washington Street continued to handle bulk items, with 100 tons of hay and 70 tons of concrete blocks unloaded there in 1904. A perusal of city directories shows the distribution of maritime-related businesses throughout downtown buildings illustrating how vital the waterfront was to the city's economy.

As waterfront activity increased, longshoremen attempted to improve their working conditions. The Stevedores, Longshoremen and Riggers Union reorganized on March 27, 1900, as the Seattle Longshoremen's Mutual Benefit Association, Local 163 of the International Longshoremen's Association (ILA). While initially formed to provide aid to injured members like many fraternal orders, it was not long before they began organizing longshoremen to bargain with the shipping companies. A two-hour work stoppage the following summer drew attention to the local's demand for recognition as the longshoremen's union in Seattle. The stoppage targeted the Pacific Coast Steamship Company, one of the largest employers of longshoremen in Seattle. The company quickly acceded to the demands and shipping resumed.

Loading logs onto a ship, circa 1880.

John Olmsted (center with pipe), of the Olmsted Brothers landscape architecture firm, was invited in April 1903 to design a park and boulevard system for Seattle. Despite the amount of industrial activity on the waterfront, he recommended three locations for recreation and public access to the water and views. Given the high demand for the limited shoreline adjacent to deep water, the parks remained on the drawing board.

Workers on coastwise ships often planned springtime strikes. This strategy delayed shipments to replenish supplies for non-Native Alaskans who did not have access to the outside world while their ports were blocked by ice and who relied on imported foods for survival.

The next summer, several newly formed unions created a mutual assistance pact to fortify their bargaining power. They tried to include the longshoremen, sailors, marine firemen, marine cooks and stewards, caulkers, steamboatmen, and shipwrights in the pact with varying success. Other efforts to unite workers included the formation of the International Longshoremen, Marine and Transportworkers' Association, which aspired to be a maritime industry-wide union. The movement toward industry-wide unions in this era was led by more radical elements of the labor movement such as the "One Big Union" movement led by the Industrial Workers of the World. The effort to unionize was resisted by many waterfront workers who tended to be more conservative in their ideologies and tactics.

In 1902, in a surprising move indicative of the challenges of attracting workers in a booming economy, the stevedoring firm McCabe & Hamilton posted a new, higher wage scale for longshoremen. The union looked to Pacific Coast Steamship Company to match the new scale, but the company refused. The longshoremen struck and negotiations began. The company and the union reached a compromise, but the Seattle local rejected it. The strike continued into February 1903 when the union settled for less than it had demanded and all the locals on Puget Sound returned to work. Not long after, McCabe & Hamilton reverted to its former wage scale. The union's power ebbed.

Top: Longshoremen unloading cargo from a freighter by hand truck, 1906.
Bottom: Pacific Steamship Company routes to Alaska, 1917.

72   WHERE THE CITY MEETS THE SOUND

Mosquito Fleet steamers played a key role in the establishment of a Seattle icon: the Pike Place Market. Farmers and customers were frustrated with wholesalers charging exorbitant prices to consumers, but paying farmers little. On August 17, 1907, farmers sold produce directly to customers for the first time on Pike Place, which the city council had set aside for the nascent public market. The public market was wildly popular, soon growing to fill the curbs along Pike Place and later the Market's arcades. Many farmers came on steamers from around Puget Sound bringing berries, poultry, butter, eggs, and other farm produce to town. They traveled up the bluff via Western Avenue, a route that provided a reasonable grade and bypassed busy downtown streets.

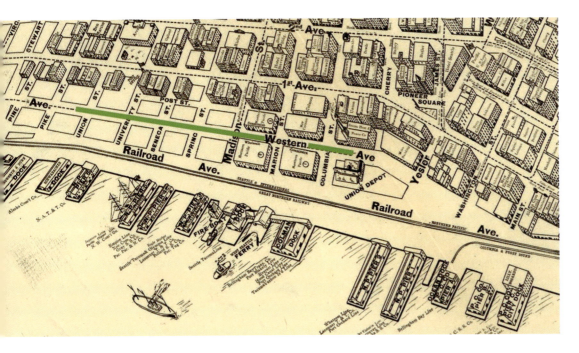

An attempt at retaining and filling along Western Avenue (green line) in 1904 was stymied by the tides running under the elevated streets. Detail from Periscopic Map Co. bird's-eye view, 1903.

After four years of relative quiet among workers and employers on the waterfront, the shipping companies, who had been informally meeting as the Bilgewaters at the Butler Hotel in Pioneer Square, officially became the Puget Sound Shipping Association. A short lockout of workers followed in May 1907. It was resolved quickly, but the next year Seattle longshoremen struck in support of striking Tacoma longshoremen. Shipping companies took advantage of the racially restrictive membership among waterfront unions and brought in Black miners to break the strike. The union lost the fight and had to accept wage cuts.

With the increased activity on the waterfront, the conflict between the north-south movement of people and goods and the east-west movement between downtown and the piers grew more problematic. After 1905, motor vehicles increased both danger and congestion. Railroad Avenue did not have any of the infrastructure needed for safety and order. Nearly every foot of its width was allocated to train right-of-way, and cars and trucks had to make their way along the tracks without benefit of lane markings or traffic lights.

Harbormaster reports for the first decade of the 20th century document the remarkable number of passengers crossing the central waterfront docks. In 1908, 4.5 million passengers traveled in and out of the city on ships and steamers. The vast majority were local passengers, coming and going from Puget Sound and Hood Canal towns and settlements. In 1909, a wooden bridge was built to allow pedestrians to pass over the chaotic waterfront. It ran along Marion Street, from the upper level of Colman Dock to First Avenue.

The increase in maritime trade also brought deep social connections. People from around the Pacific Rim came and went via the port and built a web of cultural and personal relationships. The American annexation of the Philippines brought a stream of students and workers to Seattle, along with the soldiers who maintained American control of the island nation. Japanese immigration began in the 1890s and picked up considerably in the 1900s. Residential segregation led to the development of a Nihonmachi (Japantown) adjacent to the existing Chinatown. Steamers from Alaska brought the children of non-Alaska Native settlers who were attending boarding schools in Seattle, along with workers, speculators, and businessmen heading north in the spring and south in the fall. The reciprocal influences shaped the identities of communities at both ends of the steamer routes.

To bring more structural stability to the waterfront, the city began to build a retaining wall along the western margin of Western Avenue in 1904, but construction did not proceed smoothly. In November, the contractors Stirrat & Goetz, hired to fill between Union and Columbia Streets, wrote to the city that "On account of the sea wash and the rise and fall of the tides, we have been unable to imp[rove] certain portions, along the western margins of the street, up to grade." Between April and October, they had placed more the 113,000 cubic yards of fill—the equivalent of around 750 rail cars full of soil—but much of it had washed away with the tides.

Meanwhile, teredoes and gribbles threatened the wooden infrastructure of the waterfront unrelentingly. Even with creosote treatments, the pilings weren't safe. It just took one small gap in the surface coverage of a wooden piling and pests could get into the heart of the timber and feast. They often went undetected until it was too late. This was the case on October 21, 1907, when the Ainsworth & Dunn pier at the foot of Clay Street collapsed. One man died and seven were injured. According to *The Seattle Times*,

> "Twenty men were working on the wharf when, with a crash that could be heard for blocks, the piling gave away and the north corner of the dock sank into the Sound . . . The collapse came so suddenly that almost before the men on the wharf knew what had happened, hundreds of tons of merchandise had fallen into the water."

Front page of the *The Seattle Daily Times* warns of the "Deadly Teredo," 1907.

Sargent Frances Jenkins & Rufina Clemente Jenkins, shown with their children at Fort Lawton in 1909, were the first Filipino American family in Seattle.

JENKINS FAMILY

The relative proximity of Seattle to the Philippines made it an important port for moving soldiers for the Philippine-American War and ongoing occupation of the Philippines. Many Seattleites volunteered for the war, and the US Army moved African American soldiers who served in the American West, known as the Buffalo Soldiers, to the Pacific War. Seattle's Black population would continue to grow with the arrival of 25th Infantry Regiment, which had served in the Philippine-American War and was temporarily stationed at the newly established Fort Lawton beginning in 1909. One Buffalo Soldier, Francis Jenkins, brought his Filipina wife, Rufina, and their children to Seattle. Rufina was among the first of a significant wave of Filipino migrants to Seattle following the United State's annexation of the island country. Their son, Frank Jenkins, would grow up to be a longshoreman and a union leader.

Near the same time, an existential threat to the port festering under the planked streets and buildings came to the surface on October 19, 1907, when Leong Seung succumbed to bubonic plague. Bubonic plague struck fear in city officials because it could lead to quarantine for the entire port. The Board of Health jumped into action to contain the outbreak which was quickly traced to the rats flourishing in the fetid conditions on the waterfront. Just a few days after Seung's death, the Board hired twelve inspectors to look for code violations and other conditions promoting the spread of disease. On October 25th, the Board authorized a five-cent bounty on rats "properly tagged and delivered." Just a week later, the Board increased the bounty to ten cents per rat and hired another inspector and a man to focus entirely on rat eradication.

As the winter progressed, the measures escalated. Dr. Frank Bourns became a full-time special health officer in charge of eradicating the plague. The city council authorized street improvements to fill in areas where rats congregated. By the end of 1908, 3,078 vessels had been inspected for signs of disease before being allowed to dock. The Health Department paid a bounty on 41,709 rats. City trappers caught an additional 15,500 rats. Nearly 50,000 were necropsied to check for plague.

These were just stopgap measures, however, as long as the rat-friendly conditions remained. The Board of Public Health inspectors painted a detailed portrait of the disgusting situation along Western Avenue:

> *"There is a vast amount of rotting timbers, planks, boxes, and all kinds of garbage, the waste of commission houses, restaurants, and markets. Within this district are broken sewers and cesspools. One cesspool in particular is thirty feet long, fifteen to twenty feet wide, and from eight inches to two feet deep, filled with the most horrible filth that it is possible to imagine."*

Near Cherry Street, "tons and tons of refuse from the chicken section" lay on the beach under a building—apparently a hole in the floor had served as a "garbage chute"—which was located near a "lake of sewage" from a broken sewer pipe.

The city council called for a seawall along the waterfront. The *Seattle Post-Intelligencer*, echoing that sentiment, complained that "there, and there alone, are the makeshifts of a pioneer era permitted to remain. Instead of permanent concrete docks there are temporary wharves of piling, rapidly crumbling under the ravages of the teredo." The harbormaster called for action on a seawall in his 1908 annual report, citing the availability of Denny Hill regrade spoils, the cost of continually re-planking Railroad Avenue, the railroads' trestle maintenance expenses, and the unsanitary conditions. Regardless of the many reasons to build a seawall, very few actual plans for a seawall appear in city records in the 1900s and the situation continued to fester.

Map showing sewer pipes to the waterfront at Union, Madison, and Columbia Streets, 1900.

REGINALD H. THOMSON

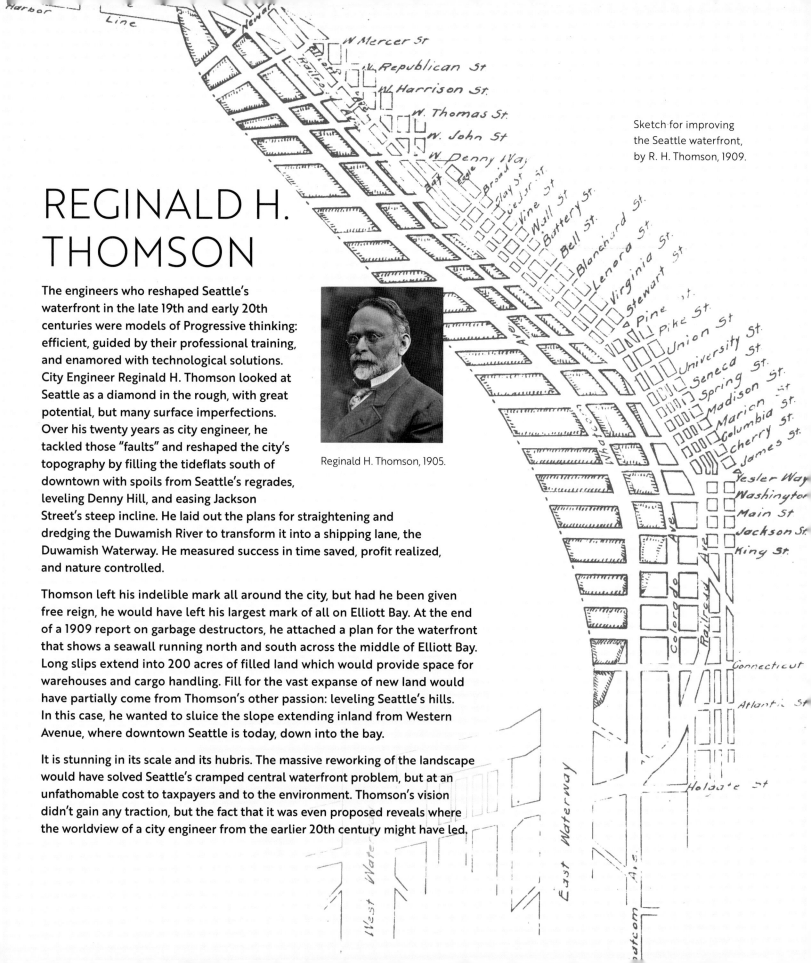

Sketch for improving the Seattle waterfront, by R. H. Thomson, 1909.

Reginald H. Thomson, 1905.

The engineers who reshaped Seattle's waterfront in the late 19th and early 20th centuries were models of Progressive thinking: efficient, guided by their professional training, and enamored with technological solutions. City Engineer Reginald H. Thomson looked at Seattle as a diamond in the rough, with great potential, but many surface imperfections. Over his twenty years as city engineer, he tackled those "faults" and reshaped the city's topography by filling the tideflats south of downtown with spoils from Seattle's regrades, leveling Denny Hill, and easing Jackson Street's steep incline. He laid out the plans for straightening and dredging the Duwamish River to transform it into a shipping lane, the Duwamish Waterway. He measured success in time saved, profit realized, and nature controlled.

Thomson left his indelible mark all around the city, but had he been given free reign, he would have left his largest mark of all on Elliott Bay. At the end of a 1909 report on garbage destructors, he attached a plan for the waterfront that shows a seawall running north and south across the middle of Elliott Bay. Long slips extend into 200 acres of filled land which would provide space for warehouses and cargo handling. Fill for the vast expanse of new land would have partially come from Thomson's other passion: leveling Seattle's hills. In this case, he wanted to sluice the slope extending inland from Western Avenue, where downtown Seattle is today, down into the bay.

It is stunning in its scale and its hubris. The massive reworking of the landscape would have solved Seattle's cramped central waterfront problem, but at an unfathomable cost to taxpayers and to the environment. Thomson's vision didn't gain any traction, but the fact that it was even proposed reveals where the worldview of a city engineer from the earlier 20th century might have led.

The fair's seal featured three women representing Alaska, Washington, and Asia, holding gold, a train, and a ship, respectively.

The Alaska-Yukon-Pacific Exposition (AYPE) was set to be held at the University of Washington campus from June to October 1909. The AYPE was unlike many world fairs commemorating historical events as it looked to the future. It promoted Seattle as the portal to Asia and Alaska markets with limitless potential.

In anticipation of the event two new transcontinental railroads began service to Seattle. The Milwaukee Road began service that year and took over Agen's pier for transferring cargo between ships and rail cars. The Soo-Seattle-Pacific Line began summer-only service from St. Paul, Minnesota, via Canadian Pacific tracks across Canada to Sumas, then south to Seattle. In 1915, it shifted its Seattle service to steamers operating from Northern Pacific's Pier 1 at the foot of Yesler to its western terminus at Prince Rupert, British Columbia.

By 1910, Seattle was a modern city. It had industry, global transportation connections, a burgeoning population, a developing hinterland, and key pieces of urban infrastructure: a park system plan, a streetcar system, a reliable water system, and a municipal power utility. The next challenge lay in taking those assets and realizing Seattle's potential. The waterfront was a key element of that potential as maritime trade continued to drive the regional economy.

YE OLDE CURIOSITY SHOP

Along with gold, travelers to the Klondike Gold Rush brought back art, artifacts, and oddities to Seattle. Interest in anything related to Alaska was high in Seattle. One early purveyor, Joseph E. "Daddy" Standley, opened a store at Second Avenue and Pike Street in 1899 to capitalize on it. The Alaska Club, dedicated to cultivating interest and investment in the northern territory, paid Standley to fill a display case at their headquarters in the Arctic Building with items to augment their efforts.

In 1901, Standley moved his shop, The Curio, directly adjacent to the docks where newcomers arrived in Seattle at the foot of Madison. Three years later, he moved to Colman Dock and renamed his store Ye Olde Curiosity Shop. Some of the items he sold were actual works of art produced in traditional styles by Indigenous artists. Many, however, were made just for the non-tribal market, in a style similar to the northern Northwest Coast tribes' traditions, even if the artists were members of other tribes.

After Standley's death in 1940, his family continued to operate the business and incorporate a broad range of items into the store, including two mummies named Sylvia and Sylvester, and items such as the Lord's Prayer written on the head of a pin, animals pickled in jars of formaldehyde, and other curiosities. The store is now located at Pier 54.

Ye Olde Curiosity Shop at Colman Dock, 1908.

"Most Unique Shop in the World," boasts Ye Olde Curiosity Shop, with items such as a "hat worn by Chief Seattle," and a 500 lb. pair of clam shells.

Wrestling with Growth

"Cut off the waterfront and shipping and the grass would be growing in Third Avenue in less than a year."

—MAYOR HIRAM GILL TO SEATTLE CITY COUNCIL, 1914

After the Gold Rush, Seattle's global connections increased, as shown by the steamship tickets available at Pier 4 between Spring and Seneca Streets, acirca 1900.

IN 1910, AS CITY LEADERS caught their breath from the first burst of development following the Klondike Gold Rush and anticipated the opening of the Panama Canal, they looked at how the city could be developed in a more rational, organized way. Important projects—the regrades that leveled hills and eased steep and uneven streets, tidelands fill, and the rapid construction of buildings in the downtown and residential districts—had proceeded without much orchestration. Big projects on the horizon—the Lake Washington Ship Canal, the Duwamish Waterway, and port terminal development—called for greater planning and coordination. Government and civic leaders tried to improve the waterfront's infrastructure, but wrangling public sentiment and realizing desired goals proved challenging. The boom times and relatively easy money of the Gold Rush era gave way to the hard work of managing population growth, infrastructure development, and social conflict.

The city council established the Municipal Plans Commission in 1910 and hired civil engineer Virgil Bogue to develop citywide plans for commercial, municipal, industrial, and residential development. Bogue was well-respected in Seattle because of his work on the Stampede Pass tunnel for the Northern Pacific Railroad's Cascade Mountains crossing. He had been involved in the Harbor Lines Commission's attempts to square up property ownership on Elliott Bay and would soon be hired by the Port of Seattle to develop its first comprehensive plan after it was voted into existence in 1911.

Bogue would never be accused of narrow thinking, nor did his faith in engineering ever waver. His *Plan of Seattle* reorganized downtown by moving the cluster of courthouses, city hall, and county offices to a civic center near the south end of Lake Union. Embodying the ideals of the City Beautiful movement that gained momentum across the country in the Progressive Era, the public buildings were large and ornate and the primary streets wide and tree-lined. One such street, a boulevard roughly along the alignment of today's Broad Street connected the civic center to the waterfront.

At the foot of the boulevard, Bogue placed one "watergate"—a formal entry into the city from the water—and another at the public dock at Spring and Madison Streets. Bogue proposed a ferry slip there, too. At the foot of Harrison, in a nod to a 1903 Olmsted plan, Bogue incorporated a power boat harbor, a recreation pier, and a pavilion. To provide a hillside viewpoint along the lines of Olmsted's recommendations, Bogue located a park at Elliott Avenue and Blanchard Street because it "offers the shortest course to the waterfront. The conditions at this proposed location are such as to afford the maximum of opportunity for a central waterfront outlook. It is peculiarly adapted

A detail of this Port of Seattle map shows the post-1889 fire angled alignment of piers east-to-west (east is up).

THE STORY OF SEATTLE'S WATERFRONT

This view of the Bell Street facility shows the pedestrian access to passenger service on the upper level.

The Port of Seattle completed their Bell Street Terminal in 1914.

Bogue's plans incorporated elevated streets, inclines, and subways (underpasses) to make Seattle's hilly topography accessible.

to the convenient assemblage of large crowds to view water spectacles." Bogue recommended shoreline fill to create space for a north-south street and increase the available frontage. And, for the first time, the idea of an elevated road along the waterfront appears in a planning document. He rejected it, however, because it would disrupt the waterfront's functioning and disconnect it from the central business district, much as later critics would argue about the Alaskan Way Viaduct.

Bogue allotted space for the ever-increasing numbers of ferries, power boats, and steamers carrying passengers and cargo. He located piers with access for smaller vessels between Yesler Way and Pike Street. A park would run on the eastern side of that small-boat harbor between Columbia and University Streets. Bogue moved most of the cargo handling south to proposed pier development at the mouth of the Duwamish Waterway.

For a variety of reasons, voters rejected Bogue's *Plan of Seattle* in March 1912. It was just the start of comprehensive waterfront planning efforts, however. His vision for a waterfront combining industry and commerce with facilities for enjoying the waterfront and its natural beauty would reappear multiple times over in various waterfront plans for the next 90 years. None of those plans succeeded either, primarily because of the ongoing commercial activities and transportation infrastructure obstacles on the waterfront. However, another plan was in development on the heels of Bogue's plan.

The Port of Seattle, formed in 1911, had just started its own planning process and hired Bogue to create a comprehensive plan for port development. In the same March 1912 election in which voters rejected the *Plan of Seattle*, they approved the Port's plan and seven bond measures to fund the first projects. These included a moorage at Salmon Bay, a deep-sea terminal at Smith Cove, a public wharf and warehouse at Bell Street, a pier on the East Waterway at the mouth of the Duwamish River, shipping terminals on Harbor Island, and a public ferry system on Lake Washington.

The Bell Street Terminal on the central waterfront was a group of structures: a two-story warehouse, a cold storage warehouse, a passenger terminal, and the Port of Seattle's headquarters. A bridge from Elliott Avenue connected to the warehouse's upper floor, or the terminal could be accessed via Railroad Avenue. It was the first pier designed for both truck and railcar loading. Pedestrians could cross a bridge from Elliott Avenue to reach a rooftop park which soon closed because its popularity with sailors and prostitutes became a "moral nuisance." The pedestrian access was the third crossing over the railroad tracks, joining the first at Marion Street and a second one at Pike Street connecting the Market with the waterfront in 1912.

When the Bell Street Terminal officially opened on May 22, 1915, it served local steamers and coastwise freight and passengers. The Port touted its use of Douglas fir girders measuring 14 inches by 33 inches

Overpasses were an essential, though not ideal, solution to the lack of waterfront access for pedestrians across Railroad Avenue.

Top: Barrels and baskets in the Seattle Hardware warehouse, circa 1917.
Bottom: Freight from *Tacoma Maru* in a transit shed, 1909.

and up to 40 feet in length. These timbers allowed the warehouse to hold up to 300 pounds per square foot. The Port also noted that soil from the Denny School block was used to fill the area inland from the pier. The Denny Hill regrade was underway and many people called for using the massive amounts of soil being sluiced into Elliott Bay to create new land on the central waterfront. Without a seawall, however, any deposited soils would wash away within a few days. With its own wharf structure serving as a seawall, the Port could protect the upland fill from tidal erosion.

The city was operating several facilities on the waterfront in addition to the Washington Street gridiron and the fire station. There were public piers at Harrison, Columbia, and Pike Streets where small boats could tie up for a short term, much like parking garages today where people leave their vehicles while they shop and conduct other business downtown.

A comprehensive solution to the seawall issue continued to flounder for topographical, financial, and political reasons. The primary issue was the seafloor. Its slope varied considerably along the central waterfront. South of Madison Street, the gentle slope allowed the city to construct a conventional seawall, with simple footings and a single concrete slab holding back the sea and protecting the fill placed behind it. The first section of wall, between Madison and Washington Streets, was completed in 1916 and extended south to King Street by 1918. Even there, with the gentler slope, the force of gravity made it difficult for the seawall to completely hold back the fill. Gravity pulled the fill behind the wall down the slope. As tidal action eroded the soil at the base of the wall on the water side, small amounts of fill escaped under the wall. By 1929, the deterioration led to the street settling between Madison and Washington Streets.

North of Madison Street, the seafloor sloped more steeply, increasing the gravitational forces pulling the fill downslope. In addition to resisting that pressure, the wall had to be able to withstand wave action on its westward side. At the western margin of Railroad Avenue, a wall needed to be tall enough to accommodate about 17 feet in tidal rise, on top of the depth of low water. That adds up to a lot of forces acting on the wall, making a conventional seawall with concrete footings insufficient. The wall could not be moved inland to shallower water without encroaching on upland cargo handling and Railroad Avenue. A conventional wall could also not be reinforced with riprap at its base because the volume of rock that would be required would encroach into the berthing areas along the piers, rendering them too short to be useful.

The biggest conundrum the city faced, however, was a funding issue. Engineers could design a wall that would solve the physical challenges, but only at significant expense. State law at that time required adjacent property owners to pay half of the cost of any improvements, such as sidewalks, paving, or a seawall. To portion out these expenses, the city formed local improvement districts consisting of all the parcels adjacent to an improvement. If more than half of the parcel owners objected to an improvement, it was blocked unless the city condemned the property and exercised eminent domain. In the seawall case, the adjacent property owners were primarily railroad companies that were perpetually in dire economic straits and had the political power to block projects, which they did repeatedly, to the chagrin of city officials.

The superintendent of streets addressed the waterfront conditions in his 1913 annual report. In addition to his reiteration of the expense and challenge of maintaining the planking on Railroad Avenue and

The seawall at Columbia Street (top) and north of King Street, (bottom) 1917.

THE STORY OF SEATTLE'S WATERFRONT **85**

Section of Railroad Avenue barricaded where an ice truck broke through, 1918.

surrounding streets, he also noted, "Increased use of auto trucks with their heavy loads has destroyed many planked streets that were built several years ago of material too light to withstand present traffic vehicles." With their higher horsepower, trucks could carry heavier loads than wagons, but this put more stress on the pilings and planks. Increasingly over the next twenty years, trucks and railroad cars periodically broke through the planking and dropped onto the beach below.

Like the seawall issue, labor conflict continued to simmer on the waterfront. Longshoremen had not regained control of hiring or wages since the 1908 strike, and their disdain for shipping companies' hiring practices and pay scales continued. The longshoremen struck on June 1, 1916, along with 21,000 West Coast dockworkers. The Waterfront Employers' Union (WEU), made up of Seattle-based shipping companies, brought in 1,400 non-union workers to break the strike, including Asian Americans and Blacks, taking advantage of the union's racially exclusive membership policy to undermine the union's power. As with earlier labor disputes where white workers refused to join forces with Blacks and Asian Americans, racial tensions rose. Historian Quintard Taylor tells of an incident on a streetcar when Horace Cayton Jr. witnessed white strikers attack a Black strikebreaker. One of the strikers used his cargo hook to grab the Black man by his neck and force him off the streetcar. Ron Magden, a labor historian, described the atmosphere during the strike: "For 127 days the Seattle waterfront resembled a battleground. Nonunion men went uptown looking for fights. Union longshoremen beat up scabs on docks and ships. There were fist fights, knife cuttings, dock bombings, pier fires, shooting duels, and murders."

The strike ended in October after a riot broke out at the foot of Seneca Street causing a breakdown in a tentative agreement with the WEU. The strikers' use of violence gave the employers the upper hand in the dispute and an open shop prevailed. The ILA, realizing the way shipping companies would continue to use the union's own racially exclusive policy against itself, integrated their union in 1918. Cayton, son of the prominent publishers and editors of *The Seattle Republican*, Horace Cayton Sr. and Susie Revels Cayton,

Longshoremen loading the *Manukai* in Seattle, circa 1925.

FISHERMEN'S UNIONS

The development of a fishermen's union paralleled the longshoremen's experience. When the industry was smaller and less capital-intensive, workers were not as organized, and work patterns developed over time as the number and size of fishing vessels grew. From the 1880s, when commercial halibut fishing began on Puget Sound, until the early 1910s, most fishing was limited to the Sound because the range was limited by the distances that could be reached under sail.

Beginning in the 1910s, diesel-powered schooners extended the Seattle-based industry's reach to the outer coast of Washington and up to Alaska. Tensions rose with the fishermen on the company-owned boats as larger seafood companies entered the market. In November 1912, disputes over share of the catch, prices paid for fish, and working conditions, along with rising danger on the open waters, led to the formation of the Halibut Fishermen's Union and a strike by the fishermen on the *San Juan*, *Independent*, and *Comet*. Fishermen from Tacoma joined the union, too. After a difficult four months, the companies met the fishermen's demands and the strike ended in mid-February. In January 1916, cod fishermen joined the union and it was renamed the Deep Sea Fishermen's Union of the Pacific.

Also similar to the labor disputes in the shipping industry, the boat owners formed an organization to represent their interests, the Fishing Vessel Owner's Association. It had offices on Pier 8 and operated a wholesale fish market there until the 1930s. More than 40 percent of the American halibut catch was landed at Seattle before 1940, but over the next decade the majority of fishing shifted north to Alaska where fish could be caught and processed, then shipped down to Seattle for distribution and export. Fish processing and selling continued on the waterfront, but on a smaller scale.

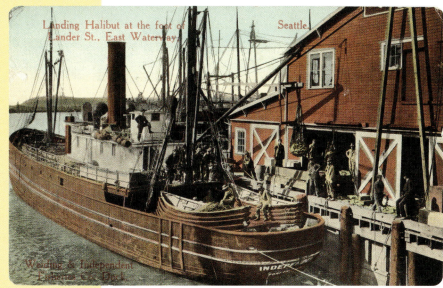

The *Independence* unloads halibut at a pier along the East Waterway, Seattle.

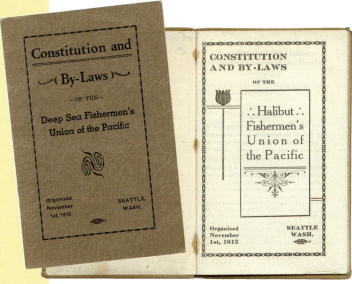

Original 1912 consitittion and bylaws of the Halibut Fishermen's Union of the Pacific, later renamed the Deep Sea Fishermen's Union of the Pacific.

joined the union and recruited other Black workers. It was a mixed experience, as Horace Jr. would later recall,

> *"We did have a black and white union, and a closed shop, and a union dispatching office. But it didn't stay that way for long. We noticed that the dispatchers were beginning to discriminate against Negro longshoremen on the pretext of union seniority. When work was slack, colored longshoremen were frozen out. Soon I lost my job and was then more convinced than ever that I'd been right, however desirable a mixed union was, you just couldn't trust any white man."*

In contrast to the very visible, public fight over labor rights, the fight over Indigenous fishing rights unfolded largely away from Elliott Bay and the Duwamish River. The Duwamish who lived around Elliott Bay had joined other area tribes in signing The Treaty of Point Elliott in 1855, ceding the majority of their traditional lands, but reserving a number of their existing rights, including fishing in their usual and accustomed places. To a degree, the state recognized those rights, going so far as stating in an 1891 state fisheries management law that, "this act shall not apply to Indians." Overfishing by non-Natives led to declining fish populations over time and later state legislatures passed several laws pertaining to licenses, restricted seasons, and prohibition of some gear, which, when applied to Native fishing practices, illegally abrogated the treaties.

The fishing restrictions were just one of many challenges tribal communities faced during the early decades of the 20th century. The effects of residential boarding schools undermined families, the Dawes Allotment Act reduced tribal land bases and opened reservation lands to non-Native ownership, and tribal governments struggled to exercise their sovereignty. To maintain their traditional ways and their connection with the land and waterways, Native people around the state protested the state's fishing restrictions and fought back through the courts. A series of cases guaranteed the tribes' access to their "usual and accustomed" fishing sites as promised in the treaties but denied their reserved right to fish freely in the state's waters using traditional methods, including nets and fish traps. Instead, the courts ruled that the Department of Fisheries could regulate tribal fishing to conserve fish populations. This not only ignored treaty rights but also held tribal fishing equally responsible for the decimation of fish populations that followed the introduction of fish wheels, canneries, and other elements of industrial fishing.

Despite these obstacles, Native people maintained their connection to dᶻidᶻəlalʼič, primarily by continuing to fish in Elliott Bay, working around the state-imposed restrictions. A *Seattle Post-Intelligencer* article from August 1907 remarked that

> *"The silver salmon are running in Elliott Bay and every evening sees a flotilla of from thirty to fifty dories trolling off the east and west waterways.*
>
> *Some of the fishermen come from the old floats at the foot of Massachusetts street and others live in shacks on the tideflats and these eke out a precarious existence by selling the fish to the local market.*
>
> *The greater number of fishermen, however, are from the Indian settlements under the bluffs of the*

Coast Salish tribal members paddling on the Sound, unknown date.

Duwamish head, south of West Seattle. There, in shacks built just above the high-water mark, a score of aboriginal families flourish and their fishing is not for the public market, but for the winter supply of food.

While the men work in the mornings and evenings out on the bay, the days are spent by the women cleaning the catch and smoking it.

Tribal sources show that Native people continued to use fish camps on Elliott Bay beaches until the 1910s when seawalls, dredging, and over-water construction obliterated shellfish beds and space for smoking the catch. After that, the tribes could still fish in Elliott Bay, but only from vessels on the water and under the state's rules.

Their reserved fishing rights would not be fully recognized by Washington state officials until 1974 when the tribal resistance movement, known as the Fish Wars, resulted in the court ruling in *United States v. Washington*, popularly referred to as the Boldt Decision. The ruling affirmed treaty-reserved fishing rights and established usual and accustomed areas for federally recognized tribes in Western Washington. Elliott Bay is a recognized usual and accustomed fishing area for the Muckleshoot Indian Tribe and the Suquamish Tribe because their enrolled members' ancestors fished there. The tribal fishers use docks reserved for them at the Port of Seattle's marinas around Elliott Bay and near Shilshole Bay in North Seattle.

"Soon I lost my job and was then more convinced than ever that I'd been right, however desirable a mixed union was, you just couldn't trust any white man."

In the 1910s, pier development in the area north of Lenora made room for businesses needing more room and fewer cross-traffic obstacles. Galbraith and Bacon moved their hardware and lumber store to Pier 10 at the foot of Wall Street. Richmond Beach Sand and Gravel operated just south of it. Roslyn Coal's dock at the foot of Cedar Street was transformed in 1920 into the American Can Company dock, with its massive warehouse and factory across Railroad Avenue. At the Dodwell Wharf at Broad Street, the Northland Steamship Company and Blue Funnel Line used Pier 14 as their terminal for ships transporting passengers and cargo to Europe and Asia. North of Broad Street, Standard Oil of California operated a fuel depot, a complex of fuel tanks extending two blocks inland and a dock where diesel-engine ships could fill their fuel tanks before heading out to sea. Its facilities stretched from Broad Street to Bay Street where the Olympic Sculpture Park is located today.

Indigenous camp on the beach in Seattle, circa 1885.

FISHING CONNECTS PAST AND FUTURE

Millennia Miller and Maryjane Miller fishing for king salmon with their dad, Henry Miller.

Louie Ungaro, a member of the Muckleshoot Tribe, fishes on the Duwamish River and on Elliott Bay. His personal connection to the waters and the land that surrounds it traces from his parents and grandparents to his great-grandparents. After a lifetime of fishing, he knows the waters and how they change with the seasons and the weather; he knows the plants and animals living in the waters; he knows the landmarks surrounding the bay. He also feels the connection fishing provides within the Muckleshoot tribal community, with the Suquamish Tribe across the Sound, and with the "sister tribes" from around the region. Beyond the immediate connection to the water and land, he also has a spiritual connection to this place that is part of his identity.

The tribes have been here since time immemorial and have no intention of moving on, so they fish, and they protect the fish populations by ensuring there is enough escapement of salmon to spawn the next generation. The tribes also tend to the upper reaches of the rivers to protect habitat and mitigate for the impacts of pollution, climate change, and population growth. Ungaro works to protect the fisheries because of the importance of fishing—it connects people to the non-human world and to other people who live here. He believes it isn't an option to break that connection and not sustain it for the next generation.

Fishing for chum salmon on Elliott Bay, 2024.

The Standard Oil facilities viewed from the roof of the American Can Company, 1934.

World War I would have a massive impact on Seattle's maritime economy, but not on the central waterfront. Shipbuilding companies built out their shipyards in the southern end of the bay, on the East and West Waterways and Harbor Island, and along the newly opened Duwamish Waterway, as the straightened and dredged Duwamish River was renamed. Likewise, the war stimulated the newest industry in Seattle, airplane manufacturing. William Boeing moved from his first workshop on Lake Union to the wide-open farm fields in the Duwamish River valley.

Passenger traffic on Seattle's piers initially declined drastically with the American entrance into World War I, dropping from nearly 3 million in 1916 to about 1.5 million in 1917. The port warden did not provide any explanation for the decline in his annual report, but the Streets and Sewers Department blamed the war for higher costs that slowed progress on the seawall south of Washington Street. The next year, the number of passengers rebounded dramatically. More than 4.7 million passengers again passed through the waterfront. There was also a dramatic increase in foreign arrivals, jumping up to 87,000 in 1918. This was higher than previous years when the average was below 10,000, excluding travelers to and from British Columbia. In 1919, passenger numbers jumped again, with 114,000 foreign arrivals, and the Harbor Department Annual Report notes that 20,000 passengers traveled to and from Alaska. This east-west movement of people between downtown and the piers, paired with the farm produce and other cargo coming into downtown from steamers, continued to clash with the north-south movement of trains and the increasing truck traffic.

Each Harbor Department Annual Report documented the types of vessels coming and going. By the 1910s, steam and motor (diesel) ships predominated. Sailing ships continued to call at the port, primarily carrying lumber, a heavy but non-perishable commodity that could be shipped cost-effectively by slower sailing ships. Natural resources continued to be a significant portion of the cargo

THE STORY OF SEATTLE'S WATERFRONT

moving through the port, including gold, nearly 35 years after the start of the Klondike Gold Rush.

As the 1920s got underway, the types of cargo moving through grew more diverse. Ships running between Seattle and Alaska, California, Hawaii, the Philippines, Indian, China, Japan, the East Coast, Europe, and South America carried raw materials and finished goods, automobiles, raw silk and silk goods from Asia, and grain from Eastern Washington farms. While the Great Northern Steamship Company ceased its regular service in 1915, numerous other shipping lines helped maintain Seattle's close connection with Asian ports.

Another strike disrupted activity on the waterfront in 1921 when the Marine Cooks and Stewards Union struck for higher wages. This union remained racially exclusive despite the lesson of the longshoremen from 1916, and Black workers were once again brought in to break the strike. James A. Roston, a Seattle realtor who had served with the all-Black Tenth Cavalry in the American-Philippine War recruited many of the Black workers as he had in the 1916 strike. They took over the majority of steward positions on passenger ships running out of Seattle for ports on the West Coast from Alaskan to California. Historian Quintard Taylor traced a shift in employment for Blacks in Seattle to the strike. They followed the stewards onto the passenger lines and took jobs as singers, musicians, cooks, dishwashers, bellhops, and telephone operators. Many of the musicians and singers also played the clubs on Jackson Street when they were in town, fueling the development of a vibrant jazz scene in Seattle.

The need for a proper seawall was obvious but one would remain unbuilt through the 1920s. Funding

Japanese silk in a waterfront warehouse, circa 1920s.

The Grand Trunk Pacific Railway added steamship service in 1910. In this image, Railroad Avenue traffic passes their dock at Marion Street, circa 1925.

WASHINGTON STREET BOAT LANDING

At Washington Street, the city replaced the gridiron with a pair of floats and a metal pergola. Christened the Naval Shore Station on July 3, 1920, it served the tenders from visiting naval ships at anchor in the harbor and launches from local military facilities such as those from Sand Point Naval Air Station, Puget Sound Navy Shipyard, and Fort Lawton. The city recognized the significant role military operations played in the city's economy and wanted to encourage its continued presence.

The port warden's office and its radio station KGL occupied a small space in the pergola. A new radio installed in 1923 could reach ships up to 3000 miles away, providing communication for local businesses with ships at sea and with harbor management, including coordinating vessel traffic and responding to SOS calls.

remained elusive with local improvement district assessments blocked. The state legislature resisted lobbying from Seattle for funding. The general sentiment towards the Seattle projects is captured by an item in the *White Bluffs Spokesman* out of Hanford in eastern Washington, "Seattle is not at all unselfish in its demands at this session. There are now pending bills which, if all enacted, would give what remains of the motor vehicle fund after the policy bills are out of the way, to that city."

Nevertheless, the waterfront remained economically vital. The 1926–1927 *Port of Seattle Yearbook* highlights all the ways in which Seattle's waterfront was operating at full capacity. It compared trade in 1906 to 1925, and the growth was phenomenal: from $10 million to $320 million in imports and from $48 million to $120 million in exports; 5,429 vessels called at the port in 1925; Hawaiian trade quadrupled and Alaskan trade doubled.

The waterfront had almost everything it needed to succeed: railroads, dozens of shipping lines regularly coming into port, the Port of Seattle, sufficient population to support trade and industry, capital to invest, a shoreline full of piers, and an upland full of warehouses and light industry. It also had bankers, insurance companies, brokers, and ship chandleries. The only real weakness was the lack of a seawall north of Washington Street. The future looked bright until the Great Depression hit in 1929.

Breakdown of Seattle's average annual foreign and domestic commerce, 1921–1930.

The Port of Seattle's Bell Street Terminal, busy as ever, but mind the gap! Circa 1920.

GEORGE BROOM, SAILMAKER

For 21 years, George Broom led renditions of "Blow the Man Down" and served hundreds of clams dug from the beds in front of his Port Madison home at an annual February party he held in his loft on Pier 8. The party drew 50 invited guests each year and was described by *The Seattle Times* as

> "captains and commodores, executives of steamship lines, members of the pilots' association, some fellows who didn't rate financially, but they were all 'good waterfront men.'"

The men would compete in the annual "lying contest," such as the one in 1935 where,

> "Captain Ernest Brinker, old-time pilot, told of a motor launch with batteries powered by electric eels. Captain Alex Peabody described an automatic seagull ejector which consisted of sharp spikes placed on ferryboat masts to keep the birds away."

George Broom working on a sail in his loft, 1935.

Broom was born near Yarmouth in Norfolk, England, in 1870 and came to Seattle in 1886. He worked first for an Irishman from Liverpool, Louis Wilton, who had made sails in the British Navy. They worked out of a loft on Yesler's Wharf until the 1889 fire swept it away. Broom shifted to the Felix Brothers' tent and awning company for a couple of years, then joined with William T. Tickle to form Broom & Tickle, sailmakers and riggers. Around 1898, after travelling back to England or to the Klondike (sources vary), Broom returned to Seattle and started his own business on Pier 6. In 1914, he moved to Pier 8, where he held his annual clam feast.

After his death in October 1935, Jackson B. Corbett Jr. wrote a remembrance in *Marine Digest*,

> "He was the perfect host, moving quietly among his throngs of old friends and yet somehow infusing the whole gathering with a glowing spirit of fellowship and good cheer and happiness. As you entered the sail loft you stepped into the past, into the old world of sea romance. You stepped into an atmosphere of sailing ship days—the aroma of sailcloth, hemp, tar, and rum in the air; walls covered with pictures of famous ships and navigators; a large ship's wheel here; and scattered about the loft a clutter of nautical instruments and gear of all kinds, and over there in the center of the loft the huge potbellied stove crackling cheerfully."

Broom brought his sons into the business before his death. George Broom's Sons relocated to the Lake Washington Ship Canal in 1946 and continues to make sails today.

Negotiating Depression and War

"This Railroad Avenue is a death trap. It is a menace to the life of all that use it. The improvement should be made because daily the hazard is run of taking human life by inaction."

—MAYOR JOHN DORE, JANUARY 1933

The waterfront, looking south from Magnolia, with several navy ships at anchor in Elliott Bay, circa 1930s.

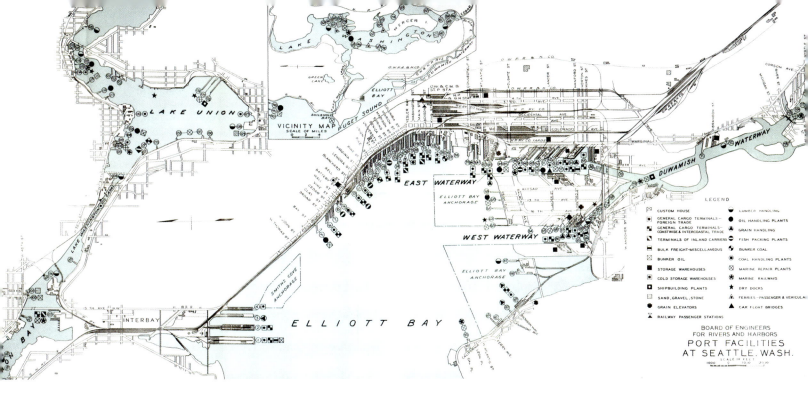

Army Corps of Engineers map of cargo handling and facilities on the Seattle waterfront, 1932.

THE CENTRAL WATERFRONT was such a fundamental part of how the city worked, that it continued to be active even during the economic recession of the 1930s. At the same time, the central waterfront's underlying challenges—not enough space in the uplands, the lack of a seawall, the limit on pier length due to the seafloor's steep slope—made other parts of the harbor, where new port facilities offered more space and better infrastructure, more appealing. As those other areas developed, the central waterfront became less "central" and began to decline. Disinvestment and changes in shipping would culminate in the piers' obsolescence for cargo handling by the late 1960s.

Newspaper articles in the 1930s describe scores of ships coming and going. There is very little mention of slowdowns or business closures. In 1930, Canadian Pacific moved its operations to a new "modern steamship passenger terminal" at the Port of Seattle's Bell Street Terminal. In 1936, the Brostroem Line began the first direct service between Seattle and Europe with the *Falsterbro* and *Fermia* steamships. The Pacific Coast Terminal Company began a major renovation of its piers adjacent to Pioneer Square in 1936. Its parent company, McCormick Steamship Company, made one pier its terminal for ships running between Seattle and California ports and mid-Atlantic ports on the East Coast. The next year, Alaska Steamship announced it would be running 21 ships between Seattle and Alaska, for a total of 170 sailings. The *Post-Intelligencer* called it the "most comprehensive and sustained service ever listed."

The Depression's impact can be seen, however, in the lack of upkeep. Few companies besides McCormick made significant improvements to their piers. The streets' planking and pilings continued to deteriorate, and the city's reduced budget could not keep up. In 1933, Mayor John Dore wrote to the city council encouraging approval of the seawall project saying "This Railroad Avenue is a death trap. It is a menace to the life of all that use it. The improvement should be made because daily the hazard is run of taking human life by inaction." He also noted,

THE STORY OF SEATTLE'S WATERFRONT   97

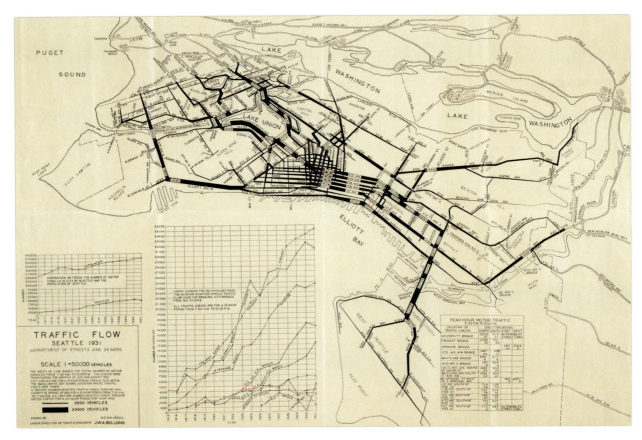

This traffic flow map from 1931 details the huge increase in vehicle traffic from 1915 to 1931.

"Another fact that should not be overlooked is that this is a public project that will ... decrease the huge toll of unemployment in this community. .... It is also of great help from the standpoint of community well-being. If in this community by public projects we do not soon get thousands to work, I hesitate to forecast the dire consequences."

As time passed with no progress, Dore grew frustrated with the railroads' and pier owners' resistance to funding the seawall. He refused to continue to drain the city budget by repairing the planking and pilings. As sections of Railroad Way fell into disrepair, he simply placed detour signs around the gaping holes that developed.

Beyond the economic troubles, other seeds of change were planted during the 1930s. The Pacific Highway had been paved between Seattle and Tacoma in 1928. In 1932, the section between Everett and Seattle was paved and the George Washington Memorial Bridge over the Lake Washington Ship Canal opened. The paved roads allowed reliable, relatively easy travel overland in a region that had long relied on primarily shipping for cargo movement between cities. Now trucks could be used for deliveries to inland areas and Seattle's preeminence as the region's market town and hub of transportation rapidly declined.

Increased use of trucks and trains for coastwise trade was felt all along the West Coast, making the already-competitive shipping industry even tougher. With ship operations and pier facility costs fairly fixed, labor was one of the few expenses that companies could reduce. They were always looking for ways to reduce the number of longshoremen needed, the wages paid, and the time ships sat idle during cargo handling. After the initial stock market crash in 1929,

Without a seawall, Railroad Avenue was a "death trap." Looking South from Lenora Steet, 1934.

Longshoremen unloading cargo, circa 1935.

fewer and fewer longshoremen found work on the waterfront as each year passed. Employment reached a nadir on February 24, 1933, when no longshoremen were dispatched to work the ships.

The shipping industry began to recover from its low point that spring and workers began to ask for restoration of higher wages. The Pacific District of the International Longshoremen's Association (ILA) represented most of the 14,000 longshoremen on the West Coast. Despite a large number of American Federation of Labor affiliated union locals nationwide (AFL), overall membership declined significantly between 1919 and 1933, from more than 4 million to about 2.5 million. This was partly because many of the locals were company unions and were operating in collaboration with employers. In Seattle, the ILA could not get shipping companies to allow union-controlled hiring. A Journalist from the *Daily Call* described the longshoremen's experiences with the shape-up process:

> *"His 'luck' [at getting hired] depended on a number of factors. Does some hiring boss have special favor for him? Has he been able to find a hiring boss willing to take a kick-back for every day's work? Has he been able to befriend a hiring boss through an occasional bottle of liquor, or through such little services of painting or repair work on his house?"*

But the longshoremen and others working in the maritime trades did not have much choice, Morris explained,

> *"Seamen called it 'piecing-off the crimp' but by any name it meant eating instead of starving. For all intents and purposes the shape-up and the chance to work was the sum total of the benefits paid-out by the company union."*

As the longshoremen's work conditions continued to decline, the Communist Party of America increased its organizing among maritime workers. Like the Industrial Workers of the World (IWW, or Wobblies) before them, the

"Seamen called it 'piecing-off the crimp' but by any name it meant eating instead of starving."

communists wanted to organize an industry-wide union affiliated with the more radical Congress of Industrial Organizations (CIO). The longshoremen tended to be more conservative than other industries' union members. However, according to historian Andrew Bonthius, the lack of leadership by the AFL unions and the horrible working conditions and low pay made CIO's message more attractive. The passage of the National Industrial Recovery Act (NIRA) in June 1933 also promoted more aggressive advocacy for workers' rights. The Act required that companies develop "codes of fair competition" for their industries. The codes addressed pricing, production quotas, and wages, with the goal of reviving the country's industrial base.

In the fall of 1933, the companies and the Tacoma ILA Local 38-3 each produced proposals for the shipping industry's labor code. The union proposed $1.00 straight pay, $1.50 for overtime, a six-hour day, and union-controlled hiring halls in place of the shape-up. The employers only agreed to $0.85 cents for the first 44 hours per week, and $1.20 for overtime. They refused to recognize the ILA.

The NIRA hearing on the code was held in Washington, DC, in late January 1934. Shipping companies opposed the terms under consideration and no agreement was reached. Shipping companies then rejected new terms proposed by the ILA's Pacific District and the union locals voted to strike. In Seattle, on May 9th, 1,500 longshoremen "hung the hook" and walked off the job. Other maritime unions, including the sailors, marine engineers, and the masters, mates, and pilots all joined the strike. The Teamsters agreed to support the strike by not carrying cargo in trucks driven by their members.

It did not take long for the shipping companies to bring in strikebreakers. By May 12th, 650 of them were working on Seattle's waterfront piers, protected by fencing on the inland side of the piers. Sensing that the Seattle longshoremen might not be aggressive enough to hold the line, longshoremen from Tacoma and Everett arrived to bolster their resolve. They strong-armed their way onto Pier 6 where they beat up two strikebreakers and threw one into the water. They then moved to Pier 1, with no resistance from the police, and continued down the waterfront to oust any strikebreakers they could find moving cargo.

Seattle's situation was different than other ports'. Seattle's docks held supplies for the canneries that needed to be ready for the salmon runs, and food and other necessary items for Alaskans, some of whom had been frozen in for the whole winter and were low on supplies. This situation gave the union some leverage in negotiations. On May 23rd, the Joint Northwest Strike Committee formed to negotiate with the Alaskan shipping companies to handle labor on the cannery supply ships. The committee agreed to allow the ships to be loaded if the longshoremen and the ships' crews were union members. Washington Governor Clarence Martin sent a telegram to the committee on May 29th "pleading for resumption of Alaska shipping," but the committee could only refer the politicians to the Waterfront Employers' Association (WEA). On June 5th, the first Alaska shipping companies agreed to the

The Northwest Joint Strike Committee in Seattle, 1934.

FILIPINO CANNERY WORKERS UNION

The annexation of the Philippines in 1898 created a pathway for Filipinos to emigrate as United States nationals and a Filipino community soon formed in Seattle. Many of the newcomers attended colleges, including the University of Washington, while others worked as laborers. The number of emigrant workers increased over time, especially after the Immigration Act of 1924 excluded Asian immigrants. By 1930, about 1,600 Filipinos lived in Seattle.

Many Filipino Seattleites started working summers in Alaska's fish canneries beginning in the 1910s. By the 1930s, more than 4,000 Alaskeros traveled north each year. The cannery workers faced discrimination in pay scales, job opportunities, housing, and living conditions. In response, they formed the Cannery Workers and Farm Laborers Union Local 18257 in 1933. It was the first local largely operated by and for Filipino laborers. The affiliation with farm workers was a natural fit because many of the cannery workers traveled to work in agricultural areas in Eastern Washington, Oregon, and California after they returned from Alaska each year.

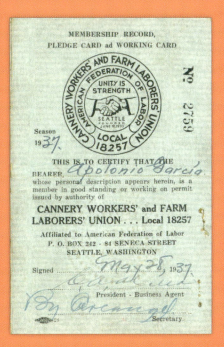

A Cannery Workers' Union card from 1937.

Filipino cannery workers heading for Alaska at Pier 40, 1939.

Cannery Worker's Union members picket along Pier 2 on the Seattle waterfront, 1939.

THE STORY OF SEATTLE'S WATERFRONT

union's terms. Five more companies followed later that day. Alaska Steamship held out for the union to agree to accept 71 of the non-union longshoremen who had been working their ships.

On June 8th, the "Alaska Agreement" was reached with the Alaska shipping companies. It granted the union control of hiring, a six-hour day, a 30-hour week, and a higher wage scale. Additionally, the strikebreakers had to join the union within thirty days. The Joint Northwest Strike Committee also required that other ports on the West Coast agree to the same terms for Alaska shipping before workers would return. Shipping companies balked at extending the agreement to other ports.

The parties having reached a stalemate, Seattle Mayor Charles Smith gave the longshoremen 24 hours to return to work or the police would open the ports in Seattle, Tacoma, Portland, and Bellingham. On June 16th, a new agreement was reached in which the ILA would be recognized, the hiring halls would be jointly operated by the union and companies, and union and non-union workers could be hired. Wages and hours were left for later resolution. Over the next two days all the union locals except for Los Angeles rejected the terms.

On June 20th, Smith called in the police to open the docks. They started at Pier 40 in Smith Cove. Three hundred police officers and special deputies confronted 200 longshoremen at Pier 40 and then 400 longshoremen at the Milwaukee Dock at the foot of Union Street. The next day, 600 union members filled the picket line at Pier 40. They covered the tracks with equipment and scrap materials found nearby and greased the rails so the trains bringing in railroad cars for cargo could not get to the pier. A melee broke out and the mayor refused to back down. The union called a halt to all Alaska cargo handling.

Violence sporadically broke out over the last few days of June. Tear gas grenades were thrown at the front door of the ILA hall. A bomb exploded in front of the Northern Pacific Railroad yardmaster's home. A striker was killed at Point Wells (near Edmonds) while investigating reports that non-union workers were handling fuel there. In early July, violence broke out in San Francisco and two strikers were killed on July 5th. A general strike was called for that city on July 16th. That evening, 3,000 union members and their allies attended a rally at Civic Auditorium in Seattle. Skirmishes erupted between strikers and the police over the next couple of days.

On July 19th, the union agreed to National Longshoremen's Board arbitration on the condition that the shipping companies also agreed. Before the process could begin, however, the Battle of Smith Cove broke out at Piers 40 and 41. Ron Magden described it:

> "At midnight on July 19. Seattle Police Chief George Howard argued with Mayor Smith over the use of force against strikers. Howard resigned. Then Smith took personal command. At 5 a.m. Tacoma, Everett, Aberdeen, and Bellingham [police] reinforcements marched in semi-military formation into the strikers' enclave in front of the pier gate. At 6:45 a.m., the mayor gave the order to drive pickets from the entrance to Smith Cove. Longshoremen in the front ranks yelled.

Armed police stationed in Smith Cove in July 1934.

102   WHERE THE CITY MEETS THE SOUND

"Come on men. hold your ground!" Police Captain George H. Comstock shouted from the top of the bridge. "All right. let 'er go!" Tear gas pellets rained down from the bridge superstructure on the pickets. A half dozen strikers with gloves picked up pellets and tossed them back on the bridge. Police on foot closed in on the strikers. shooting tear gas and wielding riot sticks against those who tried to hold their ground. A few pickets, not yet affected by the gas, threw stones at the advancing police. Their resistance was met by police clubbings. Olaf Helland, a Sailors' Union striker, fell mortally wounded from a hit in the head by an unexploded gas grenade. In fifteen minutes the police chased pickets from the gates to the railroad tracks where a last stand was made. Then mounted police chased the men up the slopes of Queen Anne Hill. As the battle ended, Mayor Smith and Chamber of Commerce President Alfred Lundin congratulated each other."

That same day, the ILA agreed to National Longshoremen's Board arbitration. The longshoremen returned to work as that process unfolded. On October 12th, the board released its decision, and the union came out on top with increased wages, a 30-hour work week, joint control of hiring halls, and union control of dispatching. The extent of the win is reflected in *The Seattle Times* headline: "Workers Jubilant; Employers Caustic." Over the next few years, the ILA membership leaned toward the industrial union movement and, in 1937, became the International Longshore and Warehouse Union (ILWU). It was led by Harry Bridges and affiliated with the Congress of Industrial Unions.

Squabbles erupted periodically between workers and employers after the 1934 strike, but the fundamental goals the labor union had strived for since the 1880s had been realized. The waterfront workers who handled cargo—the stevedores, the riggers, the warehousemen—had a foundation of dignity and security that would provide stability in port operations through the coming decades.

Striking longshoremen block train tracks at Pier 40, July 19, 1934.

ALASKAN WAY SEAWALL DESIGNS

There were two types of structures used for the Alaskan Way seawall design. Both designs utilized sheet wall piling driven into the seafloor as a foundation for the concrete slab seawall face. The concrete slab was connected to a timber structure on the inland side. The timber structure consisted of plumb pilings, driven vertically into the ground, batter pilings driven at an angle, pier caps that formed a grid that laid on top of the piles, and a relieving platform across the top of the pier caps made of wooden planks.

The relieving platform was located midway between the seafloor and the surface street and the weight of the fill on top of it counterbalanced the gravitational forces pushing the wall outward. Tie rods connected the steel sheet piling to the relieving platform.

The Type A wall design was the smaller of the two types and was used between Washington Street and Madison Streets where the seafloor was more gradually sloped. Its steel sheet piling was driven completely into the seafloor and the concrete wall was set on top of it. Its relieving platform extended 40 feet inland.

The Type B wall, built where the seafloor was steeper north of Madison Street, had a relieving platform extending 20 feet farther inland and had more pilings to anchor the pier caps. The steel sheet pilings extended above the seafloor and the entire wall was backed by steel I-beams.

Alaskan Way was built on top of the fill on both seawalls and the sidewalk cantilevered out from the top of the concrete seawall slabs. Large rocks, known as riprap, piled up against the base of the seawall on the face of the wall and on the soil along its base, protected it from most of the erosive effects of tidal action. This helped limit the amount of fill that could work its way out from under and behind the wall through cracks and at the seams between the concrete and steel portions of the wall.

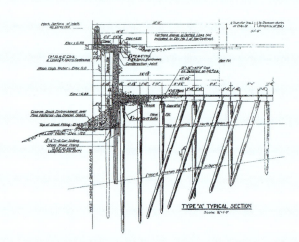

The Type "A" seawall design was used for less steeply sloped sections.

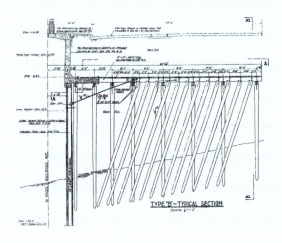

The Type "B" seawall design was needed in steeper sections with greater water depth.

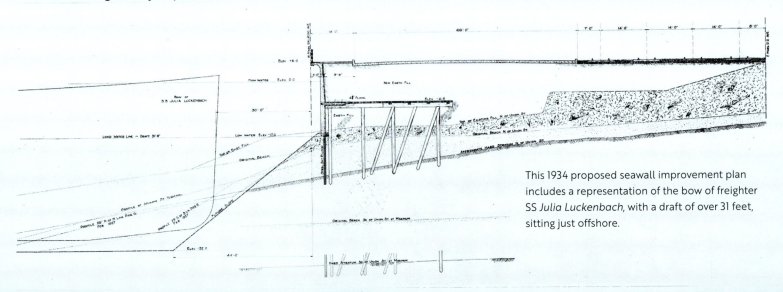

This 1934 proposed seawall improvement plan includes a representation of the bow of freighter SS *Julia Luckenbach*, with a draft of over 31 feet, sitting just offshore.

While the workers' struggles were unfolding during the 1930s, efforts to replace the trestles on the waterfront with solid ground continued. The city's engineering department completed plans for 6,040 feet of the wall, stretching from Madison Street to Bay Street. The plans included two types of seawalls, both using relieving platforms to anchor the wall to the shore. Type A was designed for the conditions from Pike Street north to Bay Street where the water was somewhat shallower. The Type B design was used between Madison and Pike Streets where the water reached its greatest depth. The relieving-platform design reduced costs by making it possible to use less-expensive construction methods and timber that was locally plentiful and relatively cheap. Instead of having to build cofferdams, temporary seawalls that would hold back the seawater and create dry space for pouring concrete footings and the wall, the concrete and steel portions of the wall could be constructed off-site and placed directly in the water.

The city estimated that building a seawall between Madison Street and Bay Street (the northern boundary of Olympic Sculpture Park today) would cost $1.4 million. In March 1932, voters approved a $600,000 bond measure, but the project also relied on a $600,000 assessment on property owners and additional state funding, which proved elusive. Property owners threatened to block the project by protesting the assessment and the mayor feared state funding would not be allocated or that, if it was, other important projects would go unfunded.

Finally, in November 1933, the funding pieces fell into place. The property owners agreed to pay $400,000 if the city secured $396,000 from the State Emergency Relief Fund. The city council stated in the project fund ordinance:

> "Widespread and acute distress exists among the unemployed inhabitants of this City to such an extent as to endanger the immediate preservation of order and the public health and safety, and it is therefore expedient and necessary that work on the construction hereby authorized be commenced at the earliest possible date in order to provide employment."

Fill being placed behind newly constructed seawall, 1934.

Paying for the labor costs with that relief funding eased the burden on the city and property owners enough to make the costs manageable and the project finally proceeded.

The city could not find a private company willing to take on the project and so it served as the general contractor, letting contracts for materials and hiring day laborers to complete the work. The first seawall construction contract was let in January 1934, the last fill was placed in August 1936, and the entire project was completed that December. In place of the cacophony of railroad tracks, a new paved roadway and three sets of tracks ran the length of the central waterfront in an orderly fashion.

The city considered naming suggestions from around the state for the new street—Cosmos Quay, Seawall Avenue, Port Strand, Bois Boolong, Salt Spray Way, Export Way—but settled on "Alaskan Way," which was suggested by a local organization the Alaska-Yukon Pioneers. The *Argus* newspaper noted that

After the seawall was completed, the city reduced the number of train tracks and moved them east of the newly constructed Alaskan Way.

the name "dignifies its importance and emphasizes its traditions as the point from which the argonauts embarked for the gold fields of the north." The name also highlighted the continued importance of Alaskan trade to Seattle's economy.

The environmental consequences of covering the tidelands passed without remark in city records or the press. The Alaskan Way seawall connected with the seawall running south to the mouth of the Duwamish River built in the 1910s. The fill behind the walls buried vast areas of the intertidal zone on Elliott Bay. They obliterated shellfish beds and thousands of acres of marine and shoreline habitat that had sustained a rich web of plants and animals. Its cultural impacts also escaped notice in non-Native communities, but the Duwamish, Suquamish, and other Coast Salish tribal members lost the tidelands their ancestors had lived on and cultivated for millennia.

The non-Native communities focused on the economic benefits the seawalls provided. The seawalls allowed the waterfront to operate on solid ground and ended the continual monitoring and maintenance of pilings and planking. Trains, automobiles, and pedestrians could navigate the waterfront more easily and safely. However, the ease of travel attracted so many vehicles hoping to avoid congested downtown streets that the Propeller Club, a maritime-commerce group, petitioned the city to address traffic issues on Alaskan Way in 1939. The petition asserted "The use of the waterfront as a traffic 'bypass' is gravely harming our most vital industry—shipping. Relief must be obtained promptly if irreparable damage to the city's maritime commerce is to be avoided."

Even during the Depression, motor vehicle registrations in King County increased. There were 115,000 vehicles registered by 1936. They had become essential, rather than novelties, and the city had to find

SEAWALL MATERIALS AND EMPLOYMENT

The scale of the Alaskan Way seawall is difficult to grasp because most of it was hidden from view once the fill was placed and covered with pavement. A May 1933 article in *The Seattle Star* catalogued the enormous volume of materials needed to build the wall:

- 50,000 barrels of cement
- 32,000 cubic yards of sand and gravel for making concrete
- 245,000 cubic yards of sand and gravel from the mouth of the Cedar River for fill behind the wall
- 5.2 million board feet of lumber
- 600,000 lineal feet of piling (about 20,000 pilings total)
- 1,775 tons of structural and reinforcing steel

In all, 5,000 men were employed in constructing the wall and its components. As the State Emergency Relief Fund intended, their wages produced a stream of revenue that flowed through the local economy and eased unemployment well beyond the project's payroll.

Construction crews used the tide to place the pier caps on top of the pilings. Sections of pier-cap grids were constructed off-site at the city's yard on Harbor Island. Each piling connection point was pre-cut according to measurements of the pilings driven into the beach. Sections were floated to the work site at high tide and allowed to drop into place as the tide receded.

Seawall under construction. Man at left is standing at the level of the future sidewalk.

IVAR HAGLUND

In the dark days of the Depression, Ivar Haglund—real estate man, folk song crooner, and showman at heart—opened The Aquarium on Pier 3 (today's Pier 54) in 1938. He brought Pat the Seal, Oliver and Olivia the octopi, and a multitude of Puget Sound's marine creatures to tanks in a space along the pier's frontage. He "declared his exhibit will not be a display of freaks, but a showing of 'fascinating' marine life of Puget Sound," but he embraced the opportunity to entertain. He put Pat the Seal in a baby carriage and took her shopping in downtown Seattle for a Christmas present for her friend Ockie, an octopus. Ivar was happy to add to his display a five-foot-long wolf eel "with a protruding jaw and a head like that of a bulldog" caught by fishermen Mike, Joe, and Jack Cricuola off Whidbey Island near Coupeville.

Ivar Haglund with Oscar, his captive Giant Pacific octopus.

Ivar lacked some basic aquarium management skills, leading to some serious mishaps. He put a 60-pound and a 15-pound octopus in the tank together without any precautions. The newspaper reported that, "Visitors at Ivar Haglund's aquarium at Pier 3 were entertained by a desperate battle." The large octopus promptly shot ink at the smaller one, which then climbed out of the tank to safety. In 1939, 233 "specimens" died when the pumps failed. In 1956, he told a *Seattle Post-Intelligencer* reporter

> "We had a steady flow of salt water pumped from right under the dock... One day I was standing in the aquarium and every fish in several tanks simply gasped and died and floated to the surface in a matter of minutes. Perhaps some chemist dumped a batch of acid in the sewer. One thing or another, it was a visual example of pollution, anyway."

Ivar seemed generally nonplussed by the mishaps, at least in his interviews with the papers. Ever aware of opportunities to draw attention to the popular octopus exhibit, Ivar set up octopus-human matches. In 1939, he held a finger-pulling contest. Finger-pulling is a Scandinavian tradition consisting of two men trying to pull each other over using only one finger, a sort of combination of thumb wrestling and tug-of-war. Ivar released a challenge "from" Oscar "to any or all of the finger-pulling champions that frequent the Fisheries Supply Company." The contest was to take place in Oscar's tank, but he was only allowed to use one tentacle.

In August 1946, Ivar staged a fight between "Two-Ton Tony" Galento, a prize fighter, and Oscar the Octopus. According to a newspaper account, they put boxing gloves on each of Oscar's tentacles and then put Tony in the tank to grapple with him. It was not much of a fight, however, and Oscar died 3 days later.

In 1946, Ivar opened the first of his restaurants, Ivar's Acres of Clams. It soon became a center of activity because Ivar was a master of promotion. He hosted an International Clam Eating Contest each summer. It

Haglund had a knack for turning any event into a media sensation—as seen here after a railcar spill of syrup, to which he brought pancakes.

was officially run by the International Pacific Free Style Amateur Clam Eating Contest Association, of which Ivar Haglund was executive secretary. The contest was held on a barge between Ivar's pier and Fire Station No. 5 and it attracted an audience and newspaper coverage. In 1947, a pipe broke on a railroad tank car delivering corn syrup to the Corn Products Refining Company, causing about 1,000 gallons of the syrup to flow across the tracks and street. Ivar pulled up a stool and sat down with a steaming plate of pancakes just in time to be photographed by the reporters on the scene documenting the mess. After introducing a new octopus to a tank with two others already in residence, he told the newspapers "I hope Miss Ballard [the new octopus] doesn't cause any trouble in that tank. But, if there's gonna be a fight, I hope it comes off when there's a good crowd in the joint."

While there had always been saloons and bars, Ivar was part of a new type of entertainment on the waterfront. Around the same time, he opened The Aquarium, the Marine Salon opened nearby with 1,500 marine photographs for sale, as did The Pilot House, a "nautical studio" selling novelties.

Ivar Haglund hosted an annual clam eating contest that drew crowds, media attention, and the always-lively Seafair Pirates.

> "The use of the waterfront as a traffic 'bypass' is gravely harming our most vital industry—shipping. Relief must be obtained promptly if irreparable damage to the city's maritime commerce is to be avoided."

a way to accommodate them. At the same time, the carnage they inflicted caused alarm. Between 1926 and 1936, 922 pedestrians and passengers in vehicles died on Seattle's streets (compared to 296 between 2014 and 2023). The need for traffic management for economic development and public safety was glaringly obvious, but the solutions proved elusive.

By the late 1930s, the traffic situation on all north-south streets in Seattle between Alaskan Way and Boren Avenue had become dire. The city installed "Thru Trucks Use Alaskan Way" signs where Highway 99 entered the city to try to ease the congestion at 4th Avenue South near Jackson Street, Dexter Avenue North near Mercer Street, and Broad Street near 6th Avenue. Waterfront businesses protested because the bypass traffic impeded trucks and trains and slowed the movement of cargo.

Other cities' transportation systems utilized a separated-grade waterfront bypass, either elevated or depressed. Chicago and New York City built them in the 1920s and 1930s and improved the traffic flow through their cities while easing congestion in their downtown business districts. Chicago's Wacker Drive ran along the river below grade and New York City's West Side Elevated Highway ran along the Hudson River. *The Seattle Times* described Wacker Drive, completed in 1926, as a "picturesque and useful thoroughfare which looks like a mezzanine floor on the river's brim."

Seattle traffic engineers considered an elevated waterfront highway as a business district bypass several times in the 1930s. After the Aurora Bridge opened in 1932, state highway engineer Ray M. Murray, who had

THE STORY OF SEATTLE'S WATERFRONT 109

directed the bridge construction project, sketched out a route for a waterfront viaduct between Wall Street in the north and 4th Avenue South near King Street in the south. The elevated structure extended over the railyard that was impeding through-vehicle traffic just to the south of King Street Station.

In 1939, city traffic engineer James W. A. Bollong proposed a viaduct for the waterfront. His version connected with a new elevated structure running along Dearborn Street (one block north of today's Royal Brougham Way) to 1st Avenue South. It crossed over the industrial district to the new tunnel through Beacon Hill that would connect to the Lake Washington Floating Bridge (then under construction). A sketch of the plan appeared in the *Seattle Post-Intelligencer*, but City Engineer Charles L. Wartelle dismissed the plan as "dream stuff." Local and state funding remained scarce during the Depression and no source of federal funding for in-city transportation projects yet existed. Once World War II began, all infrastructure projects not related to defense were put on hold to reduce demand for construction materials and workers.

The war came to Seattle's port in the early summer of 1940, when the United States began to build up facilities in Alaska rapidly following the fall of France to Germany. As with the Gold Rush, Seattle served as a supply depot for military operation in the north. In October 1940, transport of troops and materiel to mainland Alaska, the Aleutian Islands, and Canada began out of Seattle's Port of Embarkation at the foot of Atlantic Street. After the Japanese attack on Pearl Harbor on December 7, 1941, wartime activity in West Coast ports accelerated. Harry Bridges of the ILWU

Top to bottom:

Alaskan Way had become all but impassable by 1939.

It didn't help that Alaskan Way was the chosen truck bypass for even more crowded city streets.

The relatively undeveloped swath of hillside north of Pike Street, shown here covered in brambles, offered space for construction of a bypass route.

developed a plan for a shipping industry council to maximize the efficiency of the ports to support the war effort. It had representatives from unions, shipping companies, and the government. Northwest union locals were wary of ratifying the Bridges Plan at first, fearing it might have a negative effect on the workers' hard-won gains from the 1934 strike, but the demands of war overcame their wariness.

President Franklin Roosevelt's Executive Order 9066 authorized the military to designate exclusion zones from which groups of people, namely people of Japanese descent, could be excluded on national security grounds. On March 30, 1942, the US Army removed the first Japanese Americans from Bainbridge Island on the pretense that they were a threat simply because of their racial heritage. They boarded the ferry at Eagle Harbor bound for Seattle. After landing at Colman Dock, they walked across Alaskan Way to a train waiting for them just south of the terminal. It was the third time a group of people were excluded from Seattle at that location—the first being the Native people who maintained their connection to dᶻidᶻəlaličʼ on Ballast Island, and the second being the Chinese immigrants driven out of their homes to the Ocean Dock at the foot of Washington Street in 1886.

Orders to prepare for "evacuation" were distributed to Japanese Americans living on Bainbridge Island in March 1942.

Over 200 Japanese Americans from Bainbridge Island were transferred from the ferry dock to a waiting train, March 30, 1942.

Japanese Americans from Bainbridge Island were taken by truck to Puyallup, then by train to Manzanar and Minidoka camps.

The Japanese Americans from Bainbridge Island were sent by train to the Owens Valley Reception Center, later renamed the Manzanar War Relocation Center, in eastern California. Seattle's Japanese American community was taken by train to Camp Harmony at the Puyallup Fairgrounds, then on to the Minidoka Relocation Center in Idaho for the duration of the war. Many remained incarcerated there throughout the war. Others relocated to different parts of the United States or served in the military. Few would be able to return to their lives as they existed before the war because of the prejudices of white community members or because they had lost their land, homes, and businesses due to their incarceration.

Not long after, the military began to curtail all civilian use of the waterfront. On June 4, 1942, the US Navy designated the area from Bay Street to Spokane Street a restricted area, along with three other areas: Harbor Island; the East, West, and Duwamish Waterways; and Lake Washington Ship Canal, Shilshole Bay, Salmon Bay, Lake Union, and Lake Washington. Enemy aliens—anyone of Japanese, Italian, or German birth who were not naturalized citizens—were not allowed to be anywhere on the central waterfront or Harbor Island without written permission from the Coast Guard's Captain of the Port. The order also barred nonessential traffic and sightseers from most of the area and prohibited most photography. Vehicles allowed to access waterfront piers had to use the east-west streets to access the piers. Workers had to carry Captain of the Port cards or other identification with their fingerprints and photographs. Ferries and passenger liners could still use their terminal facilities on the waterfront and retail establishments between Washington and Madison Streets remained open.

Surprisingly, it would be more than a year before the military would address the chaotic state of the piers' names which had devolved into arbitrariness, duplication, and several overlapping naming conventions by the start of the war. After the Great Fire in 1889, piers south of Yesler had been designated with letters, while those to the north were numbered. Some piers were named for their owners, such as the Gaffney Dock, or for the nearest street, such as Bell Street or Lander Street Terminals. *The Seattle Times* reported that the Coast Guard had already developed its own code for naming the piers to keep them straight, but that list was not public. Longshoremen, railroad cars, and barges sometimes ended up in the wrong place at the wrong time, increasing business costs and slowing cargo movement. In September 1943, the Puget Sound Traffic Control Committee began deliberating how to resolve the confusion. The Committee, set up during the war to manage the increased vessel traffic, was made up of representatives from the US Navy, Port of Seattle, shipping companies, and waterfront businesses.

In May 1944, the Traffic Control Committee announced the new names for all the piers on Elliott Bay. The list captures the peak number of piers on the central waterfront—26. After the war, changes to shipping would reshape the entire port and make many of the piers obsolete.

BRINGING ORDER TO PIER NAMES

Spokane Street Dock	Pier 24	Pier 2, Alaska Steamship Co.	Pier 51
Hanford Street Dock	Pier 25	Colman Dock	Pier 52
Isaacson Iron Works	Pier 26	Grand Trunk Pacific Dock	Pier 53
Milwaukee Ferry Slip	Pier 27	Pier 3, Arlington Dock Co.	Pier 54
Milwaukee Ocean Dock	Pier 28	Pier 4, Fisheries Supply Co.	Pier 55
Lander Street Dock	Pier 29	Pier 5, Arlington Dock Co.	Pier 56
Stacy Street Dock	Pier 30	Pier 6, Arlington Dock Co	Pier 57
San Juan Fish Dock	Pier 31	Pier 7, City Dock Co.	Pier 58
Standard Oil Dock	Pier 32	Palace Fish & Oyster Co.	Pier 60
Telephone Pole Yard	Pier 33	Whiz Fish Products Co.	Pier 61
Associated Oil Dock	Pier 34	Pier 9, Newsprint Service Co.	Pier 62
Albers Milling Company Dock	Pier 35	Pier 10, Newsprint Service Co.	Pier 63
Pier A, Seattle Port of Embarkation	Pier 36	Lenora Street Dock, CPRR	Pier 64
Pier B, Seattle Port of Embarkation	Pier 37	Lenora Street Dock, Leslie Salt Co.	Pier 65
Pier C, Seattle Port of Embarkation	Pier 38	Bell Street Terminal	Pier 66
Pier D, Seattle Port of Embarkation	Pier 39	Pier 12, Galbraith & Co.	Pier 67
Port of Seattle (pier under construction)	Pier 42	Booth Fisheries Co.	Pier 68
Pacific Coast Coal Pier	Pier 43	American Can Company Dock	Pier 69
Union Pacific Dock	Pier 44	Pier 14, State Liquor Warehouse	Pier 70
King Street Dock	Pier 45	Pier 18, Union Oil Dock	Pier 71
Pier D, Luckenback Steamship Co.	Pier 46	Great Northern Dock	Pier 88
Pier C, Pacific Coast Co.	Pier 47	Great Northern Elevator Dock	Pier 89
Pier B, McCormick Steamship Co.	Pier 48	Pier 40, US Navy Pier	Pier 90
Pier A, Pacific Coast Co.	Pier 49	Pier 41, US Navy Pier	Pier 91
Pier 1, Alaska Steamship Co.	Pier 50		

CHAPTER 8

Old Waterfront, New Ships

"A public decision was made which helped seal the fate of the Waterfront District as the city's back alley instead of its front door."

—OFFICE OF POLICY PLANNING, 1979

Aerial of Seattle waterfront from southwest, 1951.

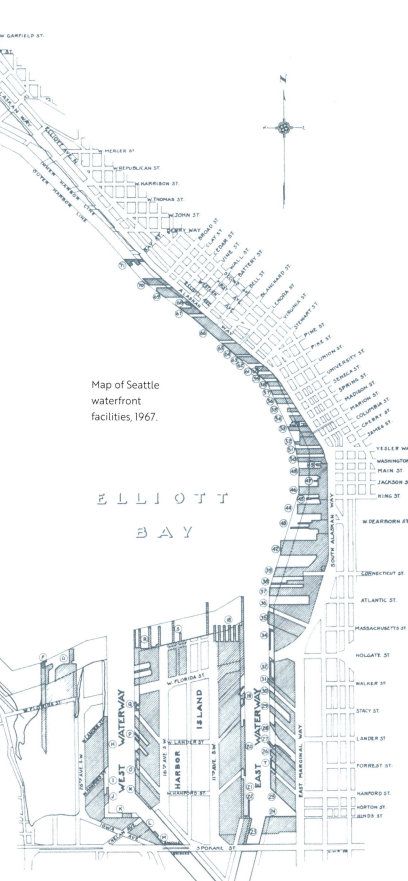

Map of Seattle waterfront facilities, 1967.

WHEN WORLD WAR II ENDED, the waterfront did not simply return to the pre-war status quo. Over the next decade, the waterfront struggled to find new purposes for its piers as business declined. Most of the piers had not been upgraded since the 1920s. Ships and the volume of cargo they carried continued to grow, making them incompatible with the central waterfront's piers and limited space. Automobile numbers increased rapidly as gas and tire rationing ended and congestion increased on city streets making Alaskan Way even more attractive as a bypass route. With regional development of highways and the emergence of suburban communities spurred by the opening of the Lake Washington Floating Bridge in 1940, fewer people traveled to Seattle via water routes. The impact of all these changes spread up and down the central waterfront and radiated inland.

For decades, Elliott Bay had been Puget Sound's center of gravity. Now, trucks could use the state's rapidly improving highway system to deliver goods to stores throughout the region and people could hop in their cars to go to the nearest town to do their shopping. This was a stark contrast to the turn of the century when nearly all regional steamer lines, several transcontinental railroads, and numerous streetcar and interurban lines ended in downtown Seattle, only one of the regional highways, Highway 10 (later Interstate 90), "ended" at Seattle after the war. Even that one provided easy connections to suburban and rural highways. The waterfront's local transportation facilities waned.

The Mosquito Fleet steamers had carried significant numbers of passengers during the war, especially shipyard workers from around the sound going to work at Puget Sound Naval Shipyard and private shipyards

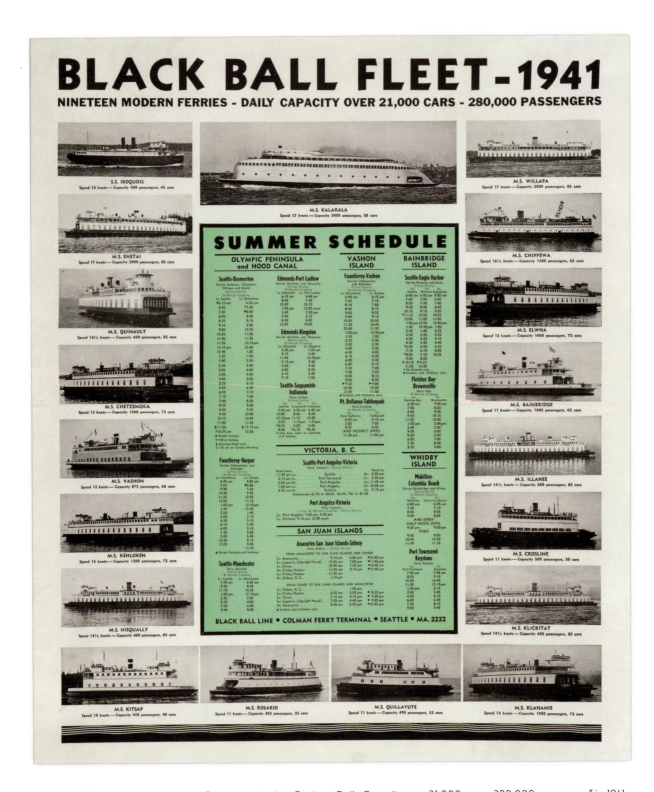

A Black Ball Fleet poster announced "Nineteen Modern Ferries – Daily Capacity over 21,000 cars – 280,000 passengers" in 1941.

in Elliott Bay. However, employment in shipbuilding declined after the war and more workers used vehicles to commute. In the 1934 city directory, four docks serve as terminals for 24 ferries operated by numerous transportation companies. By the 1940s, ferry service essentially consolidated into one company, the Black Ball Line, as the Puget Sound Navigation Company was known after 1929. Black Ball ran 15 different routes on the Sound during the war.

The Black Ball Line struggled to balance fare prices with operating costs when its ridership declined after the war. In 1951, the Washington Department of Highways bought the Black Ball Line's assets, including its ferries and terminals around the Sound, and established Washington State Ferries. Colman Dock became the last local passenger ferry terminal on the central waterfront. Long gone were the days where Seattle was the hub for routes extending north, south, and east on the Sound, out to Hood Canal, and up to Victoria, British Columbia. Ferry routes were simplified, connecting towns on either side of the Sound in pairs, serving as extensions of the state highway system. The system relied on large auto ferries that lumbered back and forth between terminals. A herd of elephants replaced the Mosquito Fleet.

Seattle's "market town" status further diminished with the post-war decline of the Pike Place Market. Wartime incarceration of Japanese Americans removed three-quarters of the market's farmers. Some farms remained, but the critical mass of farmers who worked the land in King County and on Puget Sound islands did not recover from wartime losses. Nor did the vitality that came with a robust farming community. Further, far fewer people came downtown to shop as

> Long gone were the days where Seattle was the hub for routes extending north, south, and east on the Sound, out to Hood Canal, and up to Victoria, British Columbia. Ferry routes were simplified, connecting towns on either side of the Sound in pairs, serving as extensions of the state highway system.

This view of Piers 48–50, taken from the top of the newly finished Viaduct in 1953, reflects a waterfront no longer serving the community in the same way that it had historically.

THE STORY OF SEATTLE'S WATERFRONT 117

Left: Postcard of the *Kalakala* cruising past Colman Dock (to upper left of ferry), produced from a photo taken in 1935.
Right: Art Deco façade of the Black Ball ferry terminal, 1946.

MODERN COLMAN DOCKS

In the 1920s, Puget Sound Navigation Company, then later operating as the Black Ball Line, began the transition to auto ferries. At first, it modified existing Mosquito Fleet steamers to handle cars and trucks, starting with the *Whatcom*. When California's Golden Gate Bridge and the Bay Bridge connecting San Francisco with Marin County and the East Bay were completed in 1935, Black Ball Line was able to acquire the first of a fleet of auto ferries. The first was the *Peralta*, which was renamed the *Kalakala*. It was built in a modern, streamlined style. Six more ferries soon joined the fleet.

Puget Sound Navigation remodeled and expanded Colman Dock to accommodate the new, larger ferries. The remodeled terminal opened in 1937. It had an Art Deco design in keeping with the sleek lines of the *Kalakala*.

A new terminal opened in 1966. The old pier structure was removed and replaced with a modern building with far more capacity for vehicles and passengers. A moving walkway, like a conveyor belt, carried passengers from Alaskan Way to the terminal on the upper floor. Each of the two slips had double-land loading ramps. Joshua Green, of Puget Sound Navigation Company, and later Black Ball Line, donated "Living Waters Fountain," created by artist George Tsutakawa. It was later renamed the "Joshua Green Fountain" and is currently installed on the inland side of the terminal.

That building had its charms, but by the 1990s it needed renovations. *Seattle Post-Intelligencer* columnist Jean Godden described it as having "less charm than a garbage transfer station." The building was upgraded and the exterior replaced. The interior was again remodeled in 2005.

Cover of the dedication program celebrating the opening of the new terminal, 1966.

supermarkets proliferated and more people drove to business districts near their homes for groceries. With fewer farmers bringing produce to the Market, far less farm produce passed over the waterfront's piers.

The fishing industry also underwent change after World War II. As runs declined in Puget Sound and off the coast of Washington due to overfishing, more boats went to the North Pacific and processed their catch at canneries in Alaska. Some fish processing continued on central waterfront piers, but primarily in the cluster of smaller piers at the foot of Pike Street and the nearby uplands.

Traffic volumes continued to overwhelm the central business district streets with few alternatives for traveling through the city. Much of the train traffic had moved to piers north and south of downtown and fewer people and vehicles needed to move between the piers and downtown. Cars and trucks parked haphazardly where the trains formerly ran. Many of the waterfront buildings were housing businesses that didn't need water access so much as they needed the cheaper rents offered by the underutilized transit sheds. Where it had once been the city's front porch, the waterfront became more like a "back alley."

In 1943, when the city's departments began looking forward to the end of the war and developing plans to address delayed maintenance and infrastructure development, the waterfront fell low on the list of priorities. The Alaskan Way seawall project had addressed the most pressing public need and new waterfront investment was primarily needed on privately owned properties. In a report on post-war improvements issued in 1945, the Engineering Department's Streets Division proposed a list of 31 projects including street repairs, paving projects, bridge

Cannery workers in Seattle, circa 1952.

and bulkhead construction, roadway extensions, and a viaduct on the waterfront, with a depressed (below-grade and uncovered) roadway connecting it to Aurora Avenue. The viaduct, the most expensive item on the list, ranked 29th in priority. Later in 1945, however, the viaduct project appeared at the top of a much shorter post-war-improvements list. Its promotion was possibly due to newly available funds from the Federal Aid Highway Act, which included federal funding for urban-area highway construction for the first time.

That year, the state Department of Highways and the United States Public Roads Administration (precursor to the Federal Highway Administration) initiated an origin and destination study of the Seattle area, interviewing thousands of drivers, passengers, and residents to determine traffic patterns in the region. The report, published in 1947, reiterated what several city traffic studies had already determined: a large percentage of traffic on city streets was moving through the city to destinations north and south of downtown.

Sketch of the proposed viaduct in a June, 1947 issue of the The Seattle Times

The report proposed a ring-road arrangement to solve the conflicting traffic flows. The ring road consisted of two north-south routes for traffic through the downtown core. One (later State Route 99) ran along the waterfront and the other (later Interstate 5) roughly followed 6th Avenue, and three pairs of east-west routes. The innermost pair lay close to the downtown Seattle business district. The median pair ran just north and south of the city limits, and the outer route traveled from Everett in the north, around the east side of Lake Washington and back south to Puget Sound near Burien, along the lines of today's state routes 405 and 518.

During the spring of 1947, city engineers Bollong and Wartelle developed a proposal for a waterfront viaduct: a six-lane, two-deck roadway, with downtown access ramps at Seneca and University Streets, a possible wye (a Y-shaped extension) at Railroad Way South to extend the elevated route over railroad tracks lying east of the viaduct and connect it to 4th Avenue South. In a drawing published in The Seattle Times, the viaduct appears to have been originally designed as a steel structure with concrete roadways and supports, with far less bulk than the structure that was eventually built. Wartelle also recommended that the city purchase right-of-way at Denny Way and 6th and 7th Avenues to allow for construction of a depressed roadway along Battery to carry the viaduct traffic to Aurora Avenue.

As the plans evolved, The Seattle Times sought the opinion of local architects. Paul Thiry called the project "half-baked," concerned that the viaduct would create a blighted neighborhood in its shadow and "destroy the flexibility of waterfront railroad and truck traffic." He called for a tunnel "superhighway" to handle all downtown traffic, but the costs involved deterred public officials and engineers from seriously considering it. The viaduct's costs to the neighborhood's livability and downtown's connection with its shoreline were not factors in the equation like they would be after the 2001 Nisqually earthquake.

Other architects were not so fundamentally opposed to the idea of a viaduct, though they did have reservations. John T. Jacobsen thought, "A finer solution would be a freeway—an arterial with sufficient land on either side so it wouldn't be encroached on by commercial or residential enterprises." Talbert Wegg warned that if the city built freeways to ease travel between downtown and the suburbs, more people would move to the suburbs, taking the city's tax base with them. Joshua Vogel, an architect and a planning consultant at the University of Washington, supported freeway construction and balked at the idea of a tunnel because of the expense and difficulties involved in building it.

Construction of the Alaskan Way Viaduct. Photo taken from Colman Dock in November 1951.

In January 1948, two candidates in the mayoral election, M. J. Comber and Melvin G. Tennent, ran on the promise that they would halt the viaduct project if they were elected. Neither candidate made it past the February primary and the issue does not seem to have been a prominent one in the general election. The embrace of vehicles for moving people and cargo demanded transportation facilities and overwhelmed the viaduct opposition.

When state highway engineer Oliver R. Dinsmore inquired about a viaduct's ability to withstand earthquakes, City Engineer Ralph Finke explained that "an earthquake load of .05 gravity in any horizontal direction was used in the design for the section resting on fill. This load is applied simultaneously with dead load, live load, impact, temperature and traction. Earthquake and wind loads are not used simultaneously." (The dead load of a structure is the weight of the structure itself; the live load is traffic.) On the north end, no earthquake load was applied because the single-decked portion rested on solid ground. This appears to have satisfied Dinsmore.

In the early summer of 1948, business owner. R. S. Hawley of the Central Building Company wrote to the public agencies and officials to express his multiple concerns about the cost, the effect of the viaduct on the surrounding properties, its design. He said, "it would always remain an unsightly structure along our very valuable waterfront." Someone, presumably in the Engineering Department, wrote terse refutations in the margins of the points raised by Hawley. In reply to Hawley's suggestion that the issue be further studied, the commentator wrote "We have waited too long now!"

This 1952 postcard of Seattle Harbor Water Tours, just north of Pier 54, shows the impact the Viaduct had on the view of the city from the waterfront. The Smith Tower is just visible behind the Viaduct.

The Municipal League's Floyd Naramore, an architect, wrote to the City Planning Commission to suggest that the commission look again at the viaduct plans. They had only looked at them once, in 1944, when the structure had a different design and different components. The Municipal League did not oppose the viaduct, but Naramore suggested that the commission review the effect it would have on the city's overall development and "its general appearance." The commission reviewed the plans in June 1948 and approved them because the viaduct "conforms to the accepted principle of having through traffic by-pass congested business areas," allowed access to downtown, and fit with the long-range plans for transportation in the city.

The first section of the Alaskan Way Viaduct opened on April 4, 1953. It ran between Railroad Way on the south and Western Avenue on the north. It dominated the shoreline, blocked views, and created a psychological and visual barrier between the central business district, Pioneer Square, and the waterfront. But it served its purpose well, carrying tens of thousands of cars and trucks through the city and easing congestion on city streets. Henry P. Knutsen of south Seattle wrote to the city in 1954

"I want to thank the people who help[ed] build the Battery subway [Battery Street Tunnel] it sure is wonderful. I am a truck driver [Teamsters] Local 174 and it means a lot to me. Easier driving no hills or stoplights and save[s] time and no hard pull for trucks to get on Aurora. So I want the city of Seattle to know that I appreciate the new Subway and Viaduct and will help to make it safe—as will my fellow union members."

While traffic demanded attention, a less noticeable problem was developing. As the 1950s progressed, the Port of Seattle and other pier owners around the bay grappled with changes in the shipping industry. In April 1959, KING TV broadcast a program exploring the waterfront's state called "Lost Cargo." Hosted by reporter Bob Schulman, it captured a moment in time when the transformation of the waterfront was unfolding and people were raising alarms about what could be lost. Schulman laid out the importance of shipping in Seattle's economy, "in a city like Seattle, even the gas station man who's never been on a ship numbers among his customers people who pay their bills with money that comes from waterfront businesses" and warns that "the dollars from the sea are being washed away" as shipping shifted to the Atlantic and Gulf coasts. Not only had Seattle not returned to pre-war trade volumes, but a larger percentage of the trade was bulk commodities like paper, oil, and metals. Packaged cargo, the boxes, bales, and crates handled by longshoremen, was moving to ports in California with larger local markets. Grain shipments were moving to Columbia River ports because the newly built dams made it possible to barge grain more cheaply than transporting it via railcars. And more cargo on the West Coast was being moved overland on trucks.

In addition to the shipping changes, Schulman described the port's structural issues: "pier facilities are going to hell in a bucket," "labor costs a great deal and doesn't produce enough," and Seattle has a "port personality with B.O." He also cited a lack of effective leadership and public apathy. All these problems led to empty piers, too-small berths, and pier sheds that couldn't accommodate trucks. Schulman lamented that a large section of the waterfront has become a "fish alley," with fish markets and processors filling the piers that formerly served ocean-going passenger and cargo ships. Even further south, along the East Waterway, shipping companies found the infrastructure lacking with not enough room to maneuver trucks, not enough storage, and inadequate cranes for moving cargo vans, metal boxes mounted on trailers—the newest labor- and time-saving shipping innovation.

Cargo vans were the first step toward containerization, which would radically reshape land use, pier construction, work, and the culture of the waterfront. They were first developed by Alaska Freight Lines for cargo it shipped to military installations in Alaska on barges. Trucks pulled the trailers to Seattle docks where they were uncoupled, loaded, and carried north. At Seward and Valdez, the ship's onboard cranes unloaded the trailers, and then local drivers pulled the trailers to their final destinations. The vans helped solved problems shipping companies had in Alaska with not being able to hire enough longshoremen to handle the volume of breakbulk cargo going in and out of the northern ports. Ships sat idle for too long while waiting their turns to dock and for the cargo to be moved in and out of the holds.

In 1952, Ocean Tow began service on modified LST (tank-landing) ships that had been used in WWII. The ships carried Ocean Van Lines vans in their holds to Alaska. The vans were designed by Brown Trailer Company in Spokane and were shipped without trailers attached. At Alaska ports, the vans could be placed onto trailers or onto Alaska Railroad flatcars for delivery to other parts of the state. Ocean Tow's *Alaska Cedar* and *Alaska Spruce* left Seattle twice weekly until 1953 when Alaska Freight Lines leased the vans and put them on its barges. Alaska Steamship Company

Seafair Queen Iris Adams, Mayor Allan Pomeroy, and President of the Automobile Club of Washington D.K. MacDonald (left to right), officially open the Alaskan Way Viaduct on April 4, 1953.

VIADUCT OPENING

The Automobile Club of Washington and the Junior Chamber of Commerce organized the opening celebration for the Viaduct. A procession of what the *Seattle Post-Intelligencer* termed "ancient automobiles . . . some the vintage of the first President Roosevelt" carried Seattle Mayor Allan Pomery, Seafair Queen Iris Adams, Department of Highways Director William A. Bugge, City Engineer William E. Parker, Chair of the Washington State Highway Commission Fred G. Redmon, and other dignitaries northbound in the upper deck of the Viaduct to a stage constructed on the roadway near the Pike Place Market. Radio and television stations broadcast the event to a larger audience. The Seattle Police Department color guard and drill team performed, as did an orchestra hired by Ivar Haglund. In a nod to Seattle's Alaskan connections, can-can dancers reminiscent of the Klondike Gold Rush era also performed, and Seafair Queen Adams, who had ducked away from the stage, rode up in a dog sled driven by legendary dog musher Leonard Seppala and pulled by eight Alaskan huskies.

Seattle waterfront with the new viaduct, looking south, 1956.

inaugurated its van-on-trailer service to Seward in 1955, on the steamship *Chena*.

In 1956, East Coast shipper Malcolm McLean launched a containerized cargo line, Pan-Atlantic Service, which utilized metal boxes also designed by Brown Trailer Company. The containers were slightly longer than the vans used by the Alaska shipping lines and had hardware and structural reinforcements that allowed them to be stacked on top of each other. Before long, the van and container service made steamships with hatches for loading breakbulk cargo obsolete due to their relative inefficiency.

The vans and containers changed the nature of longshoremen's work. The union rules established after the 1934 strike did not easily accommodate the changes to the work patterns required for vans. The new work was primarily crane operation by individuals rather than the team work of handling breakbulk cargo, which required physical strength and stamina. Surprisingly, given the contentious history of labor relations on the West Coast, the issue of how labor unions would work with shipping companies to introduce and adapt to the new container-ship technology was resolved by 1960. Marc Levinson recounts in *The Box*, that ILWU longshoremen assessed the situation and decided to accept a Mechanization and Modernization Agreement negotiated with shipping companies rather than fight for retaining the old work patterns and technologies.

Some members of the ILWU opposed the plan. Working condition gains had been hard-won and some felt that the longshore workers owed it to their predecessors who had fought for concessions from the shippers not to give in to the new demands. Levinson quotes Eric Hoffer, a San Francisco longshoreman, who said, "This generation has no right to give away, or sell for money, conditions that were handed on to us by a previous generation." The majority of the union members approved the agreement, however. It guaranteed jobs for all A-list men (those with priority for hiring), established a fund that shipping companies would pay into for five-and-one-half years to be

THE STORY OF SEATTLE'S WATERFRONT

distributed among the members by the union, and provided retirement pay for older workers. The union agreed to adapt the number of workers and their work methods to new container-related technologies as changes were adopted.

The relatively amicable agreement on the West Coast spearheaded by the ILWU's Harry Bridges contrasted sharply with the protracted battle over adopting containerization on the East and Gulf Coasts under the less effective leadership of the International Longshoremen's Association's Teddy Gleason. According to Levinson,

> *"Both leaders understood from the outset that automation could put tens of thousands of jobs at risk and transform shoreside labor—their members' labor—into almost an incidental expense. They ended up finding different ways to win extraordinary benefits for their members—in return for allowing the containers to reshape the long-established pattern of life on and around the docks."*

To prepare for the new ships, the Port of Seattle unveiled a $30 million terminal-building plan in 1962. It involved installing specialized cranes that could reach out over ships to load and unload containers, clearing acres of land for container storage, installing electrical lines and outlets for powering refrigerated containers, and building facilities for customs agents, shipping company personnel, and longshore workers. The first container ship, the *Hawaiian Builder*, operated by Matson, sailed from Pier 46 on January 24, 1964. Not long after, the Alaska Steamship Company's *Tonsina* set sail for Alaska. Containerized military cargo passed through Seattle to Vietnam to support military operations there, further cementing Seattle's predominance. By the late 1960s, more container facilities opened at Port of Seattle terminals.

The launch of containerized shipping in 1964 essentially sealed the fate of the central waterfront's piers, permanently shifting the critical mass of cargo handling. The change was felt in a myriad of ways throughout the city. Pioneer Square emptied of longshoremen and ship crews as the work shifted south and the time it took to load and unload ships drastically decreased. The sheds sat like barns on farms that had

Looking south along the East Waterway. Terminal 18 is under construction on Harbor Island, which would soon be a hub of container shipping.

Matson's *Hawaiian Builder*, the first container ship to sail from the Puget Sound, left the Port of Seattle for Hawaii in January of 1964.

transitioned from horses to tractors, relegating the horse stalls and haylofts to obscurity. Like many of those old barns, most of the transit sheds escaped the wrecking ball because the space they occupied was not in demand. The sheds sat either empty or only partially in use, and the warehouses on Western Avenue were slowly adapted for new uses.

The Maritime Building at Western and Madison demonstrates how the warehouse buildings' occupants evolved. In the 1910s and 1920s, the building was home to several machinery companies, including Folger Electric & Machinery, John Deere Plow Company, and Dairy Machinery Company. It also housed several food merchants selling flour, sugar, produce, and other groceries, including, T.B. Klock, who the *Post-Intelligencer* called "the big butter and egg man of Western Avenue." By 1961, it had no wholesalers and few, if any, maritime or shipping businesses. As the decade progressed, new tenants took advantage of its low rents. The Young Republicans Club and an au pair matching service set up shop in the building, as did some light industry firms, including outdoor outfitter C.C. Filson Company.

Newspaper coverage of the waterfront petered out as shipping became less integral to Seattleites' daily lives. The "Marine News" column in *The Seattle Times* went from a daily feature listing ships coming and going to each of the piers, to a bi-weekly column abruptly in the spring of 1960. The *Post-Intelligencer* shifted more slowly from full- to partial-page coverage and then to a simple listing of ships coming and going from Puget Sound ports. "Puget Sound Shipping" appeared on the business page into the 1990s, after which the phrase "Puget Sound shipping" is only found in real estate listings for homes overlooking the shipping lanes.

Despite these changes, the waterfront remained a primary feature of Seattle's identity—it was where the city started, maritime trade still played a significant role in the regional economy, and the piers still held a valued place in the community's collective memory. But the question arose—what to do with the piers? The coming decades would involve numerous plans and visions for a new version of the waterfront, but the challenges posed by the Alaskan Way Viaduct, the steep hill between downtown and the waterfront, the trains, and the difficulties in adapting the transit sheds to new uses slowed the area's makeover.

Seattle's first pier with container handling cranes, shown here in 1973, would later be subsumed into Terminal 46.

CHAPTER 9

Creating a Destination

"Despite the efforts of a small band of active dissenters, it seems inevitable that the style of Seattle's central waterfront soon will change from blue denim to silk."

—*SEATTLE POST-INTELLIGENCER* EDITORIAL, 1982

The waterfront looking north from atop the Viaduct at Pike Street, 1961.

THE EARLY 1960S brought a slew of new businesses to the central waterfront piers, many of them not water dependent. Instead, Puget Sound became beautiful scenery. This haphazard redevelopment of piers came just as business leaders were looking at how to incorporate the waterfront into plans for revitalizing downtown. Unlike in the post-war era, the waterfront was now seen as an asset in and of itself, not simply an empty space to fill with transportation infrastructure. Over the next 30 years, city leaders, planners, and community groups put forward several plans intended to connect the waterfront with downtown, protect and promote the area's maritime heritage, and provide the public with access to the water.

Downtown got a makeover as the city prepared for the upcoming 1962 Seattle World's Fair: Century 21. New trees were planted to line 4th and 5th Avenues. The monorail was extended from the heart of the business district to the fair's grounds, today's Seattle Center. Efforts to draw tourists and locals to the waterfront piers started the piecemeal transformation of the piers that would continue into the 1980s. Near Colman Dock, the Polynesia restaurant opened on Pier 51, one of the former Alaska Steamship Company docks that had been stripped of its transit shed. The restaurant's Polynesian-style building sat on the western end of the pier and the remaining expanse of open space was used for parking. To the north, at Pier 56, Trident

This 1971 map, prepared for the city's sale of Piers 55 and 56, shows the many piers that remained on the central waterfront, even as cargo handling shifted to the north and south.

THE STORY OF SEATTLE'S WATERFRONT 129

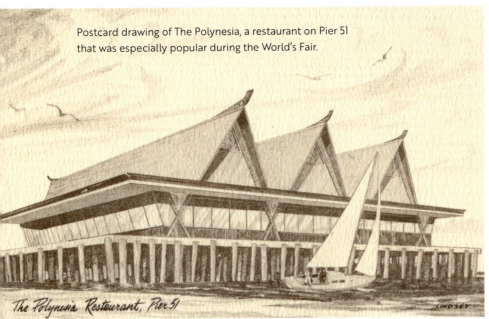

Postcard drawing of The Polynesia, a restaurant on Pier 51 that was especially popular during the World's Fair.

Hotelship *Catala* operated at Pier 58 during the 1962 Seattle World's Fair.

View looking north along Alaskan Way, with tourist-focused businesses such as Trident Imports, Seattle Marine Aquarium, The Cove restaurant, Pirates Plunder, and Harbor Tours, 1970.

Left: Postcard image of a Marine Aquarium show at Pier 56 featuring the orca Namu, circa 1965. Right: People protesting the capture and captivity of whales, 1970.

Imports opened in an empty transit shed formerly used for fish storage. Its advertisements echoed the Port's past: "If it be cork from Portugal, a space radio from Japan, a rice bowl from Hong Kong (at 19¢) or whatever, come and see us at TRIDENT." Instead of coming from ships berthed at the pier, however, the goods traversed the oceans on container ships that docked at the Port's terminals. At the north end of the waterfront, the Edgewater Inn opened on Pier 67, formerly the Galbraith, Bacon & Co.'s Wall Street Dock. It was the first (and still the only) overwater hotel on the waterfront. Three boatels, the *Dominion Monarch*, at Pier 50, the *Catala* at Pier 58, and the *Acapulco* at Pier 70, also housed visitors during the fair.

Ted Griffin opened the Seattle Marine Aquarium at the western end of Pier 56 in June 1962. *The Seattle Times* called it a "do-it-yourself museum" of Puget Sound marine life with plans to bring in octopus, sharks, and other larger creatures. Griffin aspired to create a "Marineland" for Seattle and would become infamous for capturing orcas in Puget Sound. He displayed one, Namu, in the Marine Aquarium in 1965, and sold numerous others to tourist attractions around the world. The legacy of his cruel separation of orcas from their pods resonates today with the 2023 death of Tokitae in Florida before she could be returned to her home waters. Griffin's Marine Aquarium was a small step forward from Ivar's octopus boxing match but would still fall dismally short of today's aquarium standards.

In March 1960, the Conference on Central Business District Waterfront Planning met to discuss the waterfront and possibilities for its future. Albert R. Van Sant, representing private businesses, wanted to improve downtown connections. Paul Seibert, executive vice president of the Central Association, "stressed that 'uptowners' are increasingly aware of the value of the waterfront and are eager to improve the transportation ties between the waterfront and uptown." Paul Thiry, the architect and vocal opponent of the Alaskan Way Viaduct, "declared that the relationship of uptown to the waterfront is poor; that the Viaduct has further split the two areas where they should be closer related; that far more people would visit the waterfront if properly developed." Paul Brown, the park department's superintendent, emphasized the need for a pleasant appearance and "urged that the color and character of the waterfront be preserved, including fish houses, the fishing fleet, etc."

These and other conference participants outlined the six major issues that would be the subject of planning and development efforts on the waterfront for the next 60-plus years: one, the unsuitability of the central waterfront for container shipping; two, connectivity between downtown and the central waterfront in light of obstructions such as the Alaskan Way Viaduct; three, railroad tracks; four, the steep hillside north of Seneca Street; five, shoreline access for the public; and six, protection of historical places and uses.

Federal urban renewal funding spurred the first redevelopment effort. The decline of big city downtown areas was such a widespread problem in the United States that Congress incorporated funding for urban renewal in its Housing Act of 1949 and expanded the program in 1954. The funding could be used for acquisition, demolition, and reconstruction of buildings in urban areas deemed blighted. Many urban renewal projects across the country were later regretted for their destruction of neighborhoods and historically significant buildings as well as their disproportionate impact on marginalized communities. However, the approach seemed to many urban planners to be the best solution for struggling inner cities at the time.

In Seattle, a group of businesspeople formed Seattle Urban Renewal Enterprise in 1957 to coordinate efforts to get federal urban renewal funds for several projects. The group hoped that by rejuvenating aging neighborhoods, including downtown, the city could compete with rapidly growing suburban areas. Historian John Findlay calculated that suburban areas' population grew by half during the 1950s, but that increase was less than 1 percent

Looking south past Bell Street, 1961. The separation between the city and the waterfront remained a challenge in the 1960s.

within the city's 1950 limits. Seattle's only real population growth in that decade occurred through annexation of areas north and south of the city.

In 1963, the downtown business group Central Association and the City of Seattle hired Donald Monson, a planning consultant from New York, to develop a plan that could be adopted as an amendment to the city's comprehensive plan. Aiming to help Seattle compete with suburban shopping experiences, Monson envisioned Seattle's central business district as a large-scale shopping mall. To connect downtown with the waterfront, Monson proposed replacing the original Pike Place Market's buildings. He envisioned several new office and apartment buildings, with retail space at street level, extending from Pike Street to Battery Street between the Alaskan Way Viaduct and First Avenue. Working within the urban renewal mindset, Monson dismissed any intrinsic value in the historic buildings, explaining,

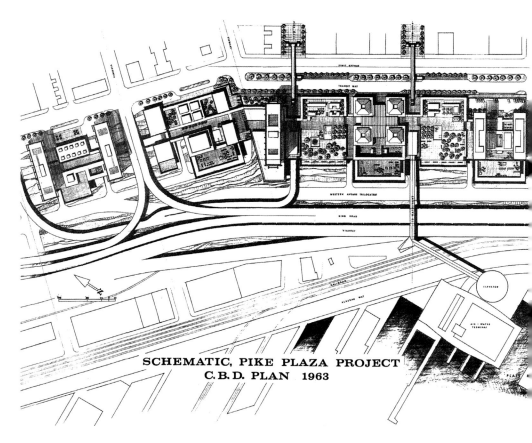

> "The charm and drawing power of the market is not in the sheds within which it now operates but in the character of the vendors, the quality of the produce sold, the attractive way in which they are displayed, and in the arrangement of the stalls and concession areas. The character of the market can be retained and reproduced under a new roof."

Monson also appreciated the potential value of the waterfront if it was redeveloped with new buildings and facilities. He wrote,

> "If a downtown area has a waterfront which can be developed as its front yard, the city is indeed fortunate. It is not necessary here to argue that Seattle's waterfront should be redeveloped as a

Top: Schematic of the 1963 Pike Plaza plan with sky bridge and heliport.
Bottom: Model of proposed Pike Plaza Redevelopment Project, 1968.

THE STORY OF SEATTLE'S WATERFRONT 133

Concept drawing for proposed Waterfront Park, 1970.

promenade connecting ferry terminus, public open areas, restaurants, marinas, boatels, and the like. Everyone knows of a city which has taken advantage of waterfront opportunities and greatly added to the attractiveness of its [city] center by doing so."

Monson incorporated a sky bridge from the waterfront to the new Pike Plaza development, mimicking the earlier pedestrian overpasses over Railroad Avenue. His drawings also show new city-owned piers with new buildings on top of them, to be leased to businesses for restaurants, concessions, and a motel. He dismissed most large-scale maritime uses of the central waterfront, including fishing and cargo handling, but he retained passenger-ship facilities in his plan. In addition to the existing ferry terminal, he added a new marina and an air-water terminal with a heliport.

The Seattle City Council adopted Monson's plan on November 26, 1963, and some elements of his proposal moved forward to more detailed planning. In 1965, the City of Seattle hired John Graham and Company, another New York-based planning firm, to refine the central waterfront plan. In his 1965 report, Graham cited San Francisco's Fisherman's Wharf and Oakland's Jack London Square as examples of the types of city-led redevelopment projects that could rejuvenate waterfronts left behind by changes in shipping. New restaurants and entertainment facilities along the shoreline, such as an aquarium, a large park on a pier, and a long esplanade along a marina, would ensure public access to the water. New, large piers would be used for parking lots, motels, and retail stores. Graham introduced a gondola-like cableway to reach the Market and a new park at the foot of Union Street. New pedestrian ramps starting on First Avenue at Columbia, Marion, and University Streets, crossed over the railroad tracks and Alaskan Way to an elevated pedestrian walkway along the shore.

Graham's planners wanted to shift traffic away from the shoreline while still giving vehicles enough access to the area to compete with the convenience of ample parking found in suburban shopping areas. They proposed vacating Western Avenue between Yesler Way and Pike Street and realigning Alaskan Way along the inland side of the Viaduct. On the water side, parking lots and a small street with bus stop turnouts would still allow drivers easy access to the piers.

As the waterfront planning process continued, a historic preservation movement emerged, partly in response to urban renewal projects. Community activists blocked plans to demolish Pike Place Market and Pioneer Square's historic buildings. Bolstered by the 1966 National Historic Preservation Act, they shifted the conversation toward restoring buildings and preserving historically significant neighborhoods. They succeeded in establishing the Pioneer Square Historic District in 1970 and a market historic district in 1971.

In 1968, community activists developed a series of bond measures known collectively as Forward Thrust. The effort was steered by Jim Ellis who had led the successful effort to clean up Lake Washington in the late 1950s. The bond measure for the new waterfront park based on Graham's planning was approved by the voters. It only stipulated the size and location of the park so the city's Design Commission hired San Francisco based Rockrise & Associates to develop a vision for the park and how it would be situated within the larger waterfront context. When the firm presented its first iteration of a plan in December 1969, the public response was tepid at best. David Brewster, then at *Seattle* magazine, wrote a lengthy critique of the plan the following February. He argued that the root of the problem lay in the Design Commission's reliance on the business community for input.

The Rockrise planners had primarily consulted with the Mayor's Waterfront Advisory Committee downtown of primarily business leaders appointed by Mayor Dorm Braman. Many civic projects in the 20th century had followed such a model that presumed what was good for business was good for the city as a whole. What resulted, however, as Brewster and others argued, was a one-dimensional view of the waterfront largely influenced by the urban renewal movement. A vocal contingent of critics objected to the plan's lack of connection to downtown, the park's "pastoral" character in an urban and quasi-industrial

Model of proposed Waterfront Park, 1970.

Waterfront Fountain by James FitzGerald and Margaret Tomkins in Waterfront Park, 1974.

Waterfront Park, 1981.

REDEVELOPMENT OF PIERS 55 TO 63

After World War II, the piers on the central waterfront between Colman Dock and Bell Street Terminal continued to house cargo handlers and fish processors, though the volume and activity decreased. The piers began to shift toward tourism as the 1962 Seattle World's Fair: Century 21 approached.

Pier 55, home to Argosy Cruises, offered shuttle service to the new Tillicum Village attraction on Blake Island and boat tours of Elliott Bay.

Pier 56 was home to the Seattle Marine Aquarium and run by Ted Griffin. In 1965, Griffin put a captive orca named Namu on display. Namu's arrival sparked protests that grew as more orcas were captured in Puget Sound for marine parks around the world. Opposition to the captures led to federal protection for orcas and other marine mammals in 1972. Namu died in captivity in 1966. The Seattle Marine Aquarium closed by the end of the decade.

Pier 57 was leased by the Seaport Fish Company for processing and freezing fish for transport into the late 1960s. The Port of Seattle bought the pier from its owner, the Milwaukee Road, for prospective World Trade Center development. Hal Griffith leased the pier in 1968 and opened Pirates Plunder, gradually expanding its operations over the next few years.

Pier 58 was a small dock built with salvaged wood from the historic Schwabacher's Wharf, which was demolished in 1952. During the World's Fair, the *Catala* tied up to the pier and operated as a boatel. The Port of Seattle then purchased this pier in the mid-1960s and tore out the remnant structure.

Voters passed the Forward Thrust parks bond in 1968 which earmarked funding for the development of a waterfront park. The Port of Seattle sold Piers 57 and 58 to the city. The city then acquired Pier 59 from a private owner and Piers 60 and 61 from the Port of Seattle. These piers were allocated for the construction of a publicly owned aquarium with a mission to educate the public about Puget Sound's marine ecology.

In 1972, the City of Seattle made one last acquisition. It paid Hal Griffith $3.8 million dollars for Piers 62 and 63 and transferred ownership of Pier 57 to him, where he operated Pirates Plunder.

When the deals were complete, Piers 54 to 56 were privately owned and operated. Pier 58 was home to Waterfront Park, which opened in 1974, and Piers 59, 60, and 61 were home to the new Seattle Aquarium, which opened in 1977. The city cleared the pier sheds off piers 62 and 63 because the sheds would require extensive repair to be usable and then maintained the piers as public open space. In the 1980s, the popular Summer Nights at the Pier concerts drew thousands of fans until the piers' structures degraded too much to permit large gatherings.

The Edgewater Inn at Pier 67, 1981.

neighborhood, its relatively small size, and its general lack of imagination. They wanted the planners to consider what removing the Alaskan Way Viaduct could do for the waterfront.

In response to the criticism, the Design Commission convened the Citizens Waterfront Task Force to provide input into the planning process. The task force included people from a wide variety of backgrounds and interests, including Philip Gayton of the National Business League; David Brewster; restaurant owner (and later a King County councilmember) Ruby Chow; labor leader Bill Olwell; architect and urban designer Lee Copeland; Boeing engineer and president of Citizens Against Freeways David C. Lefebvre; and the director of Seattle Indian Center Pearl Warren. Warren was an enrolled member of the Makah Tribe, but her organization served local tribal members as well as the Urban Indian community formed in Seattle after the Urban Relocation Program propelled members of tribes from outside the city to Seattle. Many of tribe members had developed a connection to the waterfront and Pioneer Square, and Warren served as an Indigenous voice on the task force. The city's newly formed Department of Community Development held several public meetings to gather feedback from the general public, too. This was the first time the public was given a real opportunity to shape the character and function of the waterfront since about the 1860s.

The final Rockrise plan was released in December 1971. The plan encompassed 16 acres between Piers 55 and 61. In keeping with its surroundings and the maritime heritage of the area, the park's character was urban and active, with rough-hewn planking, concrete walls and benches, and minimal plantings. Most of the park was four feet lower than the sidewalk along Alaskan Way to draw visitors closer to the water. The park also included a 1,800-foot promenade along Alaskan Way with wide sidewalks and landscaping. The promenade connected with a walkway around the outer edge of Pier 57 with benches and picnic tables so the public could take in the views from its western end. The plan also envisioned a concession center and aquacenter on Pier 57 featuring an aquarium and an aquacircus with whale and dolphin performances. In contrast to other Seattle parks, adjacent retail on Pier 55 was integrated into the park's design.

The Rockrise plan acknowledged the desirability of removing the Viaduct but planned around its presence for the near-term. It proposed pedestrian overpasses at Marion and University and a funicular (a cable railroad designed

SEATTLE AQUARIUM, 1977

On May 20, 1977, a three-day "Fishtival" marked the grand opening of the new Seattle Aquarium on Pier 59. Funded by the Forward Thrust parks bond approved by voters in 1968, the aquarium was originally planned for Golden Gardens Park in Ballard. Public opposition to the development of one of the few remaining saltwater beaches clashed with Pacific Science Center Director Dixy Lee Ray's and others' desire to have access to a natural beach habitat, as well as a clean saltwater and fresh water source for the facility. Several commissions studied alternate locations in the early 1970s, including the Union Oil fuel depot site north of Pier 70, a shoreline location near Smith Cove, near Duwamish Head, and along the central waterfront. The central waterfront didn't have clean saltwater, a natural freshwater source, or a beach, but it did have proximity to downtown, the new Waterfront Park planned for Pier 58, and underutilized and available city-owned piers. The city council chose Pier 59 for the aquarium in July 1972.

Local architect firm Fred Bassetti & Co. was hired to design the renovation of the Pier 59 transit shed and the adjacent new building replacing Piers 60 and 91. Bassetti & Co. had designed the new Federal Office Building, the Engineering Library and Loew Hall at the University of Washington, and the Frye Art Museum among other works. Like the adjacent Waterfront Park, the Aquarium buildings utilized concrete, timber, and steel to maintain the look and feel of the working waterfront.

The aquarium provided a series of experiences for visitors to learn about the region's marine life, including exhibits around four habitat types: Puget Sound salt marsh, sandy shore, mudflat, and rocky coast. Visitors could get hands-on with tidal pool inhabitants in the touch pools and experience the fish-eye view of the sound in the Underwater Dome. Salmon smolt were released from the Aquarium at the opening and over the next several years returned to their nascent waters at the Aquarium via a fish ladder.

In many ways, the exhibits and visitor experience departed from the less-educational aquarium experiences of the past on the waterfront. Director H. Douglas Kemper told *The Seattle Times*' John Hinterberger, "And once you walk through the front doors, the myths about what an aquarium is like are smashed." Hinterberger explained, "Instead of a seal tank with beach balls—a sideshow of nature's oddities—the aquarium's displays begin with exhibits of cellular biology, the formation of life in the sea and an evolution into a complex eco-system."

Top: City Councilmembers and others sing at the Seattle Aquarium Opening Day, 1977.

Bottom: Crowds gathered for the Seattle Aquarium Grand Opening, 1977.

for steep hillsides) from Pier 57 to Pike Place Market to help pedestrians climb the hill. To reduce the conflict with north-south traffic, the plan called for moving Alaskan Way under the Viaduct north of Marion Street and diverting all railroad traffic into the train tunnel under downtown. Waterfront Park on Pier 58 and the adjacent sidewalk were dedicated on October 25, 1974, and a free bus shuttle service started as part of the "Magic Carpet Service" free-ride district in downtown Seattle. The rest of the Rockrise plan remained on the drawing table.

While the plan was being finalized, a new shoreline law was working its way through the state legislature. Several cities in Washington faced the same situation as Seattle: the abandonment of old waterfront facilities and high demand for waterfront properties for non-water-dependent uses such as hotels or offices. The new businesses that opened on Seattle's waterfront for the World Fair in 1962, especially the Edgewater Inn, had raised concerns that private developments would push out water-dependent uses like the fishing industry or boating, and could block public access to the water and views if taller new buildings filled the areas previously occupied by pier sheds.

The state's Shoreline Management Act passed the legislature in 1971 and marked a significant shift in thinking about waterways and human relationships with them. Since the territorial era, waterways had been seen as tools of trade that could be rerouted, dredged, contained, or drained to meet economic needs, regardless of environmental or cultural impacts. The Shoreline Management Act required comprehensive planning for public and private shorelands and established priorities to guide planning. It explicitly stated, "Permitted uses in the shorelines of the state shall be designed and conducted in a manner to minimize, insofar as practical, any resultant damage to the ecology and environment of the shoreline area and any interference with the public's use of the water." To implement the protections, the act required cities to inventory the freshwater and saltwater shorelines within their limits and to develop shoreline master programs to guide their development.

The City of Seattle adopted its shoreline master program in 1976. The top priority, for the first time since the city's founders settled on the bay in 1851, was the protection of ecosystems, followed by protection of shoreline access for water-dependent uses such as fish processing, recreation, and ferries. Non-water dependent uses could be allowed only when water-dependent uses were not feasible. The master program also emphasized

Pike Street Hillclimb, completed in 1977, provided a pedestrian route between the Pike Place Market on the bluff and the Waterfront Park area along Alaskan Way below, including the new Seattle Aquarium.

the restoration of degraded shoreline areas and the preservation of historic resources and uses. It did not change any existing zoning laws, but it shaped how they could be applied. The program established a foundation for waterfront planning.

A park and new regulations were not enough to revitalize the waterfront, however. The area continued to struggle into the late 1970s despite nearly two decades of efforts. The Office of Policy Planning noted in a 1979 report that the "the deteriorated area is so large, it is difficult for

The return of Elliott Bay

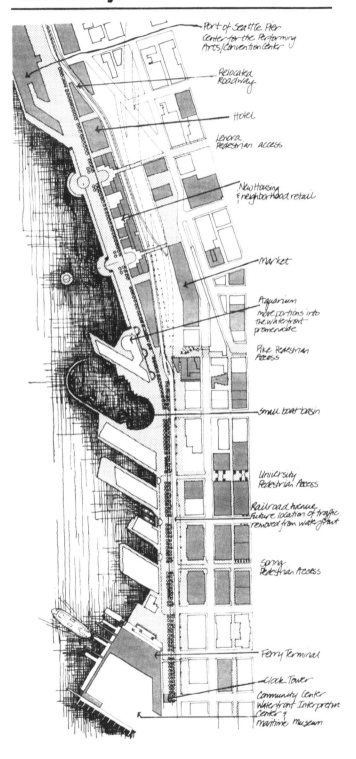

The "Gang of Five" plan published in *The Weekly*, 1982.

development to begin on a small scale. A single new building could be dominated by negative influences of the total area." The planning office recommended large-scale developments to turn the tide and noted that zoning, and the uses it allowed, had not kept up with the changes on the waterfront. Mayor Charles Royer asked the Office of Policy Planning to develop guidelines for the central waterfront area that would allow project-specific variances to the zoning rules covering the area. The new guidelines encouraged redevelopment of the large buildings along Western Avenue, formerly commission houses and factories, with a focus on residences, retail shops, and offices.

Several projects proceeded in the early 1980s under the guidelines. Cornerstone Development Company redeveloped several buildings along Western Avenue and Post Street, including the Pacific Net and Twine Building at Western and Madison. This stretch became the home of pharmaceutical company Immunex and a furniture store, Abodio. The scale of the Cornerstone project spurred other projects. Olympic Cold Storage was remodeled to house the Pacific Institute in 1986. The Oceanic Building at Western and University, a former factory, became apartments in 1987. These uses only required renovating the building interiors, preserving the historic streetscape while giving the buildings new life.

The Waterfront Park development and two other projects, the opening of the Seattle Aquarium and the construction of the Pike Street Hillclimb in the mid-1970s, reinvigorated the waterfront. But the improvements could not overcome the challenges posed by automobile and train traffic and the Viaduct noise. City planners expressed their frustration with the Viaduct, complaining that, "a public decision was made which helped seal the fate of the Waterfront District as the city's back alley instead of its front door."

While these projects were underway, another comprehensive planning process for downtown began. Discussion revealed a significant difference of opinion around what the waterfront could or should be. The

Friends of the Working Waterfront advocated for fish processing, a fishing fleet, shipping facilities, and other industrial uses even though only three of the sixteen remaining piers had water-dependent uses. Other people, represented by the Seattle Shorelines Coalition, argued for the development of recreational facilities, including bike paths, parks, and more retail stores.

In 1982, the city sponsored a symposium in conjunction with Washington Sea Grant at Seattle Center. Advocates for various visions participated in panel discussions and offered opinions ranging from some calling the waterfront an "abandoned industrial harbor," to others saying they didn't "want Seattle to copy the slicked-up waterfront facades of San Francisco and Baltimore." An editorial in the *Seattle Post-Intelligencer* concluded that: "Despite the efforts of a small band of active dissenters, it seems inevitable that the style of Seattle's central waterfront soon will change from blue denim to silk."

City planners took input from the public and the symposium participants, along with the directives of the city's shoreline master program, and developed the Harborfront Public Improvement Plan. The statement of purpose shows these numerous influences:

"To revitalize the Harborfront in order to strengthen maritime activities and enhance opportunities for public access. All reasonable efforts shall be made to encourage water dependent uses which are compatible with a high pedestrian use of the waterfront, to meet the needs of waterborne commerce and provide an active, working waterfront character. Public access on the piers shall be encouraged to the extent that such access can be designed to accommodate existing and proposed water-dependent uses. The historical and cultural significance of development in the Harborfront shall be preserved and enhanced."

Pier 65 in disrepair, circa 1980s.

Top: The city acquired Piers 62 and 63, though the sheds on them had to be demolished in 1989 and plans for them remained undetermined.

Bottom: The Alaska Marine Highway System operated its ferries out of Pier 48 from 1969 until moving its operations to Bellingham in 1989.

The plan organized the waterfront into use zones: ferry traffic from Pier 48 to the ferry terminal, retail stores and restaurants catering to tourists from piers 54 to 57, educational and recreational facilities occupying the space from Waterfront Park to Pier 65, and mixed commercial use to be retained at Piers 65 to 71.

Planners addressed the tension between north-south and east-west movement through a combination of traffic and pedestrian improvements. These included diverting all trains to the tunnel, reducing Alaskan Way to two and three lanes, and realigning ferry traffic holding lanes under the Viaduct south of Pier 48. The street ends at University, Union, Spring, and Madison were to be redesigned once again to encourage people to traverse the slope to the waterfront.

Reducing the width of Alaskan Way would create space for a 25- to 30-foot-wide promenade along Alaskan Way running north from Waterfront Park to Myrtle Edwards Park on the western side of Queen Anne Hill, amplifying the public benefit of those two parks. A brownfield was left behind when the fuel depot between Broad and Bay Streets was decommissioned in the early 1980s. While it would require a significant investment to restore the health of the landscape, it was a rare opportunity on the central waterfront to acquire a stretch of shoreline for public access not blocked by piers. It lay largely unused until waterfront redevelopment surged again in the 2000s.

The planners also encouraged the development of public or private moorages. The Washington Street Boat Landing had opened public floats in 1973 and offered temporary moorage, but planners envisioned larger facilities with more space for recreational boats. Suggestions for a marina date back to the 1903 Olmsted

Brothers' Park plan and reappeared in most later plans. Before World War II, it was hard to carve out space for recreational boats among the piers. By the 1980s and 1990s, it was difficult to fund such a large project.

A majority of the people involved in discussions about the waterfront embraced this new vision that largely excluded industrial uses. *The Seattle Times* quoted Greg Peterson of the Puget Sound Gillnetters Association discussing the feasibility of a working waterfront: "It's a nice idea . . . [but] fish buyers are at Shilshole, and most fishermen are set up to work on gear at Fishermen's Terminal. And . . . it would be dangerous to leave fishing boats unattended in such a public place."

The planners recognized efforts would need to be made to retain the waterfront's historic character as it evolved away from industrial uses as had been successfully done in Pike Place Market and Pioneer Square. The Harborfront plan called for marking historic places and events along Alaskan Way and encouraging the berthing of historic vessels along the waterfront. It called for collaboration with civic groups to increase awareness of the waterfront's role in Seattle history and to incorporate historical maritime themes in the design of public spaces, particularly Piers 54 to 59. The focus of the preservation and interpretation was on the post-settlement era, not the tribal history of the area, and tribes were not consulted as far as can be ascertained in the city's archives and other public records. The plan didn't advocate for the Viaduct's removal, but the idea was in the air. Bob Davidson, then chief of staff for Congressman Joel Pritchard, attended a "Chowder Society" event held at the time organized by David Brewster. In a 2024 interview, Davidson recalled that Paul Schell, then head of the city's Department of Community Development, spoke about the waterfront and

> "He had a model of the city, the downtown, and the waterfront, and he was talking, and he said, 'Now, here's something I'd like you to consider.' And he

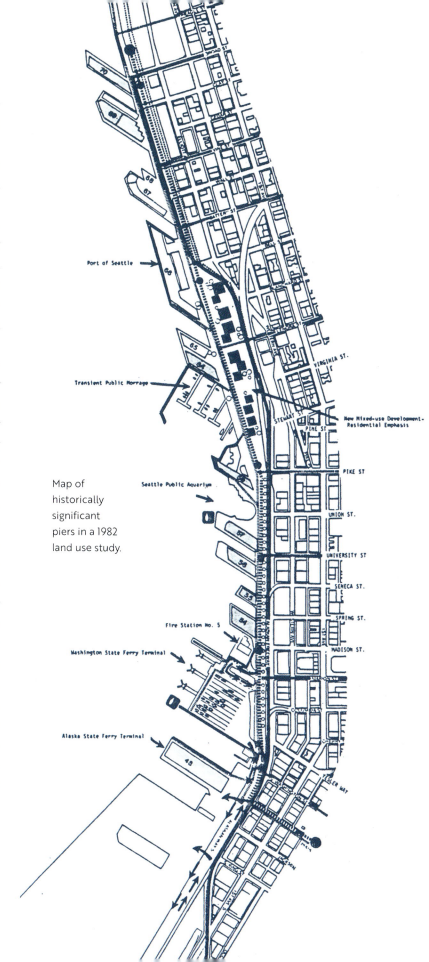

Map of historically significant piers in a 1982 land use study.

removed the viaduct from the model. And that's the first time I thought of even the notion of removing the Viaduct from the city. . . . I think there was a general skepticism that that could ever happen, but [there was] the notion that it was a good idea."

The city council adopted the Harborfront plan on June 13, 1988, but a bond measure to fund it was roundly defeated that fall. Local newspapers blamed the high cost of the project and the perception that the measure only benefited the downtown core. The city moved forward with plan elements that could be paid for out of the general fund. In 1987, city officials had signed an agreement with Burlington Northern Railroad to move its trains to the rail tunnel under downtown. Improvements were made to crosswalks and sidewalks to make the Washington Street route between the waterfront and Pioneer Square more pedestrian friendly. A parking garage added below Pike Place Market made it easier to park on the waterfront.

During the mid-1980s, the Port of Seattle was also at work on its Central Waterfront Project which it intended to integrate with the city's Harborfront Public Improvement Plan. The Port moved its headquarters to make way for development that would ultimately include a marina, new shipping berths, and a conference center, along with office, condominium, and hotel space on the inland side of Alaskan Way. The Port began by renovating dilapidated Pier 69. Stena Lines moved from there to Pier 48, where it operated alongside the Alaska System ferries for a short time, before moving its terminal to Bellingham in late 1989. The Victoria Clipper continued operating out of Pier 69. Port planners saw potential in retaining the framework of the historic structure and incorporating it into a new structure for the Port headquarters. When the Port occupied its new offices in 1993, the redevelopment of the former Bell Street Terminal (Pier 66) headquarters, along with Piers 64 and 65, into the centerpiece of its Central Waterfront Project could begin.

The new Bell Street Pier opened in 1996. It featured the 70-slip Bell Harbor Marina, a conference center, the Odyssey Maritime Discovery Center, and restaurants. It also included 11 acres of public waterfront space featuring plazas and a rooftop park more or less on the site where the Port had (briefly) established the central waterfront's first park 80 years earlier. In 2000, the Port opened a cruise ship terminal at Pier 66 and expanded it the following year. It has since grown to 275 cruise ship dockings per year.

Before demolishing the old pier structures, the Port had to move out the last two fish processors remaining on the central waterfront, Pacific Salmon and Dressel-Collins. The new building allocated space for them but the surrounding tourist-oriented development made it infeasible for them to return.

For the upland portion of the Central Waterfront Project, the Port sold a parcel of land on Alaskan Way across from the Bell Harbor Marina to Marriott International Hotels & Resorts for a new hotel. The next parcel to the south was sold to Intracorp, which built Waterfront Landings, a 20-unit condominium development. The World Trade Center complex was built to the north of the hotel.

Private development continued elsewhere along the central waterfront during the 1990s. Harbor Steps, between First Avenue and Western Avenue, opened in 1994. Like the Pike Street Hillclimb, Harbor Steps featured public seating and retail development at different levels along steps that traversed the hill.

Reducing the width of Alaskan Way proved impossible. Although regular traffic flow on Alaskan Way could be accommodated by the two- or three-lane street proposed in the plan, the existing, wide street was needed for oversize loads. Alaskan Way, Alaskan Way Viaduct, and Interstate 5 were designated truck routes through downtown. Alaskan Way was the only city street that offered an unimpeded and level-grade route for large trucks in the downtown core.

The city reiterated the goals and plans of the Harborfront plan in its 1994 comprehensive plan. Funding remained an obstacle, as did the Alaskan Way Viaduct. The elevated structure was aging, but no plans to replace it appeared feasible. The cost of replacing it just did not pencil out given that it remained functional.

The cost changed fundamentally with a 30-second earthquake on February 28, 2001.

Above: Port of Seattle's Pier 65 before redevelopment, 1985.
Below: Port of Seattle's new Pier 69, 1993.

THE STORY OF SEATTLE'S WATERFRONT

WATERFRONT STREETCAR

From 1982 to 2005, the Seattle Waterfront Streetcar ran between Pioneer Square and Broad Street, following Jackson Street and Alaskan Way. Seattle City Councilmember George Benson doggedly pursued the funding for the line, found 1920s-vintage streetcars in Melbourne, Australia, and led the effort to refurbish them with the help of hundreds of volunteers. The line was extended to Union Station in 1990.

The trolley maintenance barn was located at the former site of the Union Oil Company of California (UNOCAL) fuel depot north of Broad Street. The maintenance barn was removed when the Seattle Art Museum developed the site for a sculpture park. Some hoped it was a temporary halt to operations, but another site for the maintenance barn was not acquired, and the tracks and other infrastructure were removed during the waterfront redevelopment following removal of the Viaduct.

Waterfront Streetcar, 1982.

Crowds gather for the first day of the Seattle Waterfront Streetcar, May 29, 1982.

Salmon Homecoming, 2022.
Below: Drumming and singing at Salmon Homecoming.

SALMON HOMECOMING

One of the longest-running annual events on the waterfront is Salmon Homecoming. It started in 1992 and has been organized by the Salmon Homecoming Alliance since 1999. It is held annually during the fall salmon runs in Elliott Bay and includes canoe-welcoming ceremonies, salmon bakes, informational booths, a powwow with dancing competitions, and other activities. The event helps introduce the larger community to Native cultural traditions, including those of the Urban Indian community, which is made up of members of tribes from across the United States who live in Seattle.

Area students participate in educational programs during the event. Walter Pacheco, one of the early organizers of Salmon Homecoming and a longtime member of the Alliance's board, explained in a 2014 interview that the Alliance focuses on students because they can carry what they've learned home to their families. This helps spread awareness of what actions people can take to protect salmon habitat and restore the endangered populations.

The event was held for many years at the old Waterfront Park at Pier 58. It is now held at the rebuilt Pier 62, which has a floating dock where the tribal canoes can land.

THE STORY OF SEATTLE'S WATERFRONT 147

CHAPTER 10

Envisioning a Waterfront for All

"Fifty years ago, our civic leaders made a serious mistake. They cut off Seattle from its waterfront by building the Alaskan Way Viaduct. Now, the people of Seattle and the Northwest have an opportunity to correct this error and redirect the future of the region."

—ALLIED ARTS, 2006

WHEN THE SHAKING stopped on that February morning in 2001, many people's first thoughts were about the Alaskan Way Viaduct. Had it collapsed? Had it fallen on its side? Ivar's CEO, Bob Donegan remembered, "I was walking through the restaurant . . . and I ran to the front of the pier because I wanted to see the Viaduct come down. And Francis Ramillio, who was a busser here, grabbed me and said, 'What is wrong with you?' He pulled me under a table, so I didn't get to see anything."

Some engineers also wondered if the Viaduct was still standing. Jared Smith, then-director of the Strategic Planning Office for the City of Seattle remembered,

> "I got off [the elevator] on the second floor where my office was and just then, the earthquake hit. I began to hear things snapping in the building, so I turned to Deputy Mayor Chuck Clark, and I said, 'We need to get out of here.' So we ran down the stairs . . . out onto Columbia Street and the first thing I did was look to see what was the situation with the Viaduct, expecting that it might have collapsed. . . . Fortunately, we saw the Viaduct was still standing."

As the dust settled it became frighteningly clear how close Seattle had come to tragedy and infrastructural disaster. Before the earthquake, the city and state were already studying the Viaduct as it approached the end of its expected 50-year lifespan and several efforts had been made to shore up the seawall as wave action and other stressors weakened it. But by early 2001, no firm plans were in place for either structure's replacement. As Douglas MacDonald, the state Secretary of Transportation who started in that job just after the earthquake, would later recall that the Viaduct wasn't on the list of projects when he was considering the position in January. Prior to the earthquake, the priorities were the new Tacoma Narrows Bridge, Interstate 405, State Route 520 and its floating bridge, and the aging Washington State Ferries fleet. All enormous projects on their own. The Viaduct jumped up in priority abruptly that February. Managing the project from crisis to resolution would take nearly two decades, three governors, seven Seattle mayors, and four state Secretaries of Transportation. Tens of thousands of Seattleites would oversee the process.

To the public, the waterfront, the space beneath the Viaduct, seemed like solid ground. It didn't seem as fragile as the brick buildings in Pioneer Square, some of which crumbled as the ground moved during the earthquake.

In reality, it had been more than 60 years since the seawall's construction. It had weaknesses that made it susceptible to failure, most of which could be traced to the incessant chewing of teredos and gribbles, the same marine wood borers that had weakened the pilings supporting piers and railroad trestles on Elliott Bay since the 1850s. The Viaduct's columns were supported by untreated timber pilings and rested on glacially compacted soil, not bedrock. The soil behind the seawall which supported the columns was prone to liquefaction in an earthquake. If another one hit the area, the ground could turn semi-fluid, destabilizing the Viaduct.

City and state engineers were aware that both structures were nearing the end of their functional lives. Since the 1940s, the seawall

Mayor Greg Nickels inspecting pieces of the seawall's relieving platform damaged by wood-boring gribbles, 2002.

THE STORY OF SEATTLE'S WATERFRONT 149

A large sinkhole and void discovered underneath Alaskan Way in 1954 was an early indication of seawall weakness.

had been regularly inspected to monitor the effects of tidal action and saltwater and the structural integrity of the wall structures. Early inspections found only minor problems until 1949 when the sheet piling showed significant corrosion caused by naturally occurring electric charges in the water moving in and out of the steel. The resulting small cracks allowed more seawater to get behind the wall with each rising tide. As the tide receded, small amounts of the fill behind the wall escaped through the cracks. By the 1950s, this would lead to settling of the fill around the relieving platform, creating voids just below the untreated timbers. When the tide rose, those voids filled with water that carried marine borers behind the wall that began to eat away at the timbers. This weakened the seawall structure, leading to at least one sinkhole along Alaskan Way in the 1950s.

In 1959, a cathodic protection system was installed to reduce saltwater corrosion of the metal components. Anodes placed at various locations along the wall collected the electric charge accumulating in the wall structure and discharged it back into the water. More cathodic protection was added in 1972, and a 1979 study found it to be largely working.

Wave action and storms also caused wear and tear on the seawall. The city periodically added riprap to the base of the wall to try to reduce the amount of fill escaping from under it. In 1986, the city refaced 1,400 feet of the wall with ekki wood, a dense hardwood resistant to marine borers, that shored it up for a time.

More careful scrutiny of the Alaskan Way Viaduct began in the 1990s. The 1989 Loma Prieta earthquake in the San Francisco Bay area grabbed Seattle's attention because an elevated, double-decked highway along the Oakland waterfront, the Cypress Street Viaduct, collapsed during the earthquake. Seattleites immediately recognized that viaduct's structural similarities to the Alaskan Way Viaduct and the potential for loss of life and massive disruptions to the transportation network sent a collective shudder through the region.

The Washington State Department of Transportation (WSDOT) asked engineers from the Washington State Transportation Center at the University of Washington to assess the Viaduct's seismic vulnerability. The Center's report described differences between the Alaskan Way Viaduct and the Cypress Street Viaduct that might make Seattle's viaduct more resilient during earthquakes, including its discrete sections, with connections that could withstand more movement. Seattle's viaduct also had longitudinal girders that the Oakland viaduct did not and different underlying soil conditions.

After the Nisqually earthquake, a 1,000-square-foot section of Alaskan Way near Pier 58 settled a few inches because the wooden relieving platform had weakened. This revealed how degraded the seawall structure was and Seattle Department of Transportation (SDOT) began planning for its replacement.

The international engineering firm TYLin examined the Viaduct and issued a warning that the earthquake had weakened connections between the columns and the roadway decks, cracked the aging concrete, and shifted the structure to the east, indicating problems with the foundations. The sections near Washington Street in Pioneer Square experienced the greatest damage, most likely because the roadway curved at that point, placing more force on the connections between its sections. The report recommended that, "The Alaskan Way Viaduct should be replaced in kind with a new structure as soon as possible."

The Viaduct shifted four more times in the following months. WSDOT closely monitored its movement and installed steel bracing on the columns, along with other shoring measures, to reinforce the structure. WSDOT also instituted lane and vehicle-weight restrictions to reduce stress on it. These measures helped the Viaduct remain in operation, even as it continued to settle over the next several years. In 2004, city inspectors were surprised to find that 40 percent of the ekki wood boards had been damaged by borers. This was a significant increase from the

Relocating utilities was a significant challenge in replacing the Seawall and Viaduct.

three-percent damage rate noted just a year earlier. That rapid change raised concerns that the wall would completely fail in another earthquake, causing a chain reaction leading to the Viaduct collapsing.

Near Yesler Way, the columns settled five and one-half inches by 2009. Near Seneca Street, they settled about an inch and a half. While the scale of movement was not large, it showed intrinsic weaknesses in the structure that could amplify over time and make it more vulnerable to another earthquake. Beyond the threat to human lives, the Viaduct also served as a conduit for transmission lines from Seattle City Light, BC Hydro, and Bonneville Power Administration carrying electricity along the entire West Coast. Natural gas lines, fiber optic cable carrying internet service for the city, and sewer and water lines all ran underneath the structure and would be compromised by a seawall failure.

WSDOT and SDOT feared that structural failure would also leave a gaping hole in the region's transportation network. Even with that sense of urgency, amplified by the fear of loss of life, it would take seven years to settle on a replacement strategy and 16 years to build it due to the enormous costs

Supports and bracing were added to the Viaduct in the wake of the Nisqually earthquake.

Conceptual design of a cable-stayed/segmental bridge alternative to the Viaduct.

involved and the enormousness of the task. Replacing the Viaduct presented a tremendous opportunity to remake the waterfront as a place for people. It also raised big questions about the waterfront's history and its future, what Seattleites valued about it, and what they were willing to invest in.

The waterfront continued to have many of the same challenges that had stymied past planning efforts, along with some newly recognized issues. The hill still rose steeply north of Seneca Street, the north-south movement of people and goods still conflicted with the east-west movement of people and goods, and many of the piers had deteriorated and required expensive upkeep. Salmon that migrated along the waterfront had been listed as endangered. Tribal communities had no permanent space reserved for their use. And the question loomed: how would the city avoid the new waterfront becoming an exclusive enclave for those who could afford the high property values that would come with improvements paid for with tax dollars?

Additionally, the history of the waterfront and its meaning to people throughout the region had to

be incorporated into the planning. To Coast Salish people, it remained dᶻidᶻəlalič, despite the massive transformation to the landscape made by non-Native settlers. It also held the collective trauma of Ballast Island and exclusion from their traditional villages, beaches, fishing areas, and communities. To Asian Americans, it held memories of arrivals and departures by ship and annual migrations to Alaska to work in canneries. The long history of anti-Asian racism was embodied in the expulsions of 1886 and 1942. Waterfront workers—longshoremen, fishermen, sailors, captains, pilots, and others—traced their long struggle for fair wages, respect, and collective power to a century of organizing on the piers and vessels. Millions of people had memories of riding ferries and the streetcar; visiting shops, piers, and the Aquarium; and feeding French fries to seagulls at Ivar's.

Within that context of collective history, the long process of replacing the Viaduct and seawall and creating a new waterfront began.

Engineers at Parsons Brinckerhoff, working for WSDOT, began identifying alternatives in the fall of 2001. Among the alternatives, they looked at a retrofitting proposal from Victor Gray and Neil Twelker, two of the original engineers. Retrofitting was quickly deemed infeasible by a committee of experts because it was costly and only kicked the problem down the road. That committee included former Governor Dan Evans, who had been one of the lead civil engineers during the original 1950's design as part of the Gray and Twelker design team. Parsons Brinckerhoff assessed other alternatives according to a list of criteria: the new structure needed to meet modern seismic safety standards, improve traffic safety, provide capacity for moving people and goods both into and through downtown, connect with the regional transportation network and with downtown streets, replace the existing capacity of State Route 99 (more than 100,000 vehicles per day), and retain the existing functions of downtown and the central waterfront.

During the alternatives analysis, the committee examined 76 options, including a bridge over Elliott Bay, a floating bridge on top of the bay, and a tunnel under it. No possibility was rejected out of hand, however simply removing the Viaduct and *not* replacing its traffic capacity was not included as an option. By June 2002, the list had been reduced to five options: a new double-decker structure similar to the existing one, a bored tunnel, a single-deck viaduct, and two versions of a cut-and-cover tunnel. A cut-and-cover tunnel would require removing the existing Alaskan Way, building a below-grade roadway and seawall, then replacing Alaskan Way on top of the tunnel, as its "roof." After the initial review, cost estimates eliminated a stacked cut-and-cover tunnel and a bored tunnel.

While the engineering studies progressed, a parallel urban planning track ensued. Mayor Greg

> "Up until then I was thinking of the waterfront as north-south...but what the design professionals suggested was that the biggest opportunity was east-west... to reconnect the city in some uniquely interesting ways to the waterfront."

Nickels remembered taking the waterfront and Viaduct project to the Mayor's Institute of City Design in Charleston, South Carolina, for review and input. He recalled, "Up until then I was thinking of the waterfront as [running] north-south, and [as] a transportation corridor. But what the design professionals suggested was that the biggest opportunity was east-west . . . to reconnect the city in some uniquely interesting ways to the waterfront."

Allied Arts, a local civic organization, launched a campaign to envision what the waterfront could be *without* the Viaduct. As chair David Yeaworth explained, "Right now the Viaduct is like a fence that keeps people out. What would draw people in? A touch of Alki or Green Lake? A public swimming pool? An amphitheater for concerts? We're asking people to imagine." At a design charrette Allied Arts sponsored in November 2003, six architectural firms and students from the University of Washington presented visions for a waterfront without a viaduct. Their ideas ranged from a "Spill Hill" running from Pike Place Market to the Aquarium, to a saltwater swimming pool, to a large open lawn area at Pike Street.

Sally Bagshaw, who was on the board of Allied Arts and later served on the Seattle City Council and played a key role in the realization of the new Waterfront Park, described all the different elements that came together on the waterfront:

> *"It was the infrastructure; it was the idea that people living in Seattle could connect with the Waterfront; to retain the views from Pike Place Market; and . . . [to] make sure we could protect the salmonids that were getting chomped and devoured on their way up from the Duwamish; [to] clean up that water. We were working with the Aquarium, and God bless the Aquarium with their focus on really bringing people down to the Aquarium to see the value of Puget Sound. . . . And then I got to know Bob Donegan who's the CEO of Ivar's and the importance of the economy to the waterfront businesses, and it just all meshed."*

In March 2004, WSDOT released the first Draft Environmental Impact Statement (DEIS). Secretary of Transportation Doug MacDonald insisted that the DEIS be prepared in a reader-friendly format rather than usual, technical style for expert audiences. It laid

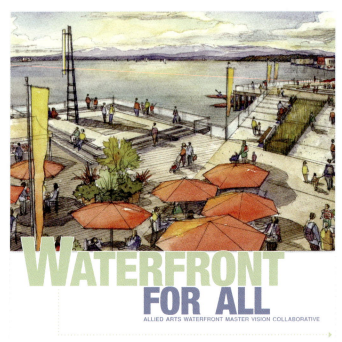

Allied Arts' "Waterfront for All" report promoted a cut-and-cover tunnel as the best alternative for replacing the Viaduct, 2006.

out five alternatives: two single-level cut-and-cover tunnel options, one with four lanes and the other with six lanes; an elevated structure; a new waterfront street paired with elevated structures at the north and south ends; and a rebuild of the existing structure with the same configuration of downtown connections with no changes to Alaskan Way. All the alternatives incorporated seawall replacement, either integrated into the design or as a separate structure.

Almost immediately, the People's Waterfront Coalition, led by Cary Moon, Julie Parrett, and Grant Cogswell, called for a no-build alternative utilizing surface streets and transit improvements to replace the Viaduct's traffic capacity. It became known as the surface-transit option. They argued that many commuters would find other ways to move around the city, and the existing street grid and Interstate 5 could handle the remaining vehicular volume. As proof, they pointed to how the city had continued to function while the Viaduct was closed immediately after the earthquake for inspections and repairs. Siting the process already underway to identify traffic management options in case of the Viaduct's failure or closure, the Coalition argued for directing investment into infrastructure that would allow more people to give up their personal cars and rely on transit, walking, and biking. The organization's website encouraged people to consider options that would not require a new highway on the waterfront.

The Coalition also released a vision of how the new waterfront could reconnect the city with the shoreline. On their website, they described the opportunity that lay before the city:

"We are a city with a densifying downtown and no place to let loose. We are a city heading a charge toward sustainable building, while pouring polluted runoff into our struggling bay. We are a city that remembers its recent wilderness, a city in love with our watery terrain, yet largely remote from contact with the water itself. We are a city that knows landscape as active and visceral, not just as scenic backdrop. How could we build a freeway along our shore without exploring the greater possibilities?"

WSDOT studied the surface-transit option and published their findings in December 2004. Their report argued that the proposal was not feasible because it would cause gridlock on downtown streets, make the waterfront unfriendly to pedestrians due to

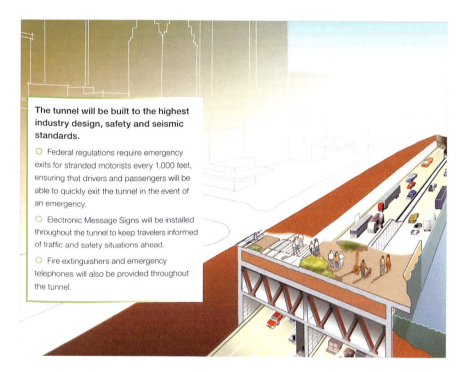

Concept from a 2004 pro-tunnel brochure.

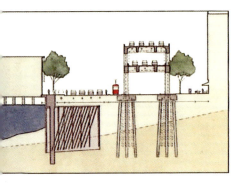 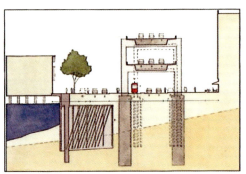 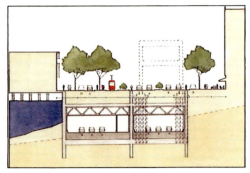
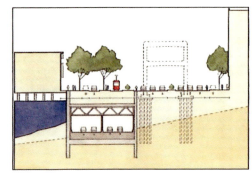 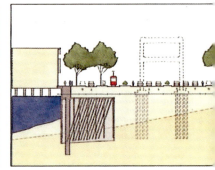

Numerous Viaduct replacement options were considered: from new elevated structures and cut-and-cover tunnels to utilization of existing surface streets and augmented transit only. All options had to address the failing seawall.

high traffic volumes on Alaskan Way, and slow the movement of cargo. Additionally, the ferry terminal, with the largest traffic volume of any of the state's ferry terminals, required significant vehicle queuing areas for vehicles waiting to board the ferries. The report did not settle the issue. The Coalition and others continued to advocate for a surface street and transit alternative for the next five years. However, several features included in the Coalitions renderings and accompanying descriptions were ultimately realized: a beach at the foot of Washington Street, a stairway at Union Street, linear green space along the shoreline, "green building strategies," and habitat improvements for marine ecosystems.

That same December, WSDOT and Mayor Greg Nickels announced that the six-lane cut-and-cover tunnel would be the preferred alternative for the Final Environmental Impact Statement (FEIS). The tunnel would run under Alaskan Way with a rebuilt seawall as its western wall. In January 2005, the city council endorsed the cut-and-cover tunnel alternative.

In most large transportation projects, the project proceeds through the Environmental Impact Statement process to determine if any design changes or mitigation are needed for the preferred alternative. Studies look at all aspects of how the proposed project will impact the environment, communities, and historical features within the project. With the Viaduct replacement project, however, the announcement of the preferred alternative triggered a robust debate before any further study even commenced. In August 2006, the Alaskan Way Tunnel Coalition commissioned a study that argued in favor of the tunnel because of the economic benefits the city would accrue from the investment in the waterfront and because it would return access to the shoreline to the community and make the waterfront Seattle's "front porch." The Congress for the New Urbanism issued a report the next month that advocated for a surface-transit solution, arguing that the traffic capacity requirement built into the argument for a tunnel was based on faulty assumptions. Cary Moon wrote in an editorial in *The Stranger*

> "This pro-tunnel enthusiasm needs to be tempered by some sobering truths: First, no city actually improves traffic by giving people incentives to drive. Second, Nickels' promise of open space dramatically exaggerates what will actually be an awkwardly shaped strip of park. And, perhaps most important, the money isn't on the way."

Waterfront businesses also formed a coalition, the Seattle Historic Waterfront Association, to campaign for other alternatives because the cut-and-cover tunnel construction would require years of business closures while the waterfront was torn up and closed to the public. Many people remembered the construction of the cut-and-cover transit tunnel under 3rd Avenue in the 1980s and feared a repeat of that level of disruption on the waterfront. Bob Donegan, CEO of Ivar's, reacted immediately to the DEIS when he read how long Alaskan Way would have to be closed for construction: a little over nine years. Concerned about how that would affect waterfront businesses, Donegan got engaged in the planning process, attending meetings, organizing business owners, serving on committees, and advocating for an alternative that would be less disruptive

As 2006 progressed, civic groups promoted investment in a tunnel because of the benefits a viaduct-free waterfront would provide. Allied Arts weighed in with their "Waterfront for All" report, issued in the summer of 2006:

> "Fifty years ago, our civic leaders made a serious mistake. They cut off Seattle from its waterfront by building the Alaskan Way Viaduct. Now, the people of Seattle and the Northwest have an opportunity to correct this error and redirect the future of the region. We have the choice of giving future generations a vibrant Waterfront neighborhood or cursing them with an even larger viaduct ripping through some of the most significant urban land in the Northwest."

Mayor Greg Nickels began a multi-pronged effort to promote the cut-and-cover tunnel option. His office released a brochure showing what a viaduct-free waterfront could look like and a tongue-in-cheek video about the "Committee to Save Big Ugly Things." He also approached the issue like a campaign, as he recalled in a 2022 interview, "We felt we needed to capture hearts and minds behind the idea. We renamed the Viaduct: it was the Dangerous Alaskan Way Viaduct, and every time we talked about it, we talked about 'This thing is sinking, it has a very limited shelf life and dammit, you don't want to be on it when it decides time is up.'"

The challenge, however, lay in reconciling the state budget for the project, which led the state to focus on a new elevated structure, and the city's demand for a cut-and-cover tunnel, which would exceed the budget. As Nickels recounted,

> "We worked the legislature. A friend, Ed Murray, who later became mayor, was head of the transportation committee in the House. And we got him to provide funding. We got him to agree on a process that would allow them to buy into a tunnel as opposed to a new aerial structure. And at the end of the 2006 legislative session, some funny things happened. And the deal that we had with Representative and Chairman Murray went away . . . The goal post was moved significantly."

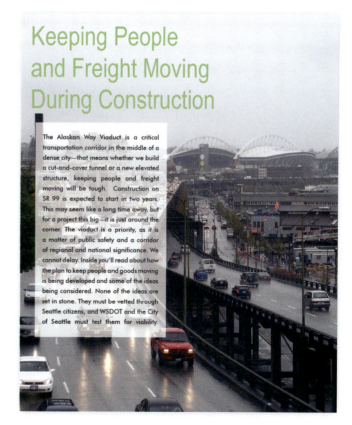

WSDOT brochure on the construction process, 2006.

Existing Elevated Viaduct at Waterfront.

Proposed Elevated Viaduct at Waterfront.

The legislation required an expert panel review to assess the feasibility of the two options. In July 2006, WSDOT and SDOT released a supplemental DEIS with both the cut-and-cover tunnel and a new elevated structure as alternatives. In September, the city council again endorsed the cut-and-cover tunnel as its preferred alternative and recommended the development of a surface street-transit alternative in case costs or other issues made the tunnel alternative infeasible. That fall and early winter, the project was mired in gridlock. The state rejected the city's plan for a four-lane, cut-and-cover tunnel because it did not meet standards for federal funding, leaving the state to shoulder the full cost.

In January 2007, Governor Gregoire summoned Mayor Nickels to a meeting attended by legislative leadership and Seattle City Council President Nick Licata. Nickels knew that Licata also supported the rebuild, given the costs and disruption associated with the cut-and-cover tunnel option. Nickels was not eager to attend a meeting with the rebuild supporters in the governor's office, but, he explained, "when the governor asks you to come, you come, you really don't have a lot of choice. And if she's going to be backed up by the entire legislative leadership, well, it's a bad day for you, but it's certainly within her purview. . . . And their purpose was to beat me over the head with a club and insist upon a public vote."

The city council approved two advisory vote measures for the March 2007 election. One measure asked if the voter preferred the elevated option and the other asked if the voter preferred the tunnel option. Voters rejected both, with 70 percent voting against the tunnel and 57 percent voting against a new elevated structure.

Meanwhile, the Viaduct continued to deteriorate. During an inspection in June, WSDOT found that the structure had settled another quarter inch, for a total of five inches of settling since the earthquake. WSDOT had set six inches as the critical point for safe use.

At an impasse, the state, county, and city signed an agreement pledging to participate in a "collaborative process." Various agencies addressed a handful of issues needing resolution regardless of which viaduct replacement option prevailed. The Moving Forward projects included stabilizing the Viaduct's footings between Yesler Way and Columbia Street, relocating

No Elevated Viaduct at Waterfront.

In addition to the state legislature, some in Seattle continued to support construction of a new elevated structure. It was less expensive than the cut-and-cover tunnel, with fewer risks. Business owners in SODO and Ballard campaigned to keep a viaduct because it more directly connected the interdependent industrial districts. A new elevated structure would retain the on- and off-ramps into downtown, too, maintaining direct access to downtown for commuters traveling from South and West Seattle. And many people just loved the idea of maintaining the view they enjoyed from the existing viaduct.

A new elevated structure would have been a behemoth. To meet newer safety standards, the structure would have to be wider to accommodate wider lanes and shoulders. Renderings showed how it would loom over Alaskan Way, creating a more pronounced barrier between downtown and the waterfront. While it certainly retained the capacity of the existing structure, it didn't meet any of the other guiding principles for the project. Civic leader and architect John Nesholm prepared a computer-generated rendering of what an elevated option would look like to help voters understand the intrusive nature of the proposed structure.

electrical lines between South Massachusetts Street and Railroad Way South, making safety upgrades to the Battery Street Tunnel, adding transit enhancements, and the replacing of the South Holgate Street to South King Street section with a new roadway.

A Project Oversight Committee was formed to facilitate the decision-making process. The committee consisted of Governor Gregoire, King County Executive Ron Sims, Mayor Nickels, the chairs of the Senate and House transportation committees, and one member each of the King County and Seattle councils. To ensure public involvement in the process, a 30-member Stakeholder Advisory Committee with members from advocacy groups, neighborhoods, business groups, and labor groups was formed in December 2007. The state legislature set December 2008 as the deadline for these groups to decide upon a solution. It also set a $2.8 billion limit for the state's contribution. An Interagency Working Group was established to facilitate the technical aspects of the planning. Staff from WSDOT, SDOT, the Federal Highway Administration, King County Metro, Community Transit, the Freight Mobility Strategic Investment Board, the Passenger Ferry District, Pierce Transit, the Port of Seattle, King County Public Health, the Puget Sound Clean Air Agency, the Puget Sound Regional Council, and Washington State Ferries made up the group.

The trio of groups proceeded with analyzing and considering eight new alternatives. These included three surface-street options and five structural options. Each of the options contained elements to make them different from the two rejected previously by voters. As part of this process, the city council directed SDOT, under the leadership of Director Grace Crunican, to develop an Urban Mobility Plan. It was intended to inform the collaborative process partners' work because the surface-transit alternative analyzed in the draft environmental impact statement was inadequate. The Urban Mobility Plan provided better and more complete data and information to inform the development of the new surface-transit alternative. One key difference with the city's plan was that it directed SDOT to find a solution that would "focus on the movement of people and goods to and through Downtown, rather than maintaining vehicle capacity of the existing SR 99

The Integrated Alternative was developed by architect Kevin Peterson to illustrate state House Speaker Frank Chopp's proposal for an elevated structure with park, retail, and office space and residential levels to replace the Viaduct on part of the waterfront.

corridor." Opponents to this strategy included business owners in the two Manufacturing and Industrial Centers (MIC) in Ballard and the Duwamish River valley. The opponents advocated maintaining vehicle capacity to ensure trucks could move easily between the two MICs.

Over the course of late 2008, two parallel processes were unfolding. The public process culminated in the Project Oversight Committee presenting two new preferred alternatives: the I-5, Surface, and Transit Hybrid option, and a new elevated structure with street and transit improvements.

The Cascadia Center for Regional Development, part of the Discovery Institute and led by Bruce Agnew, sent a letter to the committee in March 2008 urging it to also consider a deep-bore tunnel alternative and commissioned a study of deep-bore tunnels by engineering consultants at ARUP. Their report, "Large Diameter Soft Ground Bored Tunnel Review," released in late November 2008, provided an overview of newly available technology for building larger-bore tunnels, the lower costs per mile of recently completed projects in other parts of the world, and comparisons of soil types in which the other tunnels had been bored. The recently completed M30 tunnel in Madrid was cited as proof-positive of the concept's feasibility. That tunnel had a diameter of 50 feet and had room for six highway lanes.

The Cascadia Center also sent the report to the Stakeholder Advisory Committee. It was well-received by committee member Tayloe Washburn and his colleagues at the Greater Seattle Chamber of Commerce, including Charles Knutson, the Chamber's vice president of public affairs. Washburn and Knutson worked together to develop a solution that a majority of the Stakeholder Advisory Committee members could rally behind. The benefit of a single-bore tunnel was that it required just one pass with the larger boring machine, instead of two, reducing construction time and costs. Voters had turned down a twin-bore tunnel, but a single-bore tunnel was a whole new proposal and could be considered.

Governor Gregoire had set December 2008 as the deadline for choosing an alternative and the committee had expected to vote at the meeting on the surface-transit and elevated alternatives. Instead, the discussion turned to the tunnel hybrid option that Washburn brought to the meeting. It called for a deep-bore or lidded trench tunnel extending from S Royal Brougham Way to Harrison Street, with two or three lanes of traffic on the surface, as well as improvements to Interstate 5 and city streets to facilitate traffic flow. It also suggested that the seawall be separated from the project because it was no longer going to be jointly designed with a cut-and-cover tunnel, and that regional tolling be used to provide additional funds needed for the project.

Twenty-two of the twenty-five active members of the Stakeholder Advisory Committee agreed with Washburn's proposal to study the hybrid tunnel alternative in the final environmental impact statement and sent a letter to the governor announcing their preference later that month. The governor was interested in the proposal, but the budget just did not pencil out. WSDOT engineers could not get the costs down to $2.8 billion. To make it work, the governor's office brought in the Port of Seattle as an additional partner. CEO of the Port of Seattle Tay Yoshitani agreed to contribute $300 million to the project because the Port had an interest in a functioning regional transportation network for Port operations. This brought the state's contribution in line with its mandated limit.

Momentum had shifted to the bored tunnel option, but the surface-transit option advocates continued to press for inclusion of a surface-transit option in the environmental impact statement and for it to be evaluated against the standard of maintaining the movement of people and goods through the city, not necessarily replacing the vehicular capacity of the Viaduct. The surface-transit option advocates wanted to change how people moved around the region by investing in public transit infrastructure. They argued that investing billions in a new highway would reinforce the region's reliance on gas-powered, single occupancy vehicles, which would continue to contribute to climate change.

While not many people opposed transit system development, some questioned the assumptions made by the surface-transit advocates. It remained unclear if the near-term needs of the city could be met with a surface solution that would require decades to develop. For businesses requiring workers to move around the city, and for cargo from the port moving north-south through the city, gridlock would lengthen travel time and render the transportation network unreliable.

Still from video created by project engineers to illustrate the damage and mayhem a longer or stronger earthquake would wreak on the Viaduct and the city.

Furthermore, people living in less expensive suburbs coming into the city for jobs and people with mobility challenges would likely bear the brunt of the burden during the long-term build-out of a transit system. According to Greg Nickels, "At the end of Sound Transit 2 . . . we should have the capacity to carry a million people a day. . . . So, that, for our kids and our grandkids, will be a great alternative. . . . But today that isn't true and it's going to be some period of time before it will be true.

In April 2009, the state legislature voted to approve the deep-bore tunnel project. The state committed to funding the construction of the tunnel and removal of the Viaduct. The city agreed to pay for the seawall replacement project, city utility relocation, a park promenade along the waterfront, city street improvements, including Mercer and Spokane Streets, and evaluation of a downtown streetcar to facilitate transit use. King County agreed to make other transit system improvements. In legislation authorizing the state's contribution of up to $2.4 billion, the state legislature added a provision assigning responsibility for cost overruns exceeding $400 million to the "property owners in the Seattle area who benefit from replacement of the existing viaduct with the deep bore tunnel," which would be paid by toll revenue.

That decision did not end the debate about how, or even if, the Viaduct should be replaced. The 2009 Seattle mayoral election was dominated by the tunnel

Demolition of the southern portion of the Viaduct began in 2010.

The public had the opportunity to sign tunnel segments staged for installation as the Viaduct demolition continued, 2013.

decision. The election pitted a pro-tunnel mayoral candidate, Joe Mallahan, against an anti-tunnel candidate, Mike McGinn. Just prior to the election in October 2009, WSDOT released a simulation of the collapse of the Alaskan Way Viaduct and the adjacent seawall due to a seismic event. The engineers who made the video simulated an earthquake similar to the 2001 Nisqually earthquake but made to occur closer to Seattle with a slightly greater magnitude and to last longer. Experts who reviewed the technical work behind the simulation said its only shortcoming was not sufficiently depicting the likely catastrophic impacts to the surrounding downtown masonry buildings. The video was produced in 2007 but not released publicly because it was too dramatically catastrophic. It was released in 2009 because of a public-disclosure request from a member of the public.

In 2010, work began on the South Holgate Street to King Street project. Holgate to King was one of the "Moving Forward" projects that the state, county, and city agreed upon. These projects needed to be done regardless of which option—tunnel, surface, or new viaduct—was eventually chosen. It was the first section of the Viaduct to be demolished. WSDOT built a new, side-by-side roadway over the next three years to connect the existing Viaduct with the surface roadway south of Holgate. Highway 99 remained open during the entire construction project, but its alignment changed often in this section as the work progressed.

In February 2011, Seattle Mayor Mike McGinn, who had campaigned vigorously against the tunnel in the 2009 mayoral election because of its environmental impact, vetoed a city council bill that affirmed agreements with the state for the construction of the tunnel and related work out of concern that potential cost overruns could saddle the city with debt. On February 28, 2011, the city council overrode the veto by a vote of eight to one.

In March, the group Protect Seattle Now filed a referendum petition calling for a public vote on the ordinance. Protect Seattle Now argued against allowing the city to move forward with the project because the tunnel was too expensive, it lacked downtown access ramps, did not include any transit improvement elements, a proposed Pioneer Square interchange would impede the movement of buses serving West Seattle, and tolls would divert traffic to city streets and cause gridlock.

After some legal wrangling, the referendum was placed on the ballot in the August election. Voters approved the ordinance with a nearly 60 percent majority and a decision was reached more than ten years after the earthquake created the emergency situation.

After analyzing the FEIS for the deep-bore tunnel option in the summer of 2011, the Federal Highway Administration issued its Record of Decision in August, approving the Tolled Bored Tunnel Alternative. Governor Gregoire set 2015 as the deadline for opening the tunnel to traffic. As seawall project manager Jessica Murphy

The tunnel boring machine arrived by ship in April of 2013.

THE STORY OF SEATTLE'S WATERFRONT 163

A large conveyor belt carried spoils from the south end of the tunnel to barges at Terminal 46.

would later explain, "It was like being asked to sprint the marathon or people would die!"

Seattle Tunnel Partners (STP) had the winning proposal for designing and building the tunnel in 2010 and they signed a contract with WSDOT on January 6, 2011, for $1,089,700,002. The partnership was between Dragados USA, from New York, the primary contractor for Madrid's tunnel, and Tutor Perini Corporation, from California. Local companies, including HNTB Corporation, Frank Coluccio Construction Co., and Mowat Construction Co. subcontracted on the project.

An unsettling incident occurred in late 2012 at the Hitachi-Zosen factory in Osaka, Japan, where the tunnel boring machine was being built. The cutter head's rotary drive failed during testing and workers had to disassemble and rebuild it. That repair was completed, and the machine was shipped to Seattle in early 2013. After the machine was assembled at the south tunnel portal, boring commenced on July 30, 2013. To remove the excavated soils, a conveyor belt stretched backwards from the cutter head, exited the tunnel, crossed over the railroad tracks just north of Terminal 46, and ended just above the dock where barges waited to carry the soil away to be dumped in an abandoned quarry at Mats Mats, near Port Ludlow.

The boring machine was nicknamed Bertha in honor of Bertha Landes, the first, and at that point only, woman to serve as Seattle's mayor. Bertha moved forward along the tunnel route. The enormous cutter head turned under the guidance of an international team of tunnel engineers watching screens monitoring dozens of machine performance parameters and geotechnical and structural instruments installed along the tunnel route. As the soil was removed, curved sections of the tunnel wall were placed just behind the cutter head and bolted together. As the machine progressed, the weight of soil compressed the ring and secured it in place. The rings, each one packed tightly against the one before it, formed a hollow tunnel.

In December, just before reaching the 1,000-foot mark and as crews prepared to pass beneath the Viaduct, the boring machine began overheating and had to be shut down. Seattle Tunnel Partners immediately blamed the problem on a metal pipe that had been driven down into the earth as part of ground water monitoring process during preliminary investigations. No one on the WSDOT or City team, including their consultants, believed the pipe had caused the problem since the machine was supposed to be able to grind through boulders and high strength steel reinforcing bars. The metal pipe was only eight inches in diameter and made of mild steel. Jared Smith recalled that he, David Dye, Ron Paananen from WSDOT, and other project leaders, "did a construction progress tour into the tunnel the day after the boring machine encountered the pipe and saw the remnants of it on the ground. One of us commented that the boring machine had treated the pipe 'as though it was just a piece of dental floss' as it churned through it and spit it onto the tunnel spoils conveyor belt. In a later court case, the jury determined that STP was responsible for the delays and machine repair.

WSDOT engineers were faced with an enormous challenge. The machine sat 120 feet underground, below the upland area of Pier 48, under the Ballast Island site, and adjacent to the unstable Viaduct. Because the tube of tunnel wall rings had an interior diameter smaller than the cutter head, the machine could not be reversed out of the tunnel for repair. Instead, STP determined that a rescue pit could be constructed in front of the machine, the cutter head lifted out, and repairs made. Dozens of thick columns of concrete were poured in a ring just in front of the cutter head to hold back groundwater. The soil in the

The tunnel boring machine's control room, 2013.

middle of the ring was then excavated. The boring machine was fired up again and driven through the concrete ring until the cutter head was inside of it. An enormous crane lifted the cutter head out in one piece and placed it on the surface. Over the next several months, STP replaced the main bearing and made substantive improvements to the cutterhead, seals, and internal components of the boring machine. The entire retrieval, repair, and replacement operation took about two years. The machine was reassembled, tested, and then restarted in December 2015. About 16 months later, on April 4, 2017, the tunnelling machine emerged into daylight at the north end of the tunnel.

Work on the highway was finalized over the next two years. Building the tunnel and replacing the seawall were gigantic projects, happening in tandem and under great pressure. There were significant challenges and difficult interagency conflicts, but the complications were resolved, the projects were completed, and the stage set for waterfront redevelopment. Jared Smith, reflecting on the period when the tunnel boring machine was stuck, said, "Eventually, there was light at the end of the tunnel, the Viaduct came down and it was a huge relief, and there was a great celebration."

Access pit and lift for cutter head repair, 2015.

Viaduct demolition continued in 2019 when the new tunnel opened.

Crews pose with the tunnel boring machine after it reached its destination at the north end, 2017.

THE STORY OF SEATTLE'S WATERFRONT **167**

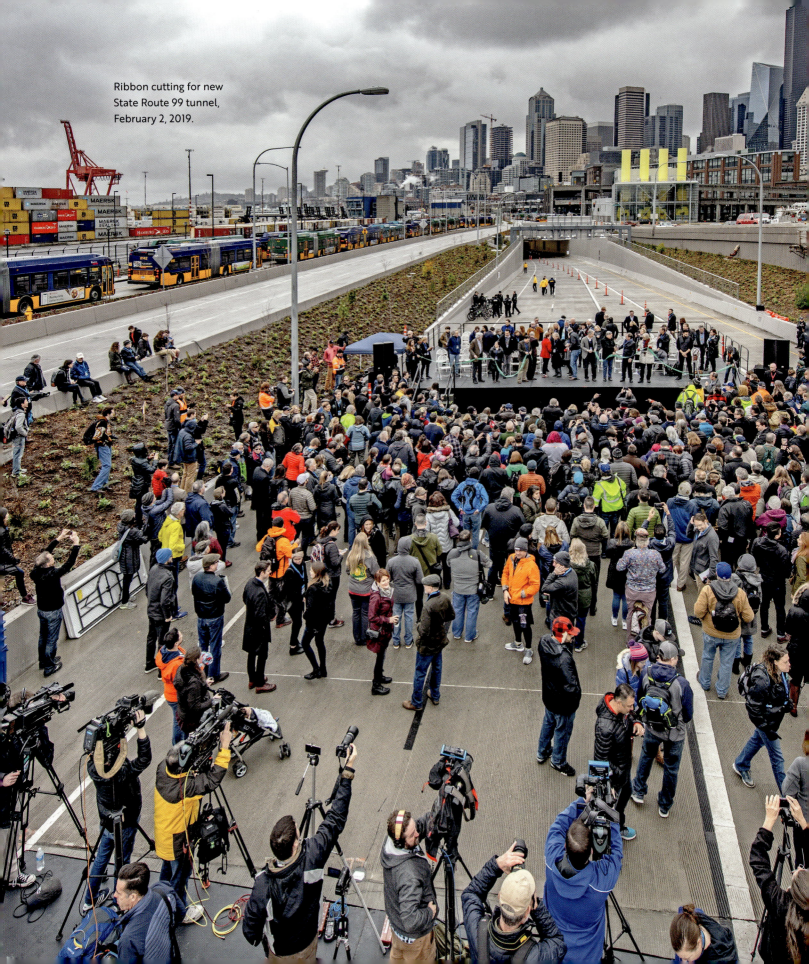

Ribbon cutting for new State Route 99 tunnel, February 2, 2019.

GOODBYE/ HELLO PARTY

Before the tunnel opened to traffic in 2019, the City of Seattle hosted an enormous Hello|Goodbye: Viaduct Arts Festival on February 2nd. The festival stretched from the southern end of the Viaduct through the Battery Street Tunnel. Participants in a 5K run followed a course from Seattle Center south through the new tunnel, then north on the Viaduct and back through the tunnel. In the afternoon, the Viaduct's upper deck was transformed into an open-air party with artists and musicians, and displays by local tribes, agencies, and others involved in the project. The tunnel opened to traffic on February 4, 2019, and demolition of the Alaskan Way Viaduct could begin.

CHAPTER 11

Becoming a Waterfront for All

I'm actually more excited to see how Seattle makes the design its own.... I want to see it grow a patina over time and take on this character that I know we can't predict.

—MARSHALL FOSTER, FORMER DIRECTOR OF OFFICE OF THE WATERFRONT
AND CIVIC PROJECTS DIRECTOR, NOW DIRECTOR OF SEATTLE CENTER

THE COMPLETION OF THE TUNNEL boring marked just one step in the process of transforming Seattle's central waterfront. The construction of portals for each end, the Viaduct demolition, and the design and building of the new Waterfront Park overlapped and intertwined for more than twenty years. It involved dozens of projects: new piers, a pedestrian overpass, green infrastructure, new streets, works of art, planting beds, and historic preservation projects. It started, however, with what Angela Brady, director of the Office of the Waterfront and Civic Projects, called the "foundation of all of it," the Elliott Bay Seawall, and ended with a new park that provides the infrastructure for a "Waterfront for All."

Planning for the new seawall started in about 2004. Replacing it was less controversial than replacing the Viaduct, but not less complicated. In all, about 3,700 feet of seawall needed to be rebuilt in the first phase. Like the old seawall, the new one had to resist wave action on its western face, remain upright, and hold back the inland fill that gravity continually pulled seaward down the beach slope it rested upon. In keeping with the guiding principles for the Viaduct replacement project, the seawall directives included minimizing environmental impact as much as possible.

Once the project was separated from the Viaduct replacement project in 2009, the city proceeded to develop a construction and funding plan. The city used a General Contractor/Construction Manager (GCCM) process because of the project's complexity and tight time schedule. This allowed City of Seattle engineers to design the wall in collaboration with consultants and contractors who had expertise in the technology that would be used, scientists who studied near-shore environments, and artists who would design public-facing elements of the project. The artwork elements were funded by the 1 Percent for Art provision in the project budget. Voters approved the seawall project's $290 million bond issue in November 2012, with 77 percent in favor, and the city hired Mortenson-Manson, a joint venture of Seattle firms,

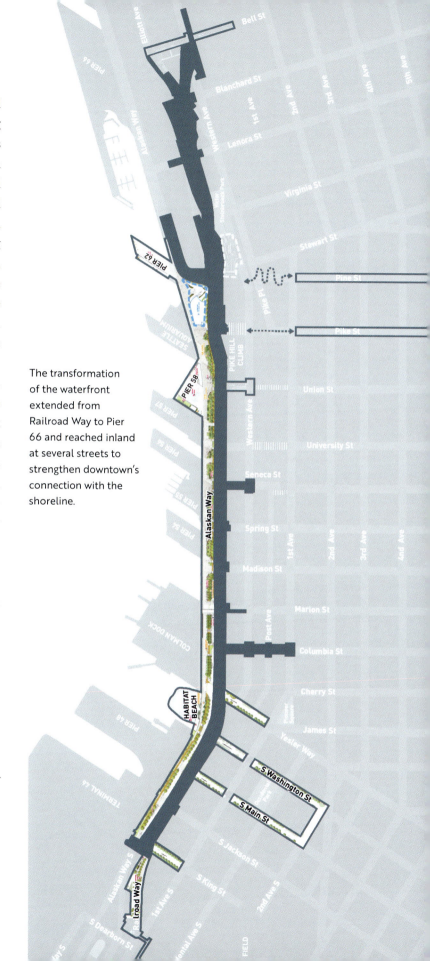

The transformation of the waterfront extended from Railroad Way to Pier 66 and reached inland at several streets to strengthen downtown's connection with the shoreline.

to serve as the General Contractor/Construction Manager for the project. Manson had a long history of working on the waterfront and one of its early projects was building the relieving platform for the portion of the seawall built in the 1930s.

Construction began in 2013. In place of the original timber, concrete, and steel structure, engineers designed a concrete seawall that is invulnerable to the biggest threat to the old seawall: the wood-boring gribbles. The new design used the liquefiable soil behind the wall and transformed it into a mass of "improved soil" that served as the foundation for the new wall and to hold back the fill on the inland side. The mass is made up of large columns of jet-grouted soil extending 40 to 80 feet deep, and up to 60 feet upland from the new seawall. Bob Donegan described it as "a Kidd Valley milkshake machine that extends down to the hard pan and it extrudes concrete." The grout mixes with the existing soils, incorporating them into the improved-soil structure. As seawall Project Manager Jessica Murphy explained in a 2024 interview,

> "It was a very smart engineering solution that fit our waterfront well. . . . [It] fit the constrained space, fit the utilities, fit the piers, fit the urban area, fit all of these unique things that we had on our waterfront because the alternative was giant drilled shafts or secant piles. So big cranes, big drilling, highly disruptive, unforgiving."

The Elliott Bay Seawall is one of the largest projects in the world utilizing jet-grout columns. Each of the 5,750 columns is three to six feet in diameter and extends up to 80 feet deep into the ground. The grout solved the issue of how to work around the existing wood pilings left behind from the old seawall's relieving

Children's coloring page featuring a gribble, the wood-boring menace to the seawall.

platform and Railroad Avenue's trestles, as well as existing utility infrastructure. Because the grout was liquid when introduced into the work area, it could conform to the available space around the obstacles. Murphy recalled how they approached the project in a 2024 interview:

> "We had this super awareness we were doing something unprecedented. We're like, 'We better figure out how some people did this and learn from others.' So we studied other cities, other mega projects, other waterfront projects, other seawalls, other jet grouting projects, trying to find lessons learned in an analogous situation. . . . We could find mega projects and we could find seawall projects and we could find jet grout projects, we could find utility projects, but not all in the same combination that we had . . . in our central waterfront: high tourist volume, largest ferry terminal by volume in the country, local and regional utilities, the Viaduct. We just had all these unique components, and we were trying to do something that had never been done before technically."

A new, four- to five-foot thick concrete support slab was poured over the top of the columns in a continuous line from Pioneer Square to Pier 62. More than 1,000 pre-cast pieces of seawall were then attached to that foundation slab. The weight of those two elements ensured the wall would stay vertical and the fill would not slide seaward, nor would the wall liquefy during an earthquake, providing stability to the whole waterfront. The wall is built to accommodate the sea level rise that is anticipated as the climate warms, but if the actual rise is higher, the infrastructure of the seawall can support upward extension of the wall.

During construction, a new sheet piling wall on the western side of the old seawall served as a cofferdam to keep the saltwater out of the work area. On the inland side, groundwater intrusion created a significant problem. The water could not be pumped out because the tunnel boring machine repair team was already trying that and seeing subsidence upland from the rescue pit that endangered buildings, roads, and sidewalks. Groundwater entering the work area also introduced the possibility that contaminated water from unknown sources would have to be treated. To prevent that, the engineers devised a way to freeze the ground just upland from the seawall work, creating a "wall of ice." Work proceeded in the channel of dry land between the two barriers. SDOT operated two water treatment plants adjacent to the construction area, one for seawater that made its way into the work area and one for stormwater that entered the construction area as rain or runoff.

The seawall, like the Viaduct, was at great risk of failure. City staff knew that it could fall into the bay, property would be damaged, transportation disrupted, and lives could be lost. Project Manager Jessica Murphy knew that there was a risk in even removing a section of the old seawall to begin construction, as she would later recount:

> "We were scared it would just unzipper [fall into the bay]. We didn't know. We had a lot of measures [in place]. We were trying to mitigate risks. We did a lot of things to mitigate it. But just like nobody can tell you when the earthquake comes, we could have had a small 3.5 [on the Richter scale] tremor that happened periodically, and that could have done it."

The Elliott Bay Seawall replacement project illustrates the radical changes in civil engineering that have taken place since the 1970s. The introduction of the environmental impact statement process and the acknowledgement of Puget Sound tribes' treaty-reserved fishing rights in the 1974 *United States v. Washington* case (popularly known as the Boldt

A disorganized mishmash of utilities filled the space under the Alaskan Way sidewalk.

The utility connections to the piers were streamlined and organized into portals built into the wall structure.

THE STORY OF SEATTLE'S WATERFRONT 173

WATERFRONT ART PROJECTS

Artists helped create the new Waterfront Park. Sculptures, carvings, castings, and more are installed up and down the corridor. Including artwork has been an integral part of the design process from the beginning of the project. Seattle's 1 Percent for Art program, enacted by voters in 1973, allocates one percent of eligible capital construction costs in the infrastructure and public building projects for the inclusion of art. This program has created a public art collection throughout the city.

The substantial funding involved in the seawall replacement and other infrastructure construction on the waterfront translated into significant funding for realizing the vision for arts and culture on the waterfront. Artists and curators developed art plans to guide artwork commissions during the design of both the Elliott Bay Seawall and Waterfront Park projects. In all, the funding provided opportunities for sixteen artists working on nine artwork projects. All the projects are site-specific, designed

by the artists for the unique spaces on the waterfront, and reflect the guiding themes of environment and community.

Pier 62 features two pieces. On the floating dock on the south side of the pier, Stephen Vitiello's *Land Buoy Bells* translates the wave action into sound. On the seawall between the pier and the Seattle Aquarium, Laura Haddad and Tom Drugan of Haddad|Drugan LLC created *Seawall Strata*, a series of seawall-facing panels with textures mimicking the shapes of sea life found at different levels of the tidal zone.

The promenade features installations interspersed along the parallel ribbons of sidewalks, plantings, bike lanes, and traffic lanes. Oscar Tuazon collaborated with carvers Randi Purser (Suquamish), Tyson Simmons (Muckleshoot), and Keith Stevenson (Muckleshoot) to create a series of longhouse-pole-like structures between Columbia and Spring Streets. Qwalsius-Shaun Peterson (Puyallup) created a group of carved, welcome figures, *Family*, at Pier 58. Adjacent to the Pioneer Square Habitat Beach, artist Buster Simpson created *Migration Stage* consisting of two elements, *Anthropomorphic Dolo*s and *SeaBearer*, evoking the working waterfront while addressing climate change issues and providing seating and play space.

On the Union Street Pedestrian Bridge, Norie Sato's *Unfurling a Gesture (The Nature of Persistence)* spans the length of the walkway. It also has two elements. One is a large, steel fern frond rising from the base of the stairs and arching over the bridge. The other is a metal screen on the bridge's south railing "that layers abstracted imagery of seagull wings over that of ferns." Sato had a studio in the 619 Western Building for a number of years and was "inspired by looking at the waterfront and how nature and the built environment interacts there."

Art from the MTK Matriarchs team is featured on the lower level of the Overlook Walk on the Salish Steps.

Seawall Strata, designed by Laura Haddad and Tom Drugan, is composed of geometric forms emulating "the life forms it is trying to attract," including barnacles, mussels, anemone, starfish, and rockweed.

The team of artists Malynn Foster, Tamela LaClair, and Kimberly Deriana represent both local tribes and Urban Natives. Their work carries on the traditions of their elders. Their large-scale, woven clam basket embodies the interconnectedness of community and invites people inside to experience the Indigenous perspective.

Extending inland, Derek Bruno and Gage Hamilton have developed a "cohesive visual language" for the Pike Pine Corridor. Along those two streets, on bicycle buffers, planters, and overpass railings, images of sine waves represent the water in the blocks nearer to the shoreline. Moving inland, triangle lines representing the hill dominate.

Near Colman Dock, as part of an agreement with regional tribes, an artwork on Habitat Beach complements the historical marker documenting the history of Ballast Island located on the overpass leading to the new passenger terminal. The artwork, *Family*, was created by Muckleshoot tribal historian Warren King George. It consists of four basalt columns representing the gathering of Coast Salish families on the waterfront since time immemorial, welcoming people ashore and wishing them well on their travels.

Suquamish carver Randi Purser created *Looking at All Tomorrows* (ʔasla?labəd kʷədi bəkʷ dadatu), featuring Chief Sealth as an infant in the arms of his mother, Sholeetsa, for installation on the north end of Oscar Tuazon's piece *To Our Teachers* (deqʷaled).

James Corner Field Operations designed the faces of the seawall panels near Habitat Beach. The geometric texture of the wall contrasts with the more organic forms of the rest of the seawall.

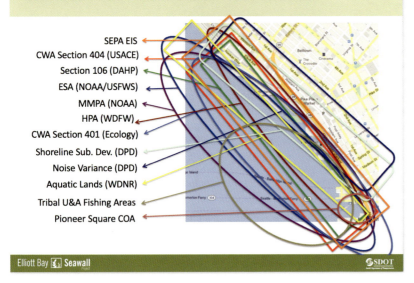

The Elliott Bay Seawall project team had to negotiate a complex web of overlapping jurisdictions and permitting processes.

Decision) changed the equation for assessing the costs and benefits of public projects. Where City Engineer R. H. Thomson had weighed his proposals solely against financial costs and benefits, today's city civil engineers also weigh the environmental and cultural costs of their proposals. They come into the profession with a broader educational background, as Angela Brady, explained in a 2024 interview, "Civil engineering is a really interesting career because you aren't pigeonholed into any one discipline. A civil engineer can do transportation engineering, they can do environmental, they can do water quality, they can do wastewater treatment, they can do structural engineering, [and] construction management."

This made the seawall replacement project both exciting and intimidating for the SDOT team that undertook it. The project had urgency because of the potentially imminent structural failure of the existing seawall. But it also had complexity. It wasn't really an option to find a solution that only addressed the need for holding back seawater. The additional environmental considerations created a project described by Brady as, "a unique project that civil engineers could really sink their teeth into, because it required all the different disciplines." The initial costs of this more holistic approach to civil engineering are high, but the long-term benefits to the health and livability of the city will pay off many times over.

During construction, the engineers had to manage the groundwater so it didn't enter the worksite and create a potential contamination issue because of possible toxic materials in the soil the water passed through uphill from the project. Dewatering, a common solution, involved pumping water out as it entered the site, but that had the potential for causing settling in the nearby Pioneer Square Historic District because the ground slumps as the water is drawn out by the pumps. The engineers also had to devise methods to keep construction debris, especially excess jet grout, out of Elliott Bay. And they had to manage any rainwater that fell into the work area so it wouldn't carry contaminants from the work area into the bay.

Additionally, engineers had to plan for the seawall's impact on the environment once it was constructed. This started with the purpose and need statement developed for the project, which Jessica Murphy summarized as "reduce the seismic vulnerability and attempt to restore some of the marine habitat loss with the construction of the original seawall." This statement guided every decision made about the seawall and the urban infrastructure constructed on top of it.

Environmental impact is part of every engineering project today, but the seawall had one significant difference: it wasn't clear that the solutions proposed to make the face of the wall more friendly for salmon would work because nothing like it had been attempted in similar circumstances. But the environmental costs of the project were known: the new wall would continue to block fish access to shallow water and have an impact on their survival rates. The engineers had to make decisions based on the best science they had so that, as Murphy explained, "everybody thinks this might work at least enough to give it a shot, [and] we're at least going to get the data that others can benefit from," for future projects, even if it doesn't work as intended.

The project also introduced stormwater management on the central waterfront to mitigate the impact of large areas of street pavement, sidewalks, and parking lots. Swales running along the sidewalk first capture stormwater and filter it, instead of letting it run untreated into the bay. That means 10 million gallons of water that used to carry pollutants from cars and streets into the near-shore habitat where salmon and other marine animals and plants live is cleaned and harmless.

In contrast to the earlier seawall and fill project, significant attention was given to providing habitat for marine life. The original tidelands and beach ecosystems could not be restored, but the seawall structure itself could be redesigned to improve the habitat along the shoreline for salmon and other marine flora and fauna.

Studies had shown that about half of the juvenile salmon coming out of the Duwamish River on their way to open water followed the shoreline along the east side of the bay up to the Smith Cove area where they moved west out to West Point and on to the ocean. Along the way, they encountered all the central waterfront's piers. Salmon do not like to go under structures because low light makes it difficult to feed and there is little food available without sunshine anyway. As a result, the fish would aggregate between the piers and swim out and around them, increasing the distance they had to travel. Swimming around also made them more vulnerable to predation by birds and larger sea life. The additional energy and risk associated with negotiating the obstacle course of piers reduced the overall survival rate of salmon, something the already-declining fish populations could scarcely afford.

Around 2005, the City of Seattle convened a team of planners and environmental consultants to consider

Elliott Bay Seawall under construction, showing the textured seawall surface (left) and the habitat bench between the wall and the pier pilings (right).

ways to design the seawall to make it as hospitable to marine life as possible. The smooth face of the 1936 seawall had provided no niches for small seaweeds and mussel larvae to attach. Without those initial colonizers, other sea life could not find habitat, and the seawall remained largely free of flora and fauna.

One of the consultants brought into the working group was Jeff Cordell from the University of Washington's Wetland Ecosystem Team. He and his colleagues, including Jason Toft and graduate student Maureen Goff, worked together to see what could be done to provide habitat for algae and animals in the hope of increasing the survival rate of juvenile salmon. According to Toft, who also worked on the Olympic Sculpture Park's beach element, "We study fish, and Chinook salmon are listed under the Endangered Species Act, which is a huge thing in our region, and that right there is the main reason why we would have a seat at that table."

Habitat Beach, the southern end of the waterfront's "salmon highway," and the renovated Washington Street Boat Landing, looking south.

The Wetland Ecosystem Team conducted several small-scale experiments with different materials and surfaces at multiple places along the central waterfront. The results revealed that a surprisingly simple and low-cost solution created excellent surfaces for plants and animals to colonize. Cordell describes the approach as "benches, beaches, and bumps. Benches . . . are those benches coming out away from the sea wall at a low intertidal level to mimic shallow water, natural habitat. The bumps are along the seawall face, something you might see in your head as like if you're at a climbing gym, something like that." The beaches are at the north and south ends of the central waterfront, at the foot of Washington Street and the Olympic Sculpture Park. The southern beach is key to drawing salmon toward the seawall and its "salmon highway."

Building on the model for a bumpy surface demonstrated by the scientists' experiments, Field Operations designed one version of the wall face with a cobbled texture. Another version was designed by Laura Haddad and Tom Drugan of Haddad|Drugan LLC for the section of wall between Pier 62 and the Seattle Aquarium, and one at the foot of University Street. Their *Seawall Strata* artwork, "creates geometric textures that mimic the marine life it is trying to attract," as the artists explained. They created magnified versions of the species found in the intertidal zone, such as barnacles and rockweed, and placed bands of each in the approximate location they would be found along the face of the wall. Small shelves jut out at intervals along the wall, increasing the variety and scale of surfaces.

A gabion, a metal cage-like structure filled with rocks, forms the habitat bench running along the seawall's base from the new beach at the Washington Street Boat Landing to Pier 62. This raised the seafloor, creating a channel of shallower water, which is preferred by juvenile salmon making their way to sea. Over time, the rocks within the metal net will accumulate sand and decaying plant matter from the wall above, creating more habitat for algae and animals. The hope is that the complexity of plants and animals will continue to grow, building upon those earliest colonizers who have gained a toehold.

The scientists also introduced light to the underside of the sidewalk, which was cantilevered over the water, in the hopes that the salmon would be more likely to follow the seawall under the piers, rather than detouring out to the ends. Glass blocks were inlaid into the new sidewalk when it was poured. This additional light proved helpful for the inter-pier spaces, too,

View along the Seawall, with light coming through the glass blocks embedded in the sidewalk along Alaskan Way.

because the new seawall is located about ten feet further inland than the old one, making the area shadier. It was not as dark as the under-pier areas, but it was dark enough to reduce food resources for salmon.

The new seawall is monitored for its impact on marine life. Preliminary results indicate that the design has been successful. The scientists found that the light blocks only increased the light by two to four percent, but that was sufficient for the salmon to feed at sufficient levels and to draw them along the wall under the piers. Algae and animals, especially rockweed and mussels, are growing on the wall and the biological productivity is higher, particularly of the microorganisms that are the building blocks of the food chain, such as harpacticoid copepods and arthropod crustaceans. Juvenile salmon feed on them, along with crab larvae in the water column and insects on the surface. Another exciting finding has been the colonization of the outer edges of the habitat bench by bull kelp, which provides important habitat for marine life. The seawall replacement north of Pier 62 also incorporates the "benches, beaches, and bumps" that have proven successful, extending the salmon highway north to the Olympic Sculpture Park.

The city team carefully coordinated the design of the seawall structure with the ongoing development of a design for the aboveground elements of the new Waterfront Park. As Angela Brady explained in a 2024 interview,

> *"There were elements of the seawall, aka the light-penetrating surface panels, that we installed for the habitat enhancements and the marine ecosystem. That whole thing went through a process with the Waterfront Design Team so that we could design something that was integral with the rest of the design for the promenade. We weren't just building a structure, we were building something that incorporated the marine habitat improvements, but also incorporated the urban design aesthetic that really blends beautifully with the rest of the promenade design."*

Planning and design for the park began in 2009, under the aegis of the Central Waterfront Partnerships Committee (CWPC). Mayor Nickels established the CWPC in October 2009 to ensure continuity and consistency in the Waterfront Park's planning and development regardless of changing mayoral administrations, or in case of unexpected challenges or proposals that were inconsistent with the vision for the new park. The Committee's mission was to "advise the city on the strategies and partnerships necessary to successfully design, develop, and manage a series of premiere public spaces . . . along the Central Waterfront." Nickels appointed former Mayor Charley Royer and park advocate Maggie Walker as co-chairs. Over the next 16 years, they would play pivotal roles in each step of the waterfront's redevelopment through their leadership, vision, and dedication.

On the city side, Mayor Nickels instituted policies to ensure robust and effective collaboration between departments. He charged Diane Sugimura, director of planning, Grace Crunican, director of SDOT, and Christopher Williams, then the acting superintendent of the Department of Parks and Recreation, with developing a partnership to ensure the planning

OLYMPIC SCULPTURE PARK

In 2007, a glimpse of the future emerged on the waterfront north of Broad Street. The Seattle Art Museum opened the Olympic Sculpture Park, a remarkable transformation of a former brownfield into a beautiful public space. The park successfully mitigated several challenges that had hampered successful redevelopment elsewhere on the waterfront. First, toxic soils were contained through remediation and capping. The original beach, which was covered in fill behind the seawall, was recreated with jetty-like piles of riprap on either side to protect it from erosion. A human-made hill with a switchback path and overpass negotiated the hill's elevation change and tied together the portions of the parcel bisected by the railroad tracks and an arterial street, Elliott Avenue. The new park also provided a link between the central waterfront and the half mile of shoreline in Myrtle Edward and Centennial parks to the north.

and implementation of Waterfront Park proceeded smoothly and to support the Committee's work. This is a fairly unusual arrangement in city government, but it was the best way to ensure the vision for Waterfront Park would be realized given its size and complexity. Nickels knew that, over time, there would be political and economic difficulties, and he wanted to ensure there was a strong foundation to help it withstand those challenges.

There was also a concern that incoming Mayor Mike McGinn would derail the park's development. McGinn had campaigned on dismantling the interlocal agreements for the tunnel project and to stop it from being constructed. His concerns were financial: that the city would be stuck with cost overruns, and ideological, that the city was investing in vehicle-centric transportation projects rather than a transit-based replacement for the Viaduct. In the end, the dual support provided by the Committee and the departmental partnerships carried the Waterfront Park development project through six mayoral administrations and numerous practical obstacles.

Nickels ensured community support by appointing people from a broad range of backgrounds and waterfront connections to the group. Looking back at those early years, former Office of the Waterfront and Civic Projects Director Marshall Foster described it as an "eyes on the prize; we defend the vision; support the city staff; make sure that this thing happens as planned" committee. In a departure from most citizen committees, the city also gave the Central Waterfront Partnerships Committee the authority to work with city staff.

Early on, the CWPC recommended the waterfront project be viewed as a whole—the seawall, the streets, and the park elements—so it could be managed efficiently and holistically. The Committee also urged the City of Seattle to hire a landscape architect at the beginning, before the engineers got to work, so, as committee member Cary Moon explained, it will be understood as "a cohesive whole and be able to figure out, how do we integrate shore ecology, parks and public life, our commitment to green infrastructure, a modest four-lane street, and how do we connect the market and all the downtown neighborhoods to the waterfront?"

The Committee also recommended that the City of Seattle hire an urban design firm before the civil engineering firm was chosen, to place the vision for

Olympic Sculpture Park, *Father and Son* fountain, 2015.

the park at the forefront of the design and construction process. Several members of the committee had been involved in planning for the Seattle Art Museum's Olympic Sculpture Park, which had benefitted from a design competition, and so the CWPC design subcommittee put out a call for submissions. Several dozen firms responded and four were chosen to present at a public meeting at Benaroya Hall in September 2010. The room was full. Maggie Walker remembers 3,000 people attending. The public was clearly engaged with the project and in thinking about what the waterfront could become. Cary Moon describes the outcome:

> "It was really clear they [the James Corner Field Operations team (JCFO)] understood how we needed to reweave urban fabric; that we needed to reconnect downtown neighborhoods to the bay; that Seattle has this rich deep relationship to our watery terrain, whether Lake Washington or the Salish Sea and the islands; and that that's a key part of our identity and it needed to be this center driving idea of the whole plan. And they understood the muscular industrial part of Seattle and how that is also part of our identity, working class, no nonsense, let's not make this too fussy and elitist, but let's make it industrial and reflective of our waterfront history and our industrial working-class history. They got all of that about our city."

James Corner hails from Manchester, England, and he recognized similarities in Seattle's waterfront to his home. He told the committee members that there is "Big nature, big city, but also, you're a working port. That's your DNA, and you need to recognize that." Charley Royer remembers that Corner "loved the grittiness of this place. And he swore that he wasn't going to make it look like LA or some other city with a lot of neon. It was going to be Seattle. And he convinced people that he knew what we were talking about when we wanted this to be Seattle, not some other city, not even Manchester."

In some ways, being from outside of the city allowed Corner to see the waterfront differently than the locals on the committee. Walker remembers how hard it was for her to see past the Viaduct, which was still in operation, and envision the potential for the waterfront. At a meeting at the World Trade Center building, they were able to see the waterfront without the Viaduct in view. As Walker remembers,

> "You're looking back at the city and you're looking at the harbor. And that actually, to me, was one of the most formative experiences, because he [Corner] kept saying to us, 'You have one of the most beautiful harbors in the world. Do you know that you have one of the most beautiful harbors in the world?' And none of us understood what he was talking about because you couldn't see our harbor from any place that made sense. And, that view from that World Trade Center across from Bell Street pier was relatively new. . . . And looking at it, you realize, 'Man, this is one of the most beautiful harbors in the world.' And he recognized that. And I don't think another designer would necessarily have been able to articulate that back to us."

The City of Seattle hired Corner's firm in 2010. JCFO worked with about 50 local firms in developing the plans for Waterfront Park. Corner and his team

Seattle's waterfront is beautiful, but not beautified, retaining its working components like the Bell Harbor marina alongside its park elements like Pier 62.

created a master plan, and the local firms developed different elements from that plan into detailed schematic designs. They all worked closely with the city's planning, transportation, parks, and utilities staff to develop and refine elements of Corner's vision.

The Central Waterfront Partnerships Committee turned in its final report to the city in late January 2011. Just a few days later, the city council created the Central Waterfront Committee, with many of the same appointees participating. The council charged the new committee with, "providing oversight of the redevelopment of the Central Waterfront, to include overseeing development of the waterfront conceptual design and framework plan, ensuring robust and innovative public engagement, and establishing the foundation for a lasting civic partnership." Committee members and city staff jumped right into gathering public input with ten public forums held in 2011 and 2012. The public was asked what they wanted to do on the waterfront, what they wanted to see and experience, and what they valued about the place.

Corner's vision for the waterfront was built on the relationships between the buildings, shoreline, and experiences of the central waterfront landscape; the urban context in which it exists; the relationships between the waterfront, downtown, Pioneer Square and Chinatown-International District, and Seattle Center; and the relationships with the surrounding areas of Elliott Bay, Puget Sound, the Duwamish River, and nearby Puget Sound islands. He and his team looked at ways to strengthen the connections within and between those levels of context so the waterfront would be embedded within its surroundings and history.

The James Corner Field Operations plan also addressed the longstanding challenges posed by the north-south and east-west movements of people and goods, which remained even after the tunnel moved highway traffic underground. It also addressed the environmental health of the bay, the steep hill separating the waterfront from downtown, and the repurposing and maintenance of pier structures.

GUIDING PRINCIPLES

The redevelopment of the waterfront presented a tremendous opportunity for a wide range of new structures and activities. To guide decision making, the city council outlined seven guiding principles:

- Create a waterfront for all
- Put the shoreline and innovative, sustainable design at the forefront
- Reconnect the city to its waterfront
- Embrace and celebrate Seattle's past, present, and future
- Improve Access and Mobility
- Create a bold vision that is adaptable over time
- Develop consistent leadership—from concept to construction to operations

The East-West Connections Project brought improvements to Washington and Main Streets that reference their history, including native plants and piling remnants that look charred like they would have been after the 1889 fire.

Several project elements were introduced to restore connectivity between Pioneer Square, Chinatown-International District, and the waterfront, and to improve connections between downtown and the shoreline. On Jackson, Main, and Washington Streets, streetscape improvements make the pedestrian experience safer and easier and promote a sense of community through more welcoming sidewalks environments. At Union Street, a new pedestrian overpass with an art installation by Norie Sato extends out from Western Avenue and stairs and an elevator carry pedestrians down to Alaskan Way. At Pike Street, the Overlook Walk crosses over Alaskan Way, using a switchback path (or an elevator) to make the grade less daunting and more accessible.

To reduce the environmental impact of urban infrastructure and activities and to restore long-absent vegetation to the landscape, new landscaping surrounds the pedestrian spaces and lines the streets. Rows of trees and planting beds filled with native plants or ornamentals, stormwater swales, and grassy areas all soften the streetscape and create spaces that are a respite from the urban environment. The planting beds also capture millions of gallons of stormwater running off the streets, removing pollutants as they pass through the soils, so the water entering Elliott Bay is clean.

Alaskan Way was realigned to follow the Viaduct's path, veering uphill at Pike Street to connect with Western Avenue (northbound) and Elliott Avenue (southbound). This adjustment leaves more area on the shoreline for park uses, including a bike lane. In 2021, the city council designated portions of Alaskan Way, Elliott Way, Railroad Way, and Union Street as park boulevards, incorporating those streets' rights-of-way into Waterfront Park and ensuring that park regulations can be enforced throughout the park. A compromise hammered out with the Alliance for Pioneer Square allowed for a wider roadway south of Columbia Street to accommodate transit uses and ferry terminal traffic. As part of the environmental impact statement process it was stipulated that those extra lanes will be removed once the Sound Transit light rail line between Ballard and West Seattle opens and fewer buses from southwest King County need to come into downtown via Alaskan Way.

The piers owned by the Department of Parks and Recreation, 58, 62, and 63, were completely reimagined. The existing park at Pier 58 was demolished and replaced with a new structure featuring a playground—the first facility of its kind on the central waterfront. Piers 62 and 63 offered enormous space for public access to the shoreline, but they would require significant funds to renovate. Pier 62 was rebuilt, with plans for Pier 63 put on hold for the near future.

Along the promenade, parallel ribbons of sidewalks, plantings, bike lanes, and traffic lanes are interspersed with art installations and interpretative signage. At the south end of the waterfront, the East West Connections project improved the streetscape on Main and Washington Streets west of Second Avenue and portions of King Street and Yesler Way for a better pedestrian experience. Using varied colors of bricks, the street and alley surfaces show the pre-contact shoreline that has since been shifted westward with construction of the seawall and fill behind it. Interpretive

Elliott Way, connecting Alaskan Way with Elliott and Western Avenues along the former Viaduct right-of-way, and the Overlook Walk under construction.

Pier 62 (foreground) filled with festival goers, and Overlook Walk under construction.

signage provides insights into how Native people have lived on Elliott Bay since time immemorial.

The Central Waterfront Committee's Finance and Partnerships Subcommittee was charged with identifying sources of funding for the enormous project. The Committee developed a plan that relied on a combination of public and private funding. The public funding came from Parks and Recreation Department's Metropolitan Park District levy capacity and transportation funding, save for the cost of demolition of the Viaduct, which was paid for by WSDOT. The private funding came from a combination of sources. The first, a local improvement district (LID), assessed a levy on properties that would increase in value with construction of the park. The Committee included a large swath of downtown in the LID, including Belltown, the Central Business District, and Pioneer Square, extending inland to Denny Way and Interstate 5. This element of the funding plan also helped answer concerns that private property owners were benefitting from public investments.

The second private funding source is philanthropy. The Friends of Waterfront Seattle (now Friends of Waterfront Park) was formed as a non-profit organization that could accept donations and use those funds for constructing, maintaining, and activating the park. Special attention has been paid to drawing residents from across the city to engage with the park, particularly those who have traditionally been marginalized on the waterfront and in other public places.

To reduce costs, a refined plan was developed and presented to the public in February 2014. Some elements were removed, others simplified. One of the most significant elements, Overlook Walk connecting

Overlook Walk is integrated with the Seattle Aquarium's Ocean Pavilion and the MarketFront building.

the waterfront with Pike Place Market, was protected from elimination even though that would have reduced costs significantly. As John Nesholm explained in a letter to his fellow committee members Gerry Johnson and Maggie Walker, "Overlook Walk provides critical access. It connects the 10 million Market visitors to the Waterfront and the 3 million Waterfront visitors to the Market. As the Aquarium contemplates its multi-phased, several-hundred-million-dollar expansion, this enhanced connectivity and the pedestrian traffic it will bring is vital." The result, however, was a better, more affordable plan.

In 2015, the Seattle Aquarium, in the midst of planning its own renovation and expansion project, realized that the Overlook Walk presented an opportunity. Instead of building an overwater extension of the existing Aquarium piers 59 and 60, they could build on the uplands at the base of Overlook Walk. Constructing the building on solid ground reduced costs for the Aquarium and marine habitat impacts. It also preserved views by building below the Pike Place Market and in front of the parking garage.

The aquarium's strategic plan calls for the development of three exhibits: Puget Sound, the Outer Washington Coast, and the Tropical Pacific. The Tropical Pacific, featuring sharks, rays, schooling fish, mangroves, nearly 30 types of coral, and many more species, is housed in the Overlook Walk structure. The Puget Sound and Outer Washington Coast exhibits will be housed on Pier 60 when the pier is renovated and expanded in coming years.

Seattle Aquarium president and CEO Robert Davidson reflected in a 2022 interview on how the Aquarium's mission, "Inspiring the conservation of our marine environment," is not adequate for the challenges on the horizon. Instead, he explained,

The Seattle Aquarium's Ocean Pavilion features exhibits with species from a reef ecosystem in the Indo-Pacific's Coral Triangle.

> "We have realized that we have a need in our own community to activate people, to be good citizens, to be good voters, to be knowledgeable in how they live in the world... Are we making the planet worse? Are we making it better? And then to take advantage of this gift, of this place, where we're building the Aquarium, which the city could have turned over to any number of corporations to do something. But they instead chose to have the Aquarium expand, and to expand in a way that—this is going to be a building that is recognized around the world as reflective of Seattle."

The new Ocean Pavilion has several elements park users can experience. From the plaza between the Overlook Walk and Pier 59, visitors can look up into the enormous tank inside the building through

THE OVERLOOK WALK PLANTINGS

Valerie Segrest (Muckleshoot) designed the plantings for the Overlook Walk. In an interview in 2022, she described her vision:

> "The design concept of the Overlook Walk plantings is about telling a landscape story that stretches from 'white cap to white cap,' from the summit of Mount Rainier, Tahoma, to the shores of the Salish Sea. Along this expanse, a vast diversity of ecosystems exists, from which our ancestors harvested and maintained over 300 different kinds of foods annually. This stands in stark contrast to the modern American diet, which typically consists of only 12 to 20 foods consumed each year. That diversity of foods is essential for our bodies to maintain health. Access to a wide range of nutrients not only supports our wellness but also keeps us deeply connected to the lands and waters that sustain us. In this way, 'white cap to white cap' stitches together the story of the land.
>
> On the rooftop of the aquarium, you'll find a native berry garden with salmonberry, thimbleberry, huckleberry, and more. Along the Salish Steps, a camas prairie showcases chocolate lily, wild onion, and yarrow, beautifully framing the view of the waterfront.
>
> As you ascend the steps toward Pike Place Market, you'll encounter a wetland ecosystem featuring cattails, willow, and vine maple. At the top of the steps, plants representing the floor of old-growth forests, including salal, ferns, Douglas fir, and western red cedar, await—just before you reach Pike Place Market."

a round window, the oculus. The rooftop is open to the public as part of the Overlook Walk. Visitors can see native plantings on the rooftop designed with guidance from traditional ecological knowledge-keeper Valerie Segrest (Muckleshoot) and sandblasted images created in collaboration with Owen Oliver (Quinault/Isleta Pueblo).

One project, technically an auxiliary to Waterfront Park, but one with a significant role in its success, is the Pike Place MarketFront Building at the top of the Overlook Walk. It was built on the lone empty lot within the Pike Place Market Historic District where a 1974 fire leveled the Municipal Market Building. The Great Northern tunnel runs directly under the site and made new construction prohibitively expensive. The project became more feasible once it was partially paid for with funding provided by the City of Seattle to mitigate the impact of removing hundreds of parking spaces under the Viaduct that could not be replaced within the right-of-way of Alaskan Way. The MarketFront Building connects at its top level with the Desimone Bridge to the Pike Place Market's main arcade and sits on top of a three-level parking garage built into the hillside. Architects from Miller Hull worked with JCFO to integrate the new building seamlessly into the Overlook Walk. Along the western face of its Western-Avenue-grade level, walkways connect the Overlook Walk with a newly renovated Steinbrueck Park, also known as Native Park.

In a 2022 interview, Director of the Office of Planning and Community Development Rico Quirindongo highlighted how the MarketFront's western side answers the resistance some had to losing the Viaduct because of its beautiful views. As he explained,

> "How do you, without a dollar to spend or $10 to buy a sandwich, how can you come and spend time at the market and get a benefit that is a benefit to all, that 180 degree view, which didn't exist there before and used to be only afforded . . . by 'folks that were driving on the Viaduct' while it still existed? We created an opportunity for that vista view and place of gathering, which doesn't come at a dollar value."

That sentiment about the waterfront as a whole was echoed by John Nesholm, who served on both citizen committees: "We'll consider the project successful if a family can come down for the afternoon and have a good time and not spend any money."

Southwest view from the MarketFront building showing the Overlook Walk's varied pathways down the hillside.

The rebuilt Colman Dock ferry terminal features a new building that reestablishes the frontage of the original Colman Dock along Alaskan Way.

COLMAN DOCK REPLACEMENT

The replacement of the Washington State Ferries terminal and the dock on which it sits took seven years to complete—and the terminal remained open throughout. Begun in 2017, the project involved replacing 2,000 wood piles with 500 steel and concrete piles to ensure the dock would remain standing in an earthquake.

A new passenger terminal, designed by Seattle architects NBBJ, is made up of two buildings connected with an elevated walkway, one along Alaskan Way and one adjacent to the ferry slips. The street-front building is a rectangle structure echoing the original Colman Dock's orientation and function, with space for retail businesses. The waterside building is the passenger terminal. Its expansive west-facing windows capture the remarkable views across the water.

An overpass from the south side of the pier to the new passenger terminal is open to the public and provides access to those same views. It also features interpretative signage sharing the story of Ballast Island located south of the terminal under the Pier 48 uplands.

A section of the old dock was removed north of the new terminal. Washington State Ferries took out 7,400 tons of creosote piles, some dating to 1938. In their place, more than 30,000 tons of sandy gravel was set to cap pollutants.

The passenger waiting area's floor-to-ceiling windows provide views out across the water and back toward the city.

After Ed Murray won the mayoral election in the fall of 2013, Central Waterfront Committee members Charley Royer, Maggie Walker, Gerry Johnson, and John Nesholm wrote to the mayor-elect and his staff and advocated for a new Office of the Waterfront to lead the waterfront project and coordinate its contracts, timelines, staffing, public engagement, and interactions with the JCFO design team. The alternative, asking each of the numerous departments to manage their elements of the project and only consult with other departments as necessary, would be, they argued, "multi-layered and expensive." They cited similar projects such as construction of City Hall, the Libraries for All levy-funded projects, and the Pike Place Market Preservation and Development Authority.

Mayor Murray agreed and established the Office of the Waterfront in early 2014, with Jared Smith as its first director. Smith had set up a similar multi-departmental effort in 1997 when the city started planning the alignment options and station locations for the Sound Transit light rail program. The halt to tunneling in December 2013 stalled all other work on the waterfront, so Smith got the new office established and then passed the reins to Marshall Foster who was then the planning director at the Department of Planning and Development. Angela Brady, an SDOT civil engineer who had recently completed leading the work on the Mercer Corridor transformation in South Lake Union, stepped in as lead engineer. Foster described the Office of the Waterfront team as "this really unusually nimble and interesting group of public servants who care deeply about the city and are deeply invested, and some of the most creative people."

The Office of the Waterfront model has been studied by other cities preparing to embark on large infrastructure projects. Foster explained in a 2022 interview that the idea of interdisciplinary, interdepartmental collaboration on design projects is fairly common and expected. What makes Seattle's project unique is the "blending of the design with finance with the political layer and being able to do all those things under one roof, because we're often having this crazy interplay between those different aspects." In 2017, the office was designated as the Office of the Waterfront and Civic Projects, expanding its scope to include projects such as Climate Pledge Arena.

Seawall construction between King and Pike Streets finished in 2017, the same year that Bertha emerged in the north portal near Seattle Center. Once the tunnel was ready for use, the city held a party to say "hello" to the tunnel and "goodbye" to the Viaduct on February 2, 2019. Thousands of people participated in a day of public activities and enjoyed the unique view from the structure one last time. The next Monday, demolition began.

Over the next six years the Viaduct was removed, Alaskan Way realigned in its footprint, and new Waterfront Park elements steadily emerged from the construction dust. The first, Pier 62, opened in September 2020 and proved to be a vital resource for the city during the COVID-19 pandemic. Its wide-open spaces allowed for virtual events, and then in-person events, to be held safely. Friends of Waterfront Seattle programmed the space to draw residents and tourists to the waterfront. It offered the opportunity to put the first guiding principle of the waterfront's redevelopment, "Create a waterfront for all," into practice. This principle gained even more resonance in light of the Black Lives Matter movement, when more people realized equity of access and sense of belonging would require proactive

> Foster described the Office of the Waterfront team as "this really unusually nimble and interesting group of public servants who care deeply about the city and are deeply invested, and some of the most creative people."

BUILDING A FOUNDATION FOR THE FUTURE

Throughout the more than 15 years she co-chaired the Central Waterfront Committee, the Central Waterfront Partnerships Committee, and the board of the Friends of Waterfront Park with Charles Royer, Maggie Walker helped solve multitudes of problems. She provided extraordinary leadership in realizing the community's vision for the new Waterfront Park and ensuring its future success by establishing a strong financial and institutional foundation.

During the pandemic, Walker was hearing from people about the despair they felt over the impact the pandemic was having on downtown Seattle. While she was giving tours of the waterfront, as she explained in a 2022 interview, people were saying, "This is going to save the city. This is going to recreate what this city is." She saw this repeatedly in 2021 and 2022 as

> *"[people on the tours] realized that this was Seattle reimagining itself and thinking about itself in a different way. What we were proposing was a model of taking care of the city that was different than the one that was operating, frankly, through most of the rest of the downtown. . . . Because I think everybody lost confidence that we could actually deal with what we were faced with. And of course, we can deal with it. There's no question. It's just a question of being open, willing to have these conversations, and also willing to have principles about things, and doing what we can to solve the problems.*

Maggie Walker (center, facing camera) leads a waterfront tour, March, 2025.

The Washington Street Boat Landing's pergola was reinstalled at its historic location after an extensive renovation.

engagement, not just an absence of barriers. Friends of Waterfront Seattle developed Pier 62's programming with artists from all parts of the community and invited cultural communities to gather and share their stories, art, and experiences on the pier.

The Office of the Waterfront and Civic Projects and the Friends of Waterfront Park started the process of building a sense of a community around this new version of a place that has played a significant role in the long history of disputes and violence around differences in race and class. Interpretive signs document the stories of how people have shaped the central waterfront and how different groups have had radically different experiences there. Intentional programming that invites everyone to build a connection to the new spaces and includes a broad audience in planning decisions will help mitigate these historic harms into the future.

One of the most profound changes has been the recognition of the uninterrupted and ongoing cultural significance of dᶻidᶻəlaličh to Native people whose ancestors have made this shoreline their home since time immemorial. While regulatory requirements include consultation with tribes and protection of cultural resources, the reality of large infrastructure projects has often been superficial processes leading to damage to culturally significant places and tribal communities. With the earthquake came a new opportunity to transform the waterfront and to do it in a more inclusive and sensitive manner. Tribal consultation has been integral to the planning and development project. Space has been carved out for traditional and new tribal cultural practices, including representation through artworks and cultural facilities, as well as environmental enhancements that support salmon populations and strengthen the long-term

Muckleshoot Indian Tribe Vice Chair Donny Stevenson speaks at the unveiling of *Honoring Our Muckleshoot* by Muckleshoot carvers Tyson Simmons and Keith Stevenson, February 2025.

viability of tribal fishing on Elliott Bay. The tribal-city relationship still has room to grow, but it is more effective now than it was in the 2000s when the redevelopment began.

In a 2022 interview, Valerie Segrest (Muckleshoot) spoke about her experiences on the waterfront and how the design process unfolded:

> "I think it's telling of our time that we are included in the planning process for the Waterfront redesign. When they started breaking ground, a lot of people in my community predicted that if we were to make contributions, they would be a 'check the box' process. But in my experience, what has taken place throughout this process has been transformative and collaborative.
>
> True collaboration is an ongoing commitment that requires willing hearts, teamwork, and a shared sense of purpose. When diverse communities come together with mutual respect, they create a foundation of trust where collaboration can truly thrive. This is the story unfolding on the waterfront, where the Indigenous work groups have been working alongside architects, planners, biologists, historians, artists, and design firms in perhaps one of Seattle's most ambitious projects to date.
>
> Meaningful collaboration with Coast Salish communities has spanned program development, ecological restoration, art installations, and even species relocation with the Seattle Aquarium. This ongoing partnership weaves Indigenous knowledge into every aspect, from exhibit design and public art to cultural relationships across the Indo-Pacific. The result will be a welcoming place, one that honors these collaborations and invites visitors from around the world to witness this vision brought to life."

The 2001 Nisqually Earthquake literally and figuratively shook up Seattle's central waterfront. Like the Great Fire in 1889, it provided an opportunity, to "do over" how the city related to its shoreline. Unlike other transformations over the years, this one looks back to the city's history as much as it looks to its future. James Corner and his team tapped into the sense of connection Seattleites feel with their waterfront and sought a balance between introducing new elements to solve long intractable problems like the steep hillside, the challenges of connecting the public with the water, and the environmental impacts of the urban infrastructure while striving to honor and maintain the essence of the large piers, but at a human scale. The new Waterfront Park and the Elliott Bay Seawall supporting it are the latest and grandest transformations of an often-transformed space that has two through-lines: the past is deeply embedded in people's sense of connection to the central waterfront, and it remains at the heart of the city's identity, defining its character. What remains to be seen is how *this* iteration of the waterfront will reshape the city.

Acknowledgments

I AM GRATEFUL for the opportunity to write this book about Seattle's central waterfront. My thanks to Marie McCaffrey, co-founder and executive director of HistoryLink who developed the Waterfront History Project, and to the project's funders and supporters: the state Department of Archeology and Historic Preservation, formerly led by Dr. Allyson Brooks; King County Executive Dow Constantine; the Port of Seattle; the Seattle Office of the Waterfront and Civic Projects; and the Friends of Waterfront Park. We are indebted to John and Laurel Nesholm, Maggie Walker, and Jared Smith for their contributions and their assistance in raising funds from numerous generous individuals and businesses.

Over nearly two decades of research, I have talked to too many people about their work, memories, and relationships to the waterfront to list them all here. I am grateful to each and every one of them for sharing their knowledge and experiences. My own understanding of and relationship to the waterfront has been immeasurably deepened through my conversations with them. I hope I honored the complexity of their connections to the waterfront and the layered meanings it has had in their lives with this book.

In addition to many informal conversations, I was lucky to have had the opportunity to conduct interviews with a wide range of people who have lived, worked, studied, and advocated for the waterfront, including Sally Bagshaw, Angela Brady, Tony Chinn, Jeff Cordell, Grace Crunican, Bob Davidson, Leonard Forsman, Marshall Foster, Dennis Frair, Ben Franz-Knight, Christine Gregoire, Paula Hammond, Warren King George, Gerry Johnson, Bettie Luke, Douglas MacDonald, Mike McGinn, Jay Mehzer, Cary Moon, Jessica Murphy, John Nesholm, Greg Nickels, Mike Omura, Ron Panaanan, Rico Quirindongo, Mike Rigsby, Charles Royer, Norie Sato, Valerie Segrest, Jared Smith, Jason Toft, Maggie Walker, Marie Rose Wong, and Teresa Woo-Murray.

The archivists and librarians who maintain and share our region's history are treasures. There is an embarrassment of riches in their collections. Much of it is digitized due to their diligent efforts and all of it is made more accessible by their expertise and generous assistance. In particular, I'd like to thank Anne Frantilla and the stellar staff at the Seattle Municipal Archives, Ann Ferguson and the dedicated staff of the Seattle Room in the Seattle Public Library, the Washington State Archives, the Washington State Department of Transportation Library, and Special Collections at University of Washington Libraries.

Thank you to HistoryLink board member Jean Sherrard for sharing so many beautiful photos of the waterfront, including the gorgeous cover shot.

My thanks to the numerous readers who read all or parts of the manuscript for this book, especially Warren King George, Elisa Law, Priscilla Long, Lynn Schnaiberg, Jared Smith, David Williams, and Ruri Yampolsky. My deep gratitude to the excellent editors at Documentary Media, Petyr Beck and Tori Smith. You all helped me make this enormous story more manageable and coherent. Any mistakes that made it into print are mine alone.

Finally, a huge thank you goes to my family and friends who have supported me through this project. Your excitement for the book and interest in this history propelled me forward, especially when my confidence flagged and the deadlines seemed impossible.

This book, so beautifully designed by Marilyn Esguerra under the guidance of Petyr Beck, is my gift to each of you and to everyone who feels a connection to Seattle's remarkable waterfront.

—*Jennifer Ott*

Credits

1	Museum of History and Industry, shs7338
2	Seattle Municipal Archives, 9517, Series 2613-07
5	Seattle Public Library, spl_saw_1811222
6	Courtesy Washington State Department of Transportation
8	Jean Sherrard
10 top	Library of Congress, Geography and Map Division
10 bottom	Petyr Beck
11 top	Courtesy Washington State Department of Natural Resources, Washington Geological Survey
11 bottom	Courtesy the Burke Museum
12 top	Courtesy National Oceanic and Atmospheric Administration
12 bottom	University of Washington Libraries, Special Collections, UW22170
13	Adapted from the Waterlines Project Map, Burke Museum
14	Museum of History and Industry, 88.33.115
15 left	Smithsonian, National Museum of the American Indian
15 right	University of Washington Libraries, Special Collections, NA1546
16 top	James Cole
16 bottom	James Cole, adapted from design by Greg Colfax
17 top	Library of Congress, 98687163
17 bottom	Museum of History and Industry, SHS321
18–19	Washington State Archives, Digital Archives, AR-28001001-ph002117
19 top	US Coast and Geodetic Survey, 1875
20 top	University of Washington Libraries, Special Collections, SEA1352
20 bottom	Library of Congress, 2010589747
21	Museum of History and Industry, 2002.3.549
22 top	*Seattle Gazette*, Volume 1, Number 10, 16 February 1864
22–23	Courtesy Paul Dorpat
24 top	Museum of History and Industry, SHS11765
24–25	Washington State Archives, Digital Archives, AR-07809001-ph004557a
26	Wikimedia Commons, courtesy Seattle Public Library
27 top	Museum of History and Industry, SHS4000
27 bottom	*The Daily Intelligencer*, Volume 9, December 01, 1880
28	Courtesy Wing Luke Museum
29	*Seattle Weekly Gazette*, Volume 1, Number 43, 4 March 1865
30 top	Library of Congress, 75696660
30 middle	Courtesy Paul Dorpat
30 bottom	University of Washington Libraries, Special Collections, NA1490
31	Seattle Public Library, spl_shp_22855
32	Library of Congress, 75696661
33	Museum of History and Industry, SHS5907
34	Washington State University Libraries Digital Collection, wsu177; HE2791.S42 1874
35 top	Seattle Public Library, spl_shp_5190
35 bottom	Courtesy Paul Dorpat
36	Library of Congress, 75696661
37 top	University of Washington Libraries, Special Collections, BAB43
37 bottom	University of Washington Libraries, Special Collections, UW12061
38 top	Courtesy Puget Sound Maritime Historical Society
38 middle	Seattle Public Library, spl_shp_12027
38 bottom	Washington State Historical Society, 1994.123.9
38 bottom	Seattle Public Library, spl_shp_22898
39 top	Seattle Municipal Archives, 105457, Series 0207-01
39 middle	University of Washington Libraries, Special Collections, SEA1200
39 bottom	University of Washington Libraries, Special Collections, CUR1760
40 top	Washington State Archives, Digital Archives, AR-270-B-000109
40 bottom	Seattle Municipal Archives, TF17_137
41	Library of Congress, 75696663
42	Library of Congress, 75696661
43	Museum of History and Industry, 1980.6967.40
44	University of Washington Libraries, Special Collections, PNW00508
45 top	*Harper's Weekly*
45 bottom	Museum of History and Industry, SHS3486
46 top	University of Washington Libraries, Special Collections, UW6995
46 middle	University of Washington Libraries, Special Collections, NA680

46 middle	Museum of History and Industry, SHS2210		Collections, UW6575
47	Seattle Public Library, SPL_SHP_23054	61	*The Commonwealth*, Vol. 2, No. 11, May 23 1903, p. 3, courtesy Paul Dorpat
48	Courtesy Paul Dorpat		
49 top	Museum of History and Industry, 2000.107.096.06.01	62	Library of Congress, 75696663
		63 top	University of Washington Libraries, Special Collections, 1988.33.234
49 middle	University of Washington Libraries, Special Collections, SOC1597		
		63 bottom	Courtesy National Oceanic and Atmospheric Administration
49 bottom	University of Washington Libraries, Special Collections, NA1500		
		64 top	University of Washington Libraries, Special Collections, SEA2676
50 top	White River Valley Museum Collection, PO-00126		
50 middle	University of Washington Libraries, Special Collections, MOHAI 90.45.11	64 bottom	University of Washington Libraries, Special Collections, UW38959
50 bottom	University of Washington Libraries, Special Collections, 1983.10.PA2.1	65 top	Museum of History and Industry, SHS2500
		65 top	University of Washington Libraries, Special Collections, ADV0375
50 bottom	Courtesy Paul Dorpat		
51 top	Courtesy Paul Dorpat, Michael Maslan	65 bottom	Public Domain
51 bottom	Museum of History and Industry, 008.54.31	66–67	Courtesy Paul Dorpat
52	University of Washington Libraries, Special Collections, COBB3603	67 bottom	Washington State University Libraries Digital Collection, wsu527; F899 S44 T7 1905
53 top	University of Washington Libraries, Special Collections, UW1093	68 top	Museum of History and Industry, 1983.10.10106
		68 bottom	Museum of History and Industry, 1980.6967.6
53 bottom	University of Washington Libraries, Special Collections, 2013.58.15	69	Library of Congress, 75696665
		69 bottom	University of Washington Libraries, Special Collections, UW5229
53 bottom	Museum of History and Industry, 1983.10.10556		
54 top	University of Washington Libraries, Special Collections, 2011.76.2	70	Museum of History and Industry, LIB1991.5.78
		71 top	Puget Sound Maritime Historical Society, 1741-169
54 middle	Museum of History and Industry, 1983.10.7485	71 bottom	Seattle Municipal Archives, 31004, Series 5801-01
54 bottom	University of Washington Libraries, Special Collections, CUR240	72 top	Museum of History and Industry, SHS7490
		72 bottom	Museum of History and Industry, 2019.3.60
55 top	*The Washington Historian*, Vol. 2, No. 1, October 1900, p. 54	73	University of Washington Libraries, Special Collections, UW443
55 bottom	*Seattle Post-Intelligencer*, Vol. 17, No. 156, April 5 1890	74	Library of Congress, 75696665
		75 left	*The Seattle Daily Times*, October 23 1907, p. 1
55 bottom	*Seattle Post-Intelligencer*, Vol. 7, No. 131, March 8 1885	75 right	Filipino American National Historical Society
56	University of Washington Libraries, Special Collections, A. CURTIS 05900	76	Seattle Municipal Archives, 1552, Series 2613-01
		77 left	Washington State Archives, Digital Archives, AR-28001001-ph001701
57 top	Courtesy Paul Dorpat		
57 bottom	Seattle Municipal Archives, 11950, Series 2613-07	77 right	Seattle Municipal Archives, 1802-G2_1_2
58 top	*The Electrical Engineer*, Vol. 23, 1897, p. 155	78	University of Washington Libraries, Special Collections, UW25966z
58 middle	Seattle Municipal Archives, 130374, Series 0207-01	79 top	University of Washington Libraries, Special Collections, A. Curtis 11656
58 bottom	University of Washington Libraries, Special Collections, 1978.6585.2		
		79 bottom	Courtesy Boston Public Library, The Tichnor Brothers Collection, 64147
59 top	Courtesy Paul Dorpat		
59 bottom	Wikimedia Commons, University of Southern California	80	Seattle Public Library, spl_shp_22637
		81	Seattle Municipal Archives, 930
59 bottom	*The Traffic World*, Vol. 35, Issue 6, 7 February 1925, p. 387	82 top	Seattle Municipal Archives, 626
60 top	Courtesy Paul Dorpat		
60 bottom	University of Washington Libraries, Special		

82 left	Seattle Public Library, spl_pc_50028
82 right	Courtesy HistoryLink
83 top	Seattle Municipal Archives, 46552, Series 2625-10
83 middle	Seattle Municipal Archives, 2717, Series 2613-07
83 bottom	Seattle Municipal Archives, 4872, Series 2613-07
84 top	University of Washington Libraries, Special Collections, SEA2889
84 bottom	University of Washington Libraries, Special Collections, UW7978
85 top	Seattle Municipal Archives, 1222, Series 2613-07
85 bottom	Seattle Municipal Archives, 1221, Series 2613-07
86 top	Seattle Municipal Archives, 12533, Series 2625-10
86 bottom	Museum of History and Industry, 1983.10.209.1
87 top	Seattle Public Library, spl_pc_09017
87 bottom	Courtesy Deep Sea Fishermen's Union
88	Courtesy Vaun Raymond
89	University of Washington Libraries, Special Collections, SHS 2,174
90 top	Henry Miller
90 bottom	Tyson Simmons
91	Seattle Municipal Archives, 8956, Series 2613-07
92 top	Puget Sound Regional Branch, Washington State Archives
92 bottom	Museum of History and Industry, 1983.10.3225.1
93 top	Seattle Municipal Archives, 2705, Series 2613-07
93 bottom	Seattle Municipal Archives, 1802_G5_1923
94	Courtesy Port of Seattle
95	Museum of History and Industry, PI23950
96	US National Archives and Records Administration, Box_302_30-N-42-712
97	Report "The Ports of Seattle..., Board of Engineers for Rivers and Harbors," War Department, U.S. Shipping Board, Vol.1, 1932, p. 235
98	Museum of History and Industry, 2016.44.1
99 left	Seattle Municipal Archives, 8924, Series 2613-07
99 right	Museum of History and Industry, PI24030
100	University of Washington, Ross Rieder Collection
101 top	University of Washington Libraries, Special Collections, PNW01215
101	Courtesy Fred and Dorothy Cordova, National Pinoy Archive, Filipino American National Historical Society
102	Museum of History and Industry, PI24007
103	Museum of History and Industry, PI24001
104	Seattle Department of Transportation
104 bottom	Seattle Municipal Archives, 9362, Series 2613-07
105	Seattle Municipal Archives, 8919, Series 2613-07
106	Seattle Municipal Archives, 77093, Series 1802-0P
107 top	Seattle Municipal Archives, 8835, Series 2613-07
107 bottom	Seattle Municipal Archives, 8900, Series 2613-07
108	Courtesy Paul Dorpat
109	Courtesy Ivar's
110 top	Seattle Municipal Archives, 77106, Series 1802-0P
110 middle	Seattle Municipal Archives, 77109, Series 1802-0P
110 bottom	Seattle Public Library, spl_shp_40855
111 top	US National Archives and Records Administration, 48566387
111 bottom	Museum of History and Industry, PI28058
112	Museum of History and Industry, 2000.107.098.21.01
114	Museum of History and Industry, 1983.10.17365
115	Washington State University Libraries, Digital Collections, wsu sc001-472
116	The Huntington Digital Library, 325584
117	Courtesy Paul Dorpat
118 left	Courtesy Paul Dorpat
118 right	Museum of History and Industry, 1983.10.12301
118 bottom	Courtesy Paul Dorpat
119	University of Washington Libraries, Special Collections, SOC3567
120	*The Seattle Times*, June 7 1947, p. 3
121	Seattle Municipal Archives, 43505, Series 2613-07
122	Courtesy Paul Dorpat, Ron Edge
123	Museum of History and Industry, 2000.107.189.04
124	Seattle Public Library, spl_shp_21634
126	Port of Seattle
127 top	Courtesy Matson
127 bottom	Port of Seattle
128	Seattle Municipal Archives, 201326, Series 1204-01-P
129	Seattle Municipal Archives, 848, Series 5804-06
130 left	Seattle Public Library, spl_pc_02007
130 right	Courtesy Paul Dorpat
130 bottom	Seattle Municipal Archives, 76085, Series 5804-04
131 left	Courtesy HistoryLink
131 right	Courtesy Paul Dorpat
132	Seattle Municipal Archives, 199000, Series 1204-01-P
133 top	Seattle Municipal Archives, Doc_1171, Series 1801-92
133 bottom	Seattle Municipal Archives, 33344, Series 1628-02
134	Seattle Municipal Archives, 76067, Series 5804-04
135	Seattle Municipal Archives, 76065, Series 5804-04
136	Courtesy Paul Dorpat
137	University of Washington Libraries, Special Collections, PH Coll 541
138 top	Seattle Municipal Archives, 195159, Series 2613-07

138 bottom	Seattle Municipal Archives, 194949, Series 2613-07
139	Seattle Municipal Archives, 192444, Series 1629-01
140	*The Weekly*, February 24–March 3, 1982, pp. 23–25, courtesy Seattle Public Library
141	Courtesy Port of Seattle
142 top	Museum of History and Industry, 2000.107.171.34.01
142 bottom	Seattle Municipal Archives, 73014, Series 2613-07
143	Seattle Municipal Archives, 13265, Series 1801-92
145	Courtesy Port of Seattle
146 top	Seattle Municipal Archives, 78498, Series 4614-05
146 bottom	Seattle Municipal Archives, 78497, Series 4614-05
147 top	Courtesy Salmon Homecoming Alliance. Photo by John Loftus.
147 bottom	Danita Delimont / Alamy Stock Photo
148	Courtesy Washington State Department of Transportation
149	Seattle Municipal Archives, 130096, Series 0207-01
150 top	Seattle Municipal Archives, 45836, Series 2613-07
150 bottom	Seattle Municipal Archives, 45847, Series 2613-07
151	Courtesy Washington State Department of Transportation
152 top	Seattle Municipal Archives, 113883, Series 0207-01
152 bottom	Courtesy Washington State Department of Transportation
154	Courtesy Allied Arts of Seattle
155–156	Courtesy Washington State Department of Transportation
157	Seattle Municipal Archives, 8907, Series 1801-92
158–159	Courtesy LMN Architects
160	Kevin Peterson
161–167	Courtesy Washington State Department of Transportation
168	Jean Sherrard
169	Courtesy Washington State Department of Transportation
170	Jean Sherrard
171	Courtesy Seattle Office of the Waterfront and Civic Projects
172	Courtesy Washington State Department of Transportation
173 top	Courtesy Seattle Department of Transportation
173 bottom	Courtesy Seattle Office of the Waterfront and Civic Projects
174	Courtesy City of Seattle
175 left	Randi Purser
175 right	Courtesy Seattle Department of Transportation
176–177	Courtesy Seattle Department of Transportation
178	Courtesy Friends of Waterfront Park
179	Courtesy Seattle Office of the Waterfront and Civic Projects
181	Seattle Municipal Archives, 194852, Series 4600-01
182	Jean Sherrard
183	Courtesy Seattle Office of the Waterfront and Civic Projects
184	Courtesy Seattle Department of Transportation, Tim Rice Architectural Photography
185	Erik Holsather, courtesy Friends of Waterfront Park
186	Courtesy City of Seattle, Tim Rice Architectural Photography
187	Jean Sherrard
188	Courtesy Seattle Office of the Waterfront and Civic Projects
189	Jean Sherrard
190 top	Courtesy Seattle Department of Transportation, Tim Rice Architectural Photography
190 bottom	Courtesy Washington State Department of Transportation
192	Emily Ferrer, courtesy Friends of Waterfront Park
193	Courtesy Seattle Office of the Waterfront and Civic Projects
194	Courtesy Muckleshoot Tribe
195	Jean Sherrard
197	Washington State Archives, Digital Archives, AR-270-B-000109
208	Courtesy Washington State Department of Transportation

Selected Sources

Articles

Brewster, David. "Whatever Happened to Elliott Bay?" *Seattle* (February 1970): 26–31.

Bonthius, Andrew. "Origins of the International Longshoremen's and Warehousemen's Union." *Southern California Quarterly* (Winter 1977): 379–426.

Brown, Giles T. "The West Coast Phase of the Maritime Strike of 1921." *Pacific Historical Review* (November 1950): 385–396.

Conger, Kay. "Alaskan Way Viaduct Opened to Traffic." *Department of Highways News* (May 1953): 2–4.

Corbett, Jackson B. Jr. "George Broom: His Life and Character." *Marine Digest* (October 26, 1935).

Finger, John R. "Seattle's First Sawmill 1853–1869: A Study of Frontier Enterprise," *Forest History Newsletter* (January 1972): 24–31.

Frank, Dana. "Race Relations and the Seattle Labor Movement, 1915-1929." *The Pacific Northwest Quarterly* (Winter 1994/1995): 34–44.

Friedheim, Robert L. and Robin Friedheim. "The Seattle Labor Movement, 1919-20," *The Pacific Northwest Quarterly* 55, no. 4 (October 1964): 146–156.

The Gang of Five. "The Water Liberation Front: Free Alaskan Way! Power to the Pedestrians! Save our Seawall." *The Weekly* (February 24, 1982).

Goldberg, Joseph P. "Containerization as a Force for Change on the Waterfront." *Monthly Labor Review* (January 1968): 8–13.

Melder, F. E. "History of the Discoveries and Physical Development of the Coal Industry in the State of Washington," *Pacific Northwest Quarterly* (April 1938): 151–165.

Nash, Linda. "The Environments of Seattle's History," *The Pacific Northwest Quarterly* 107, no. 2 (Spring 2016): 56–71.

Parham, Vera. "These Indians Are Apparently Well to Do: The Myth of Capitalism and Native American Labor." *International Review of Social History,* (December 2012) 447–470.

Park, Sohyun. "Prescriptive Plans for a Healthy Central Business District: Seattle Downtown Design, 1956–1966." *Pacific Northwest Quarterly* (Summer 2007) 107–114.

Sherburne, Philip. "Wasteland Along the Waterfront," *Puget Soundings* (January 1976) 18–20.

Books

American Institute of Architects, Seattle Chapter. *Action: Better City*. Seattle: American Institute of Architects, May 1968.

Asaka, Megan. *Seattle From the Margins: Exclusion, Erasure, and the Making of a Pacific Coast City*. Seattle: University of Washington Press, 2022.

Bogue, Virgil Gay. *Plan of Seattle: Report of the Municipal Plans Commission*. Lowman & Hanford Co., 1911.

Bohan, Heidi. *The People of Cascadia: Pacific Northwest Native American History*. Seattle: Heidi Bohan, 2009.

Cayton, Horace R. *Long Old Road*. New York: Trident Press, 1965.

Cudahy, Brian J. *Box Boats: How Container Ships Changed the World*. New York: Fordham University Press, 2006.

Denny, Arthur A. *Pioneer Days on Puget Sound*. Seattle: C.B. Bagley, 1889.

Edwards, Paul. *Official Port Book of the City of Seattle Harbor Department*. Seattle: City of Seattle, 1923.

Kimeldorf, Howard. *Reds or Rackets: The Making of Radical and Conservative Unions of the Waterfront.* Berkeley and Los Angeles: University of California Press, 1988.

Levinson, Marc. *The Box: How the Shipping Container Made the World Smaller and the World Economy Bigger.* Princeton: Princeton University Press, 2006.

Magden, Ronald E. *A History of Seattle Waterfront Workers, 1884–1934.* Seattle: ILWU Local 19, 1991.

Markholt, Ottilie. *Maritime Solidarity: Pacific Coast Unionism, 1929–1938.* Tacoma: Pacific Coast Maritime Committee, 1998.

Oldham, Kit and Peter Blecha. *Rising Tides and Tailwinds: The Story of the Port of Seattle, 1911–2011.* Seattle: HistoryLink and University of Washington Press, 2011.

Port of Seattle. *Seattle: Container Gateway Port for Japan and the Far East.* Seattle: Port of Seattle, 1966.

———*Seattle Maritime Commerce and Its Impact on the Economy of King County.* Seattle: Port of Seattle Commission, 1971.

Seattle Public Library. Seattle City Directories Collection, Seattle Public Library.

Seattle (Wash) Board of Park Commissioners. *Parks, Playgrounds and Boulevards of Seattle, Washington.* Seattle: Pacific Press, 1909.

Taylor, Quintard. *The Forging of a Black Community: Seattle's Central District from 1870 through the Civil Rights Era.* Seattle: University of Washington Press, 1994.

Thrush, Coll. *Native Seattle: Histories from the Crossing-Over Place.* 2nd ed. Seattle: University of Washington Press, 2017.

Tomlan, Michael A. *Tinged with Gold: Hop Culture in the United States.* Athens: University of Georgia Press, 1992.

Troost, K. G. and D. B. Booth. "Geology of Seattle and the Seattle Area, Washington." In *Landslides and Engineering Geology of the Seattle, Washington, Area*, edited by Rex L. Baum, Jonathan W. Godt, and Lynn Highland. Boulder, CO: Geological Society of America, 2008.

Trotter, Joe William. *Workers on Arrival: Black Labor in the Making of America.* Oakland: University of California Press, 2019.

Washington Department of Highways. *Origin-Destination Traffic Survey, Seattle Metropolitan Area.* Olympia: Washington Department of Highways, 1947.

Waterman, T. T. *Puget Sound Geography.* Edited by Vi Hilbert, Jay Miller, and Zalmai Zahir. Federal Way, WA: Lushootseed Press, 2001.

Newspapers

Port of Seattle Reporter

Seattle Daily Journal of Commerce

Seattle Post-Intelligencer

The Seattle Star

The Seattle Times

Online Resources

People's Waterfront Coalition, Wayback Machine, Internet Archive, accessed July 22, 2024 (https://web.archive.org/web/20040415143218/http:/www.peopleswaterfront.org/transportation.html).

Reports

Alaskan Way Viaduct and Battery Street Tunnel, Seattle, King County, WA. Historic American Engineering Record, WA-184, Library of Congress.

Alaskan Way Viaduct Replacement Project History Report. Seattle: Seattle Room, Seattle Public Library, 2009.

City of Seattle Landmarks Preservation Board. *Central Waterfront Piers: Piers 54, 55, 56, 57, and 59.* Report on Designation, 2007.

City of Seattle. *Mayor's Recommended Harborfront Public Improvement Plan*. March 1987, Seattle Room, Seattle Public Library.

City of Seattle. *Shoreline Master Program, as Adopted by the City Council, City of Seattle, Approved by the Washington State Department of Ecology*. October 8, 1976. Seattle Room, Seattle Public Library.

Comprehensive Plan for Central Business District, Seattle. Seattle: Seattle Room, Seattle Public Library, 1963.

Curti, Giorgio H., Dr. Dayna Bowker Lee, and Cassandra Manetas. *Ballast Island*. National Register of Historic Places Nomination Form, Washington, DC: US Department of the Interior, National Park Service, 2020.

Department of Community Planning. *The Seattle Central Waterfront: A Study for Its Future Comprehensive Development, 1968–1971*. Seattle: Department of Community Planning, 1972.

Federal Highway Administration. *SR 99: Alaskan Way Viaduct & Seawall Replacement Project Draft Environmental Impact Statement*. Olympia, WA: Federal Highway Administration, Washington Division, 2004.

Higday, Hamilton. *Notes on the Early History of Activities Leading to the Creation of the Seattle Port District*. 1918. University of Washington Special Collections.

Larson, Lynn L. *Traditional and Historical Use of the Seattle Waterfront by Muckleshoot Indian Tribe Ancestors*. Prepared for the Muckleshoot Indian Tribe, August 18, 2021.

Proposal for Core Area Development Plan, Seattle, Washington. Submitted to Core Area Development Association, August 5, 1965. Seattle Room, Seattle Public Library.

Treadwell, George T. *The Port of Seattle: A Case History in Public Port Development*. [ca. 1965?]. Typed manuscript, Seattle Room, Seattle Public Library.

Washington State Department of Transportation. *Alaskan Way Viaduct Replacement Project: 2010 Supplemental Draft Environmental Impact Statement*. Seattle: Washington State Dept. of Transportation, 2010.

Washington State Department of Transportation. *Alaskan Way Viaduct Replacement Project: Final Environmental Impact Statement and Section 4(f) Evaluation*. Seattle: Washington State Dept. of Transportation, 2011.

Unpublished and Archival Materials

"Central Waterfront Partnerships Committee" Papers. In the possession of John Nesholm, Seattle, Washington.

Geoghegan, John Herbert. "The Migratory Worker in Seattle: A Study in Social Disorganization and Exploitation," MA thesis, University of Washington, 1923.

Jackson, Joseph Sylvester. "The Colored Marine Employees Benevolent Association of the Pacific, 1921–1934, or Implications of Vertical Mobility for Negro Stewards in Seattle," MA thesis, University of Washington, 1939.

Kellogg, David. "The Making of a Medicine Man." Letter to Vivian Clark, May 20, 1912. MOHAI, Manuscript Collection, MS.COLL.208.

Seattle Municipal Archives Collections. Papers, letters, reports, and yearbooks. Seattle.

Tobin, Caroline Crane. "Planning For the Urban Waterfront: A Historical Case Study of Seattle's Waterfront." MA thesis. University of Washington, 1977.

"Waterfront for All." Campaign papers. In the possession of Sally Bagshaw, Seattle, Washington.

Index

1962 Seattle World's Fair: Century 21 (World's Fair), 129–131

2001 Nisqually earthquake, 6–7, 120, 144, 149–153, 163, 194

1 Percent for Art, 171, 174

Ainsworth & Dunn, 50, 55, 69, 74

Alaska Steamship Company, 55, 64, 68, 97, 102, 113, 122, 127, 129

Alaskan Way Seawall design, 6, 104–106, 171–181

Alaskan Way Viaduct, 6–7, 82, 117 to end

Alaska-Yukon-Pacific Exposition (AYPE), 78

Allied Arts, 122, 149, 154, 157

aquariums, 109, 131–147, 153–154, 174–179, 186–188, 194

babaqʷəb, 13–14

Bagshaw, Sally, 154, 196

Ballast Island, 45–49, 111, 153, 165, 175, 190

Bell Street Terminal, 82–84, 94, 97, 136, 144

Bill Olwell, 137

Black Ball Line (Thompson Steamboat Company), 67, 116–119

Boston Fishing Company, 55, 69

Bridges, Harry, 102, 110–111, 126

Broom, George, 95

Burke, Thomas, 36, 41, 44

Canfield, Thomas, 33

Carriere, Ed, 48

Cayton, Horace, Jr., 87

Central Waterfront Partnerships Committee (CWPC), 180–193

Chinese Exclusion Act of 1882, 45

Chlopeck Brothers, 52–55, 69

Chow, Ruby, 137

Citizens Waterfront Task Force, 137

City Dock, 67, 113

Coast Salish people, 7–17, 21–26, 46–51, 88–90, 106, 153, 175, 193–194

Colman Dock (originally Hatfield–Colman Dock), 7, 66–67, 74, 79, 111–113, 117–121, 136, 176, 190

Colman Dock, 7, 51, 66–67, 74, 78–79, 111–121, 129, 136, 175, 190

Colman, James, 35, 41, 66

Copeland, Lee, 137

Crunican, Grace, 159, 180, 196

David Brewster, 135, 137, 143

Dawes Allotment Act, 88

de Soto, Alexander, 61

Denny Party, 20–21

Denny, Arthur, 20, 33

Design Commission, 57, 135–137

Donegan, Bob, 149, 154–157, 172

Dragados USA, 164

Duwamish River, 11–16, 29, 36, 47, 77, 83, 88–91, 106, 160, 177, 183

dᶻidᶻəlalʼič (Dzidzilalich), 7, 9, 13–17, 26–29, 45, 51, 70, 88, 111, 152

Elliott Bay Seawall, 171–177, 194

Evans, Dan, 121

Exact, 21

Fairy, 25

fire stations, 57, 84, 108

Fish Wars (United States v. Washington, Boldt Decision), 89, 173

Fishing Vessel Owner's Association, 52, 87

Fletcher, Dave (Dave the Shiner), 55

Frank Coluccio Construction Co., 164

Friends of Waterfront Park (first known as Friends of Waterfront Seattle), 186, 191–193

Galbraith and Bacon, 69, 89, 131

Gayton, Philip, 137

Gen, Woo, 28, 44,

George Broom's Sons, 95

George, Gilbert King, 48

George, Warren King, 16, 47–48, 173, 196

Gilman, Daniel, 36

Gray, Victor, 153

Great Northern Railway, 41, 58–59, 65–70, 113

Great Northern Steamship Company, 67, 92, 113, 189

Green, Joshua, 118

Gregoire, Christine, 158–163, 196

Haddad|Drugan LLC, 174, 179

Haglund, Ivar, 7, 108–109, 123

Halibut Fisherman's Union (later Deep Sea Fishermen's Union of the Pacific), 87

Harbor Lines Commission, 39–41

Harborfront Public Improvement Plan, 141–145

Hill, James, 41, 58, 68

HNTB Corporation, 164

Hock, Chun Ching, 27–28

Idaho, 61

Interagency Working Group, 159

International Longshoremen, Marine and Transportworkers' Association, 72

International Longshoremen's Association (ILA, later International Longshore and Warehouse Union), 71, 90

James Corner Field Operations (JCFO), 173, 182–183, 189–194

Kikisoblu (Princess Angeline), 38, 70

King Street Station, 68, 110

Klondike Gold Rush, 59–64, 78, 80–81, 110, 123

Knights of Labor, 44

Knutson, Charles, 160

Lake Washington Coal Company (later Seattle Coal & Transportation Company), 29, 34–35

Larson, Lynn, 14–15

Lefebvre, David, 137

Licata, Nick, 158

longshoring, longshoremen, 7, 43–44, 55–59, 71–74, 86–88, 92, 99–103, 113, 122–127, 153

Louie Ungaro, 90

Lushootseed, 14

MacDonald, Douglas, 123, 149, 154, 196

Marine Cooks and Stewards union, 92

Maynard, Doc, 20–21

Mayor's Waterfront Advisory Committee, 135

McCabe & Hamilton, 58, 72

McGinn, Mike, 163, 181, 196

Miike Maru, 59, 63, 67

Monson, Donald, 133–134

Moon, Cary, 155–156, 181–182, 196

Mortenson-Manson, 171

Mowat Construction Co., 164

Muckleshoot Tribe Reservation, 26

Municipal League, 122

Murray, Ed, 157, 191

Naramore, Floyd, 122

Nesholm, John, 159, 187–191, 196

Nickels, Greg, 158–161, 180–181

Nippon Yusen Kaisha (NYK Line), 59, 67

Northern Pacific Railroad, 33–36, 41, 65–70, 81, 102

Ocean Dock, 44–47, 111, 113

Office of the Waterfront and Civic Projects (first known as the Office of the Waterfront), 170–171, 191–193, 196

Olmsted Brothers (1903 Olmstead Brother's Park Plan) 71, 81, 142

Olwell, Bill, 137

Olympic Sculpture Park, 7, 89, 105, 177–183

Oregon Improvement Company, 45–48, 54, 61, 66

Overlook Walk, 7, 174, 184–189

Pacific Coast Steamship Company, 59, 64, 71–72

Pacific Net & Twine Company, 52, 69, 140

Parsons Brinckerhoff, 153

Peabody, Charles, 64, 67

People's Waterfront Coalition, 155–156

Pike Place Market, 7, 52, 70, 73, 117, 123, 133–135, 139, 143–144, 154, 187–191

Pioneer Square Beach Habitat, 7, 174–178

Pioneer Square, 7, 12–13, 44–47, 56, 64, 68, 74, 97, 122, 127, 135–137, 143–151, 163, 172–186

Pirates Plunder, 130, 136

Polynesia restaurant, 129, 130

Port Madison Reservation, 26

Port of Seattle, 59, 81–83, 113, 122, 126–127, 136, 144–145, 159–161, 196

Portland, 63

Princess Angeline (see Kikisoblu)

Project Oversight Committee, 159–160

Protect Seattle Now, 163

Puget Sound Navigation Company, 55, 65–67, 117–118

Puget Sound Shore Railroad, 36–38

Railroad Avenue, 36–41, 47, 55, 65–76, 83–92, 96–99, 134

Railroad Way, 68, 98, 120, 158, 171, 184

regrades, 76–77, 81, 84

Rockrise & Associates, 135–139

Ruby Chow, 137

San Juan Fish Company, 54–55, 69, 113

Sato, Norie, 174, 184, 196

Schwabacher Brothers & Company (Schwabacher's), 31, 38, 59, 63–69, 137

Seattle & Walla Walla Railroad, 32–36, 41

Seattle Department of Transportation (SDOT), 151–159, 172–180

Seattle Historic Waterfront Association, 157

Seattle Tunnel Partners (STP), 164–165

Seattle, Lake Shore & Eastern, 36–37, 41

Shoreline Management Act, 129

Si'ahł, 26

Sims, Ron, 159

Smith Cove, 41, 68, 83, 102, 139, 177

Smith, Charles, 102–103

Smith, Jared, 149, 165, 191, 196

Snoqualmie, 57

Stakeholder Advisory Committee, 159–161

Standley, Joesph, 78

Stevedores, Longshoremen and Riggers Union, (later Seattle Longshoremen's Mutual Benefit Association, Local 163 of the International Longshoremen's Association, or ILA), 44, 71–72, 86, 99–103

Stevens, Isaac, 23–26, 33

Suquamish Tribe, 89–90

Suquardle, 26

Swan, James, 33

Taylor, Quintard, 86, 92

Təqʷuʔməʔ (Mt. Rainier), 11, 16

Thompson Steamboat Company (Blackball Line), 67, 116–118

Treaty of Point Elliott, The, 25–26, 88–89

Treaty War on Puget Sound, 26

tunnel boring, 163–167, 171–173

Tutor Perini Corporation, 164

Twelker, Neil, 153

US Army, 75, 111

US Navy, 112–113

Villard, Henry, 36

Wa Chong Company, 27, 28, 44

Walker, Maggie, 180–193, 196

Warren, Pearl, 137

Washburn, Tayloe, 160–161

Washington State Department of Transportation (WSDOT), 151–165

Washington State Ferries, 6, 117, 149, 159, 190

Waterfront Employers' Union (WEU), 86–88

Waterfront Park, 7, 134–147, 154, 171–174, 180–195

Wilson G. Hunt, 31, 33

Ye Olde Curiosity Shop (The Curio), 79

Yesler Way, 22, 30–31, 41, 46, 55, 61, 69, 78, 82, 113, 135, 151, 158, 184

Yesler, Henry, 21–30, 38, 44

Yesler, Sarah, 61

Yesler's Mill, 21–30, 54

Yesler's Wharf, 22, 24–30, 51, 66–67, 95

Yoshitani, Tay, 161